LIBERAL SOCIALISM

Carlo Rosselli

LIBERAL SOCIALISM

Edited by Nadia Urbinati

Translated by William McCuaig

in collaboration with
Fondazione Rosselli of Torino

PRINCETON UNIVERSITY PRESS

PRINCETON, NEW JERSEY

PUBLISHED BY PRINCETON UNIVERSITY PRESS, 41 WILLIAM STREET,
PRINCETON, NEW JERSEY 08540
IN THE UNITED KINGDOM: PRINCETON UNIVERSITY PRESS, CHICESTER, WEST SUSSEX

LIBRARY OF CONGRESS CATALOGING-IN-PUBLICATION DATA

ROSSELLI, CARLO, 1899–1937.

[SOCIALISMO LIBERALE.   ENGLISH]

LIBERAL SOCIALISM / CARLO ROSSELLI ; EDITED BY NADIA URBINATI ;

TRANSLATED BY WILLIAM MCCUAIG.

P.   CM.

INCLUDES BIBLIOGRAPHICAL REFERENCES AND INDEX.

ISBN 0-691-08650-8 (CLOTH : ALK. PAPER)—ISBN

0-691-02560-6 (PBK. : ALK. PAPER)

1. SOCIALISM.   2. LIBERALISM.   I. URBINATI, N. (NADIA), 1955–

II. TITLE.

HX72.R6713   1994   335—DC20   93-42365   CIP

PUBLICATION OF THIS BOOK HAS BEEN AIDED BY A GRANT FROM THE ROSSELLI
FOUNDATION

THIS BOOK HAS BEEN COMPOSED IN LINOTRON PALATINO

PRINCETON UNIVERSITY PRESS BOOKS ARE PRINTED ON ACID-FREE PAPER
AND MEET THE GUIDELINES FOR PERMANENCE AND DURABILITY OF THE
COMMITTEE ON PRODUCTION GUIDELINES FOR BOOK LONGEVITY OF THE
COUNCIL ON LIBRARY RESOURCES

PRINTED IN THE UNITED STATES OF AMERICA

1   3   5   7   9   10   8   6   4   2

1   3   5   7   9   10   8   6   4   2
(PBK)

To Norberto Bobbio

CONTENTS

PREFACE

THE EXPRESSION "liberal socialism" may sound a little odd to an American reader. It sounded odd to the Italians when Rosselli published this book in 1930. Liberal socialism had, and indeed has, a strange sound to many who are accustomed to current political terminology. Even more strange may be the idea of presenting socialism, as Rosselli did, as a medium for promoting democracy. Nonetheless, in western Europe, socialism was the actual path of development whereby the process of democratization was anything but natural. Compared with the previous utopias of ideal cities, the novelty of modern socialism lie in the fact that it became a true school of democracy for those people who had always been kept out of civil and political life, who did not have a voice to denounce injustice, but only hoped for charity; and who, in the very moment they received charity, were deprived of full citizenship. They needed to invent a language of social rights. This language conveyed a strong sense of dignity, because it did away with relationships based on *noblesse oblige* benevolence. Social rights were not an aberration of the liberal state, but a consequence of the liberal state developing into a democratic one. Socialist movements contributed to this evolution. It was, as Rosselli said, a "specification of democracy," because it did not stress the limits of democracy, but its potential. In this sense, socialism was a "like exigency" to that expressed by liberalism in its constitutive era.

After sixty years, these words sound all but outdated. Yet *Liberal Socialism* remains a powerful text that compels us to rethink both the notions and roles of liberalism and socialism. In the face of the crisis of socialist ideology, as well as the unsatisfactory performance of our democracies, Rosselli's book might suggest useful theoretical and political clarifications. Confronted with the triumph of fascism and the crisis of the 1930s, when the old was dead and the new was unable to come to light, Rosselli was able to extract the spirit of both liberalism and socialism from the history of previous centuries. He challenged his fellow citizens by asking them to commit themselves to that spirit and renounce the search for the certainty of truth. There was a good deal of voluntarism and perhaps a grain of the pleasure of action in his message. But it was necessary. As far as the western world is concerned, the Cold War did not end fruitlessly. Proposals for widening the areas of political activity as well as dissociating socialism from Marxism and perceiving it as a constitutive part of the democratic tradition, are a way of keeping alive the socialist ideal nowadays, and also strengthening our democracies.

This book has been made possible by the generous help of Isaiah Berlin, Amy Gutmann, Albert O. Hirschman and Michael Walzer, who recommended it to Princeton University Press, and by the Fondazione Rosselli in Turin—in particular its Director, Riccardo Viale, and Maddalena Bafile—which has generously supported its publication. I wish to express my most sincere gratitude for this support. I worked on this book at the Institute for Advanced Study in Princeton where I greatly profited from the supervision and the comments of Michael Walzer, Albert O. Hirschman, Wendy Brown, James Rule and Monique Canto-Sperber. To Peter Euben, George Kateb, Alan Ryan, Mary L. Shanley, and Danilo Zolo who have discussed liberalism and socialism with me, my sincere thanks. I owe a special debt to William McCuaig for his accurate translation, which captures both the letter and the spirit of Rosselli's text; and to Dalia Geffen, Ruthe Foster and Ann Himmelberger Wald for their patient editorial advice.

The idea of translating Rosselli's book into English occurred to me in Princeton—but my interest in liberal socialism originated in Italy, where I discussed this project with Franco Sbarberi, whom I would like to thank for his advice and his friendship. Maurizio Viroli deserves a special mention, for without him, this English edition of Rosselli's book would have perhaps remained merely a desire.

But the inspiration for this book came from Norberto Bobbio, who has been an invaluable teacher over the years, and has read and commented on the introductory essay. Recalling the relevance Rosselli's intuition had for many of his generation, Bobbio recently wrote that those who have committed themselves to the ideal of a liberal socialism have always experienced a condition of exile: for its founders, during the Fascist regime, it was a political exile; for its followers, during the decades of the Cold War, a moral exile in their own country. *Liberal Socialism* is a book for those who, in various ways, lived in or experience a state of exile. I cannot but dedicate the first English edition to Norberto Bobbio.

Princeton, April 1993

INTRODUCTION
ANOTHER SOCIALISM

Nadia Urbinati

A Short Memorable Life

> Indubitably there are circumstances in which new wills
> . . . can only fructify by becoming aware . . . of their
> antagonism with previous wills. Such a case always arises
> when a new generation has an active wish to differentiate
> itself from the older generation by assigning another goal
> to its life. . . . For then people are *thinking* differently,
> because they are *feeling* differently; they are *feeling*
> differently, because they want to *be* different.
> (*Henri De Man, 1926*)

C arlo Rosselli was a socialist before becoming a liberal socialist. He was a sui generis socialist, because from the beginning socialism for him was a moral ideal, free of Marxist orthodoxy. Rosselli's first explicit adherence to socialist ideas goes back to 1921, when he attended the Congress of the Italian Socialist Party in Livorno (where the Communist wing led by Antonio Gramsci and Amedeo Bordiga seceded). In a postcard to his mother he wrote that he "felt a new being vibrating within [him]self."[1] From that point on, Rosselli devoted his intellectual and political efforts to providing the socialist movement with a new perspective, one that would replace the deterministic vision of Marxism largely adopted by the Continental socialist leaders at the end of the nineteenth century. His efforts bore fruit during the opposition to fascism, but their roots have to be sought elsewhere, in his family, in the cultural life of Florence in the 1910s and 1920s, and in the experience of the First World War.

Carlo Rosselli was born in Rome on November 16, 1899, to a Jewish family with strong Mazzinian and liberal traditions. Some members of his father's family, the Rosselli-Nathans, had been exiled to London, where they became close collaborators of Giuseppe Mazzini, who died in Pisa in 1872, in the house of Rosselli's great-uncle Pellegrino Rosselli. Carlo's mother, Amelia Pincherle, brought into the family the liberal tradition of the Risorgimento. Her influence on her three male children was profound, particularly after she left her husband and moved from Rome to Florence in 1903.

Amelia Rosselli was a talented and well-known playwright, an assid-

---

[1] Nicola Tranfaglia, *Carlo Rosselli dall'interventismo a "Giustizia e Libertà"* (Bari: Laterza, 1968), pp. 11–12.

uous habituée of the nationalistic circles and avant-garde literary clubs that flourished in Florence during the first years of the century. Like many Italians, Amelia saw World War I as the fulfillment of the Risorgimento epic, the chance to complete the unification of the country by bringing in the northeastern regions of Trento and Trieste. Her patriotism was also affected by the liberation of the ghettos, which was promoted by the government of Rome. Like other Jews of her generation, Amelia experienced the first period of assimilation as a moment of great liberation, and for this reason she could not be anything but a strong supporter of the Italian constitutional monarchy. "We are Jewish," Amelia wrote to Carlo, "but *first of all* Italian."[2] Her "sentimental nationalism" left traces on her son, who acknowledged having become a socialist "in the conviction that the emancipation of the workers has to rest on an unshakable moral basis and to recover and integrate the tradition of the Risorgimento, which, until now, remained the patrimony of the few."[3]

According to Amelia Rosselli, the Hebrew religion had to remain an inner and private experience; it must be kept "within the heart" and have a uniquely moral character: "This was the only religious education I gave my children."[4] Religion should have the function of only keeping alive the faith in human dignity and solidarity. But was it not Christianity that instilled this formidable faith? So why, Carlo asked his mother, should we still be Jewish when Hebraism preaches "a differentiation among human beings"? Why not instead, answered his mother, combine the best of both religions—the universalism of Catholicism and the innerness of Judaism?[5]

Rosselli had never been a Zionist, even if in his youth he admired the idealism of young Zionists who were able "to sacrifice their whole

[2] From Amelia Rosselli's unpublished diary, quoted in Tranfaglia, *Carlo Rosselli*, p. 13. The Jews' faithfulness to Rome's governments also explains their substantial support for Mussolini's regime until the enforcement of the racial laws. Carlo Rosselli's generation broke this tradition. See Alexander Stille, *Benevolence and Betrayal: Five Italian Jewish Families under Fascism* (New York: Summit Books, 1991), particularly the first two sections, dedicated to the Ovazzas and Foas of Turin.

[3] From the letter Rosselli sent to the judge who was in charge of his trial in 1927, when he was arrested for having organized Turati's escape in France (see ahead); Carlo Rosselli, "Lettera al Giudice Istruttore," in Rosselli, *Opere scelte*, vol. 1, *Socialismo liberale*, ed. John Rosselli (Turin: Einaudi, 1973), pp. 492–93.

[4] In a speech delivered at the Hebrew Conference of Livorno in 1924, his brother Nello Rosselli said that he was a Jew only in the sense that he was "thirsty for religiosity"; "Ebraismo e Italianità," *Il Ponte* 13 (1957): 865.

[5] Amelia Rosselli to Carlo from Florence, January 31, 1919, in *Epistolario familiare: Carlo, Nello Rosselli alla madre (1914–1937)*, ed. Zeffiro Ciuffoletti with an introduction by Leo Valiani (Milan: Sugar, 1979), p. 92.

intellectual and material life to the attainment of an ideal that seems unattainable to me."[6] Echoes of this religious inner travail may still be heard in this book, particularly in Rosselli's effort to present the liberal socialist ideal, its longing for freedom and justice, as part of Western historical and cultural tradition: "Greek rationalism and the messianism of Israel. / The first contains a love of liberty, a respect for autonomies, a harmonious and detached conception of life. / In the second the sense of justice is entirely down-to-earth; there is a myth of equality, and a spiritual torment that forbids all indulgence" (p. 6).

From his mother Carlo also inherited a strong attachment to liberal ideals. Amelia had deeply absorbed Ibsen's heroic morality of modern times: the repugnance toward all forms of social convention, the insufferableness of every moralistic restriction on individual expression, the belief in women's liberation and in the centrality of individual consciousness, and, finally, the deep devotion to voluntarism and idealism.[7] Within the individual will—Rosselli learned in his youth—is the origin of both evil and good.[8] "We have a great need to create! To create and believe. Yes, if one does not believe one is unable to create. In every field, faith is the necessary premise of action." So Amelia wrote to Carlo after the war ended, when President Woodrow Wilson for a while seemed to represent the faith in a new solidarity among the peoples: "I hope Wilson doesn't go back to America."[9]

Voluntarism, antideterminism, and Bergsonism were the traits of Florentine cultural life at the time. Florence had been a true philosophical and literary workshop since the turn of the century. Here one could detect the earliest signs of the intellectual revolt against positivism and participate in the diffusion of Croce's idealism, James's pragmatism, and Bergson's and Sorel's voluntarism through the journals *Il Leonardo* and *La Voce*, founded by Giovanni Papini and Giuseppe Prezzolini. Here the critique of governmental liberalism, parliamentarism, and Marxist socialism took its first and decisive steps in Gaetano Salvemini's *L'Unità*, while Enrico Corradini's *Il Regno* spread the nationalistic delirium with the Nietzschean myth of the cleansing and rejuvenating function of war. Common to these enterprises was "the defense of all human dimensions, of spiritual life and human activity." Their enemy was scientistic ideology, the imprisonment of human reality in meta-

---

[6] Rosselli to his mother from London, Sept. 26, 1924, in *Epistolario familiare*, p. 235.

[7] Aldo Garosci, *Vita di Carlo Rosselli* (1946; reprint, Florence: Vallecchi, 1973), vol. 1, p. 8.

[8] From the lessons Luigi Russo delivered to the soldiers, among whom was Rosselli, in 1917; Tranfaglia, *Carlo Rosselli*, p. 21.

[9] Amelia to Carlo from Florence, January 31, 1919, in *Epistolario familiare*, p. 91.

historical and fixed structures.[10] These Florentine movements cultivated the idea that culture should play a political role by representing
the "anxiety for renewal," the intellectual open-mindedness and moral
freedom, and the civic passion felt especially by a young generation
anxious to participate fully in the destiny of its society, ready to go to
war. These intellectual movements grew up amid civil society, outside
official institutions and universities, where philosophy was "treated
merely as material for an antiquated educational program,"[11] and they
were able to infuse new life into cities, now teeming with clubs, cafés,
and magazines where young people coming from different social strata
and cultural backgrounds interacted and debated.[12]

Benedetto Croce, with his usual mastery, described the prewar decade as an age of idealistic restoration.

> The result of this restoration was a widening of the spiritual horizon.
> Great ideas which had been obscured shone once more with their former
> brightness, fertile lines of thought were again pursued, courage and zeal
> for speculation was reborn, the books of the great philosophers both
> ancient and modern were reopened, including even such special objects
> of detestation as Fichte and Hegel. Philosophy was no longer obliged to
> make excuses for itself or to conceal itself. . . . To those who remembered
> the stifling sense of oppression which marked the age of positivism, it
> seemed as if they had emerged into fresh air beneath a clear sky and amid
> green fields.[13]

The prewar decade was an age of both idealistic restoration and deep
and widespread antidemocratic sentiments, ambiguously open to
many contradictory solutions, an age in which the discovery of irrational factors in human action easily converted the young intellectuals
to irrationalism.[14] Echoing Freud without knowing it, Vilfredo Pareto
was planning to demonstrate that rationality was a "patina" covering

[10] Eugenio Garin, *Cronache di filosofia italiana, 1900–1943* (Bari: Laterza, 1955), p. 25.

[11] Benedetto Croce, *A History of Italy, 1870–1915*, trans. Cecilia M. Ady (Oxford:
Clarendon Press, 1929; 1st Italian edition, 1928), pp. 238–39.

[12] A fine description of Florence's cultural life before the war was given by one of its
protagonists, Julien Luchaire, director of the Institut de France in Florence, founded by
the University of Grenoble: *Confession d'un Français moyen*, 2 vols. (1945 and 1950; reprint,
Florence: Leo S. Olschki, 1965), vol. 1, pp. 161–65.

[13] Croce, *A History of Italy*, p. 238. "Being rich and independent, Croce could (in his *La
Critica*, the most luxurious among the Italian journals) mercilessly demolish old re-
nowned scholars and elevate new ones; he used to do so in a less adventurous way than
my young Florentine revolutionaries, because he was armed with an immense erudition" (Luchaire, *Confession* 1:187–88).

[14] Norberto Bobbio, *Profilo ideologico del Novecento* (1968; new ed., Turin: Einaudi,
1986), pp. 37–38.

an ocean of impulses, passions, and instincts that were waiting to be brought to the surface. Meanwhile, Giovanni Papini, the leader of the young irrationalists, ridiculing those "enlightened philanthropists" always ready to take care of their fellows, liked to think of human beings as shadows, worthy of the love a card player feels for cards. He invoked the manlike God to awaken his contemporaries from the lethargy induced by a decent, civil, and placid liberalism: "Dare to be crazy. Be brave, audacious, reckless, foolish. . . . Let us look for the terrible problems," leaving behind the sweat stink of the working class and the weak and debilitated democracy.[15]

The war masked conflicting dreams and hopes for a new society, for a new moral heroism, for a new world order based on the liberation of the poorest countries, for the revolution of all the oppressed people of the globe. The war also meant generosity, the will to sacrifice oneself, which transcended class interests, and finally the rejection of the Italian Socialist party's obstinate devotion to pacifism. On the contrary, wrote Rosselli in a youthful Florentine journal, war would start a new international brotherhood: Wilson, "the man more than human," revealed the "great and immense side of the war," that is, brotherhood among all the peoples of the earth.[16]

Moved by this spirit, Rosselli went to war in 1917, after his oldest brother had already been killed. The war was for him—as for many Italians of his generation—a decisive and terrible experience that converted hope into disillusion, passion into skepticism. The suffering and fear in the trenches had the power to equalize soldiers, who came from social classes that had never had the chance to interact before. Many intellectuals discovered the existence of another nation, extremely poor and illiterate, a nation of which only the socialists had spoken. "Departing with an abstract ideal . . . they have been placed in a position of understanding many things that otherwise, given the isolation of their class and profession, would certainly have eluded them."[17]

The war did not turn Rosselli into a socialist. It left him in a deep spiritual crisis, tired of the "old swollen world" and casting about for an ideal, shocked by so much violence and blood. Given his faith in will and action, his Mazzinian sense of duty, his intoxication with the masses, he could have become anything, as many of his age did: Fascist

---

[15] Ibid., chs. 3 and 4. The rise of nationalism is sketched by Luchaire, *Confession* 1:192–93.

[16] Rosselli's article "Wilson" appeared in the journal *Noi giovani* (We the young) on May 17, 1917; quoted in Tranfaglia, *Carlo Rosselli*, p. 20.

[17] Carlo Rosselli, "Inchiesta sui giovani (Guerra e fascismo)" (*Libertà*, May 15, 1924), quoted in Tranfaglia, *Carlo Rosselli*, p. 23.

or socialist, nationalist or democrat. He discovered he had only one certainty: the young generation could no longer accept the way of life, politics, and ideals of the period before the war—neither the old liberalism with its conservative paternalism nor the old socialism with its messianic waiting for a new humanity.

He was disoriented and still unable to take—as he wished to—a political position. Years later, writing to his mother from his forced seclusion on the island of Lipari, Rosselli compared those former days with the present ones: "Who knows how long the wave that is submerging us will be? . . . Certainly, it feels odd to think now of what my former life was. . . . A spiritual condition a little bit similar to the one I felt immediately after the war. . . . Do you remember? But today, unlike then, I do not feel upset and discouraged by the idea that an exceptional and necessarily transitional state of affairs is ending."[18]

The postwar period was characterized by political unrest, Fascist violence, and ineptitude on the part of parliamentary parties. For a while Rosselli suspended his search for a political commitment and directed his energies toward scholarly work. In 1921 he graduated in economics from the Institute of Social Sciences in Florence; in 1923 he received a degree in law at the University of Siena (both dissertations were on syndicalism, but whereas the first was devoted to a political analysis, the second focused on the economic theory of the trade unions). In this period he became friends with Julien and Jean Luchaire, two important figures in the international democratic movement (several years later, the latter would become "one of the worst German agents in Paris,")[19] and Gaetano Salvemini, the most prominent and open-minded Italian intellectual of the time and the moral educator of a whole generation, from Rosselli and Piero Gobetti to Antonio Gramsci. Salvemini represented a new, emerging socialism deeply devoted to democratic ideals and strongly critical of Marxist

[18] Rosselli to his mother from Lipari, March 15, 1928, in *Epistolario familiare*, p. 407.

[19] Garosci, *Vita di Carlo Rosselli* 1:13. The reasons that led Jean Luchaire to fascism were depicted well by his father, Julien; they can be broadened to include all those among the generation who experienced the First World War and embraced antidemocratic ideologies: "So, when I thought of my son and his friends, I realized that they have but a contemporary culture, that they lack those sensibilities and scruples that come from a familiarity with the past. . . . My son never knew the generation of liberals among whom I had my friends. And his 'realism' made him less sensitive to the moral aspects of a political regime [fascism] that I could not stand" (Luchaire, *Confession* 2:239–40). In the 1920s, Julien Benda had identified the glorification of what is "practical" as one of the characteristics of twentieth-century intellectuals: "Nothing could show better how profound the modern 'clerk's' desire to exalt the real, the practical side of existence, and to degrade the ideal is" (*The Treason of the Intellectuals*, trans. Richard Aldington [1928; reprint, New York and London: Norton, 1969, 1st French edition 1927], pp. 100–101).

philosophy, which, for him, had become an arid and dogmatic system, useless for political action. "Marxism," wrote Salvemini, "is a marvelous filter with which to wake up sleeping souls. But he who engages in excess becomes foolish."[20]

After his graduation, Rosselli taught economics at the University of Turin, then at the Bocconi University of Milan (where he became acquainted with Piero Sraffa),[21] and finally in Genoa. During these years (1923 to 1926) he wrote several important essays against free-market ideology (whose Italian leader was Luigi Einaudi), which he distinguished from liberalism; the latter he interpreted—along with Piero Gobetti—as an "ethical conception" able to have an emancipatory effect on the workers.[22] His most significant experiences in these cities came from outside the university. His stay in Turin (then the major Italian industrial city) between 1922 and 1923, years of great social and political tensions, was particularly important. Here, a long and hard season of strikes was ending (1919–1921). Gramsci had already elaborated his version of workshop democracy (*consigli di fabbrica*) and founded *L'Ordine Nuovo*, one of the most original political journals of the time, marked by the spirit of sacrifice and search for freedom of its founder—a man, wrote Gobetti, motivated by "the spiritual necessity of those who have rejected and repudiated a native innocence."[23]

It was not Gramsci, however, who interested Rosselli the most, but the intellectuals gathered around Piero Gobetti and his journal *La Ri-*

[20] Gaetano Salvemini, "Una pagina di storia antica," *Il Ponte* 6 (1950): 131. At the end of his description of Salvemini's cultural activity during the war years, his friend Julien Luchaire wrote: "Ten years after, the 'Barbarian,' as we used to call Salvemini [because of his indomitable polemic spirit], gained exile instead of laurels. And he deserved it. Indeed, being a liberal revolutionary is a wager that no prudent man has to risk" (*Confession* 1:190).

[21] Sraffa, who was teaching at the University of Perugia, elaborated on his critique of the classic theory of market competition, which "probably marked Rosselli's economic thought deeply" (Tranfaglia, *Carlo Rosselli*, p. 135).

[22] Carlo Rosselli, "Per la storia della logica. Economia liberale e movimento socialista" (1923); "Contraddizioni liberiste" (1923); "Luigi Einaudi e il movimento operaio" (1924); and "Il liberismo di Giretti" (1926), now in *Opere scelte* 1: 29–61. According to Rosselli's critique of the theories of Walras and Pareto, neither pure competition nor monopoly was able to portray the real condition of present society, within which the two theories were blended: "Without using the expression that would become famous, Rosselli seems to mean something analogous to 'monopolistic antagonism,' on which, following a previous essay by Piero Sraffa, Joan Robinson and Edward H. Chamberlain would write in the 1930s" (Tranfaglia, *Carlo Rosselli*, p. 231).

[23] Piero Gobetti, "Gramsci," *La Rivoluzione Liberale. Saggio sulla lotta politica in Italia* (1924), now in id., *Opere complete*, vol. 1, *Scritti politici*, ed. Paolo Spriano (1960; reprint, Turin: Einaudi, 1969), p. 1003.

voluzione Liberale (Liberal revolution),[24] an unorthodox group that, contrary to the traditional interpretation of liberalism, considered the working class, then aiming to become an autonomous political actor, as the modern expression of the "liberal spirit." Gobetti tackled the relationship between theory and politics in a way that Rosselli certainly must have appreciated. In an article with the provocative title "Elogio della ghigliottina" (In praise of the guillotine), Gobetti denounced the Enlightenment tradition for its abstractness and its tendency to conceive of politics as a matter of implementing rational principles while underestimating the importance of beliefs and tradition. The Enlightenment regarded the social and historical world as identical with an intellectual world "stiffly conceived, made by clear and distinct ideas, not dialectical and without nuances or shadows."[25] When the French revolutionary armies invaded Italy to turn it into a republic, they "imposed the revolution on a people from the outside"; as a result, they caused the Italians to hate both republican institutions and their principles.[26] For Gobetti, political ideals were not "abstractions to be materialized"; they were modeled on the concrete reality of a people and could not but be regulative ideas (*idea-limite*). The same reasons motivated Gramsci to write *Against "Capital"* and Rosselli to dissociate socialism from Marxism. Both liberals and socialists were reaffirming the humanism of Italian political thought. In the country of Machiavelli and Vico, wrote Norberto Bobbio, it would have been hard to subordinate political action and historical creation to some abstract model or to ironclad laws.[27]

In Gobetti's magazine in July 1924 Rosselli published the article "Liberalismo socialista" (Socialist liberalism), in which he anticipated

[24] Piero Gobetti (1901–1926) was one of the most original and brilliant intellectuals of his time. He was born in Turin to a poor petit-bourgeois family who owned a grocery store. Deeply attached to his regional cultural traditions, he absorbed a liberal-democratic ideology from the Florentine journals *La Voce* and *L'Unità*. Strongly opposed to all kinds of paternalism, he interpreted liberalism as an untiring conflict and an overcoming. He was against protectionist policies and prized class conflict as the best liberal expression of modern industrial society. He admired Giovanni Gentile's idealistic interpretation of Marxism and saw in the Communists led by Gramsci the first modern political movement of Italy. In his short life, from the time he was a high school student, Gobetti founded important journals, among them *Energie Nuove* (1918) and *La Rivoluzione Liberale* (1922). They were the leading expressions of the political and intellectual climate of those creative years. In September 1924 he was wounded in an assault by the Fascists; he died two years later in Paris.

[25] Piero Gobetti, "Elogio della ghigliottina" (1922), now in *Le riviste di Piero Gobetti*, ed. Lelio Basso and Luigi Anderlini (Milan: Feltrinelli, 1961), p. 291.

[26] Piero Gobetti, "Manifesto" of *La Rivoluzione Liberale* (1922), ibid., p. 101.

[27] Norberto Bobbio, Introduction to Rodolfo Mondolfo, *Umanesimo di Marx: Studi filosofici, 1908–1966* (Turin: Einaudi, 1968), pp. xlvii–xlviii.

themes developed subsequently in the book *Socialismo liberale*.[28] That year he began his militant socialism (after Giacomo Matteotti was murdered by the Fascists in 1924, he enrolled in the social-democratic party known as Partito Socialista Unitario) and antifascism.

In Florence, which Rosselli never left even while teaching in the north, Salvemini was the most energetic inspirer of the earliest anti-Fascist cultural activities. In 1921 he had founded the Circolo di Cultura (a study circle), which in 1923 Rosselli transformed into a cultural association devoted to discussing historical, economic, and sociological problems and "open to all the free mainstreams of modern thought." The Circolo was the first important antifascist association to which Rosselli committed himself, along with his brother Nello, by then a brilliant historian and author of the book *Mazzini e Bakunin*. At the Circolo Rosselli met his future wife, Marion Cave, a young Englishwoman who, so she said then, had come to Italy to contribute to "the socialist revolution" and "die on the barricades."[29] Demolished by the Fascists—who also pillaged Rosselli's house—the Circolo was permanently closed by Mussolini's regime in January 1925, when "special laws" were instituted to suppress all forms of political and intellectual opposition.[30]

It is almost impossible to separate Rosselli's intellectual life from his political one. His dissertations on syndicalism show his interest in the labor movement, particularly its self-governing organizations, such as cooperatives, mutual societies, trade unions, and guilds. Unlike Croce, Rosselli never felt enthusiastic about opening the books of Fichte and Hegel. His inveterate aversion to German idealism was as proverbial as his admiration for English empiricism and liberalism, which inspired a strong interest in English socialism and led him to mistrust the theorists and followers of German professorial socialism. Rosselli's antidogmatic critique of Marxist socialism followed his journeys to England.

Rosselli went to England three times, in 1922 (to improve his English), 1923, and 1924, the last two with the explicit purpose of enrich-

[28] The year before, in the journal *La Critica Sociale* Rosselli had published another article under the same title (both are now in Rosselli, *Scritti politici*, ed. Zeffiro Ciuffoletti and Paolo Bagnoli [Naples: Guida, 1988]). Both articles indicate that Rosselli conceived of the project of a liberal socialism immediately after his participation in the socialist congress of Livorno as an alternative to the party's poverty of ideals. Rosselli worked on this project for many years, through discussions, articles, and readings that testify to the fact that the formula "liberal socialism" was not an abstract intuition, but the result of a spiritual and cultural travail and reflection on the concrete conditions of Italian society.

[29] Garosci, *Vita di Carlo Rosselli* 1:37.

[30] The story of the pillaging of both the Circolo di Cultura and Rosselli's house is narrated by Salvemini in "Il regno del manganello," in id., *Opere*, vol. 6, *Scritti sul fascismo*, t. 1 (Milan: Feltrinelli, 1961), pp. 111–12.

ing his knowledge of economics at the London School of Economics and studying the evolution of socialism, especially cooperation and guild socialism. In August 1923 he participated in the Fabian fortnight; on this occasion, through R. H. Tawney—who had been in Florence several months before to lecture at the Circolo di Cultura—Rosselli became acquainted with the Webbs and G.D.H. Cole.[31] He then participated in the Annual Congress of the Trade Unions (1923) and the Congress of the Labour Party (1924).

He wrote important articles and several fine letters to his mother about his English experiences; in those letters he told of the astonishing impression the "modern life" of the industrial city made on him, where public services worked perfectly and the masses of hurrying people made one feel like a god.[32] He appreciated the deep empiricism of the English socialists but was annoyed by their parochialism: "Here they care about fascism as much as they care about Kemal Pasha's insurrection."[33] He felt the same ambiguity when he met the Webbs, whom he described as interesting but superficial. He had read and appreciated *Industrial Democracy*, a "magnificent study" that, along with Sorel's writings on syndicalism, had been the main source for his dissertations. He found the Webbs' attempt to connect liberalism and socialism in the name of J. S. Mill particularly interesting.

Rosselli was not the only admirer of English socialism in Italy.[34] But G.D.H. Cole's guild socialism and the Webbs' cooperation were for him two important examples of the evolution of the reformist method within both the political and the economic socialist movement. Indeed, given the bureaucratic statism in both Soviet collectivism and Fascist corporatism, English socialism represented for him an alternative because of its concern for social movements.

Precisely because of his aversion to all kinds of centralism, Rosselli thought that guild socialism was superior to the Webbs' cooperation. He never committed himself to Fabian socialism, primarily because of its adherence to a positivist view of moral and social progress, a grad-

[31] Rosselli also met Keynes, on whose *Tract on Monetary Reform* he wrote an article for the journal *La Riforma Sociale*. See "Keynes sulla riforma monetaria," now in *Opere scelte* 1:264–68.

[32] "If the individual, submerged by the masses like a little straw in the universe, does not count for anything from an objective point of view, from a subjective one he is a god" (Rosselli to his mother, London, July 28, 1923, in *Epistolario familiare*, p. 175).

[33] Ibid., p. 177.

[34] See Maurizio Degli Innocenti, "Carlo Rosselli e il movimento sindacale: Dalla tesi di laurea a 'Socialismo liberale,'" in *Giustizia e Libertà nella storia antifascista e nella storia d'Italia: Atti del Convegno Internazionale organizzato a Firenze il 10–12 giugno 1977* (Florence: La Nuova Italia, 1978), pp. 54–56.

ual evolution toward a higher stage of organic society.[35] His mistrust of the Webbs' socialism gradually increased over the years, until he was not surprised to discover their tendency to undervalue democratic institutions. In 1936, commenting on their book *Soviet Communism*, Rosselli wrote: "I remember that the Webbs, years ago, secretly admired even [Fascist] corporatism, which they studied through the laws passed by Minister Rocco."[36] Contrary to the Webbs, Rosselli did not feel any attraction for a society regulated from the top; nor did he cultivate the myth of efficiency and planned happiness. On this argument his position was similar to that of his close friend Elie Halévy, who clearly discerned the two contradictory roots of socialism, the libertarian and the authoritarian.[37]

The Fabian undervaluation of democratic institutions was indeed the main reason that English and Italian socialists disagreed. In 1927 Salvemini engaged in a harsh polemic with George Bernard Shaw, who perceived only two political alternatives—perfect democracy and oligarchy—and concluded that, given the impossibility of the former, between the British and the Italian oligarchy, the latter was preferable, because at least it presented itself explicitly as an oligarchy. "But a chair, an elephant, and a tiger," commented Salvemini, "which indeed all have four legs, are not the same thing."[38]

Still, in 1933 and 1936, when Rosselli went to England to lecture and obtain support for the League of Nations' sanctions against Mussolini's

[35] See Carol Seymour-Jones, *Beatrice Webb: A Life* (Chicago: Ivan R. Dee, 1992), ch. 7.

[36] Carlo Rosselli, "Stampa amica e nemica" (*Giustizia e Libertà*, February 14, 1936), quoted in Garosci, *Vita di Carlo Rosselli* 2:351. Alfredo Rocco, Mussolini's minister, wrote the Fascist criminal code; he was the most prominent theorist of Fascist corporatism. The identification of syndicalism with corporatism was one of the reasons that led some foreign observers to appreciate Mussolini's social polities. On Rocco's Fascist idea of the state, see Silvio Trentin, *Aux sources du fascisme* (Paris: Marcel Rivière, 1931), pp. 112–20. On Giustizia e Libertà's judgment of Stalinism, see Santi Fedele, *E verrà un'altra Italia. Politica e cultura nei "Quaderni di Giustizia e Libertà"* (Milan: Franco Angeli, 1992), pp. 72–79.

[37] Elie Halévy, *Histoire du Socialisme Européen* (Paris: Gallimard, 1948, 1st. ed. 1940), pp. 19–23. But whereas Rosselli believed in the possibility of bringing about socialism within the liberal-democratic institutions, Halévy never resolved his doubts concerning the socialist "enigma." See also Elie Halévy, *L'ère des tyrannies. Etudes sur le socialisme et la guerre* (Paris: Gallimard, 1938), pp. 213–27.

[38] Gaetano Salvemini, "G. B. Shaw e il fascismo" (1927), now in id., *Opere*, vol. 6, *Scritti sul fascismo*, t. 2 (Milan: Feltrinelli, 1974), p. 316. Salvemini alluded to an article by Shaw published in the *Manchester Guardian* (October 28, 1927), where he had written that Mussolini had brought order after chaos and compelled the Italians to go to work. Indeed, for him a government's main purpose was to help society get along, "freedom or no freedom"; quoted in Salvemini, "Il 'bolscevismo' italiano negli anni 1919 e 1920," in id., *Opere*, vol. 6, *Scritti sul fascismo*, t. 3, p. 136.

government, he was disappointed by the attention the socialists paid—even G.D.H. Cole—to corporatism. Many of them had to experience the Spanish civil war before they could understand the essential role of democracy in socialism and, more generally, in any reformist project.[39]

Liberal socialism wanted to be an alternative to statism, in both its Bolshevist and Fascist versions. This was also intended for the so-called third way (*terza via*), the most important political and theoretical legacy of Giustizia e Libertà (Justice and Freedom, the movement founded by Rosselli) to the Party of Action (Partito d'Azione), the clandestine anti-Fascist party that was born in Rome in 1942, several years after Rosselli's assassination, and that disappeared at the beginning of the Cold War. The liberal-socialist third way integrated Rosselli's revision of socialism with a revision of liberalism just as profound. As one of the founders of the Party of Action wrote, the critique of free-market ideology had been the core of corporatism, through which fascism wanted to establish its theoretical and political superiority to liberalism. The ideology of corporatism, which reached its greatest popularity in the 1930s, helped to emphasize economic factors that in the end appeared to be no less fundamental for the Fascists than for the free-market theorists. Moreover, by identifying the ideology of the free market with liberalism, fascism left intact—inadvertently—the ideal dimension of political liberalism, which little by little contributed to unveiling the bureaucratic and materialistic character of Fascist corporatism.

The rediscovery of the moral value of liberty and political activity by the generation of intellectuals who grew up after the collapse of liberal institutions had the extraordinary effect of pressing them to address the relationship, now no longer between free market and collectivism, but between liberalism and socialism, that is, not between a free market and a planned economy, but between the values of liberty and equality and their concrete impact on everyday life.[40] During their search they found in Rosselli an illuminating guide, even though they perceived that they had to go farther.[41] Indeed, Rosselli came from within the socialist movement, and his major problem was ridding it of Marxist economism. The intellectuals who founded the Party of Action and called themselves liberal-socialists undertook a similar

[39] Gaetano Salvemini, "L'opinione pubblica all'opera" (1936), in id., *Opere*, vol. 3, *Preludio alla Seconda guerra mondiale*, t. 3 (Milan: Feltrinelli, 1967), p. 512.

[40] Guido Calogero, "Ricordi del movimento liberalsocialista" (1944), in id., *Difesa del liberalsocialismo* (Roma: Atlantica, 1945), pp. 193–94. Guido Calogero and Aldo Capitini were the major interpreters of the liberal-socialist ideology of the Party of Action.

[41] Guido Calogero, "Il socialismo liberale di Carlo Rosselli" (1945), in ibid., p. 125.

revision of the liberal tradition,[42] in particular that represented by Benedetto Croce.[43] Yet they were driven by the same impulse that had motivated Rosselli's revisionism: an awareness that the political moment had a value superior to the economic one. This was the main reason Rosselli intended liberal socialism to be both antistatist and antibureaucratic, so as to combine the best of the liberal and socialist traditions.

Echoing Mill's famous statement in *On Liberty*, Rosselli wrote in 1935 that "universal socialization would be deleterious. A State that leads the whole economy would be a monster of oppression, even though its representatives were elected and controlled." According to Rosselli, the social sector should remain autonomous, articulated, and pluralistic, because its multiplicity constituted "a providential safeguard against the power of the State and social groups. . . . A partial socialization is a guarantee of freedom. Universal socialization is the cause of slavery."[44] This allows us to understand Rosselli's insistence on the "moral factor," his idea that "the proof of [socialist] effort must be found not in the history of the party, . . . but in the life of the cooperatives, the rural circles, the mutual and cultural societies," that is, in civil society, where the political and moral emancipation of the largest majority began.[45] His polemic was against a state—the Fascist state—that nullified the autonomy of civil society by incorporating its movements and associations but did not go so far as to become a new version of free market liberalism. Liberal socialism intended to combine various solutions, such as free enterprise, cooperation, and state intervention, to secure public services. Its antistatism was directed in particular against the state running the economy, not against the state providing for social services. Here Rosselli's originality emerges once more: just as the antidemocratic years before and after the war had made him a

[42] They intended to combine the two substantives liberalism and socialism, so as to mark the fact that they came to that conclusion from both directions. The liberal-socialist movement "was born as a post-Fascist antifascism," that is, not by vindicating the old liberal ideals and institutions of the pre-Fascist era. One of its major centers was the Scuola Normale Superiore of Pisa, the prestigious institution for advanced studies reshaped by Giovanni Gentile, the spiritual leader of Fascist ideology. See Calogero, "Ricordi del movimento liberalsocialista," pp. 191–93.

[43] Croce's role in the growth of antifascism within the young generation was extraordinarily important especially after he subscribed to the manifesto against fascism in 1925. "There was a time when Croce was the *livre de chevet*, the secret reading, of the best Italian youth. For them the ponderous volumes of Croce had the same fascination that a forbidden romance would have in other times" (ibid., p. 193).

[44] Quoted in Garosci, *Vita di Carlo Rosselli* 2:342.

[45] Carlo Rosselli, "Filippo Turati e il socialismo italiano" (*Quaderni di "Giustizia e Libertà*," June 1932), now in *Scritti politici*, p. 244.

voluntarist but not an antidemocrat, the reaction against statism made him a defender of civil society but not a free-market ideologue.

The deep connection that Rosselli perceived between liberty and justice was certainly the result of his reflections on fascism. From this his critique of Marxist socialism originated as well. As one of the protagonists of Italian revisionism wrote in 1923, Marxism underestimated the importance of human rights, the fate of human liberty, which is either individual liberty or merely a "new mockery that follows the many others suffered by the individual throughout history."[46] What made Italian socialism original—and this may also be true for the Communist party after World War II—was the fact that its renaissance in the twentieth century was deeply marked by reflection on the Fascist phenomenon and the understanding that the defeat of liberal democracy was also a defeat for socialism. Thus, as Rosselli stressed, socialism needs political and civil liberties; in turn, these liberties need a politics of social justice to remain alive.

Rosselli personally experienced the consequences of the devaluation of civil and political liberties. His voluntarism inspired in him the belief that the only way to take a stand against oppression was by active resistance. "The will of a man who puts his stamp on a dull environment changes the environment in the very moment that it changes the man."[47] In the first issue of *Non Mollare* (Don't Give Up) (1925) one reads: "They do not concede freedom of speech: we will take it. In the title is our program."[48]

From 1925 onward, Rosselli's life was an impressive odyssey of clandestine initiatives. Immediately after the Fascists had destroyed the Circolo di Cultura, he founded two journals, *Non Mollare* and *Il Quarto Stato* (The Fourth Estate), the latter with Pietro Nenni, the future leader of the Italian Socialist party. With other friends (among them Sandro Pertini, who in the late 1970s became president of the Italian Republic, and Ferruccio Parri, the prime minister of the first government after the Second World War) he led a clandestine organization with the purpose of helping the most prominent anti-Fascist leaders to escape from Italy.

In 1927 (the year after Gramsci was jailed), having made possible the emigration of Filippo Turati, the father of Italian socialism, Rosselli and and his comrades were captured and confined first to Ustica, then Lipari, two small Mediterranean islands. On Lipari, between 1928 and 1929, he wrote *Socialismo liberale*. "Even a superficial reading of *Socialismo liberale*," wrote Aldo Garosci, "is enough to prove Rosselli's will

[46] Arturo Labriola, "Socialismo e libertà" (1923), in Tranfaglia, *Carlo Rosselli*, p. 165.
[47] Garosci, *Vita di Carlo Rosselli* 1:56.
[48] Ibid., p. 42.

not to finish his days in Lipari. This is a book that leads naturally to action."[49] As Rosselli himself said of his days in Lipari, "Here I have many friends. Life is not too bad. I read, study and, in secret, write. But I am sick, already sick of the island, sick to death of this chicken-coop existence, of this false appearence of liberty. . . . No, no, I wasn't born to live in a chicken coop."[50]

Rosselli and his friends escaped in the summer of 1929. The flight was memorable, worthy of the best tradition of romantic adventure. It created a sensation all over Europe, and thanks to Francesco F. Nitti's book *Escape*, in the United States as well.[51] The manuscript *Socialismo liberale* was purloined in Paris by Rosselli's wife when she left the island with their first child.[52]

In Paris, in October 1929, Rosselli and his friends founded Giustizia e Libertà—"among all the Italian anti-Fascist movements . . . the only one that was born and grew up after the advent of fascism."[53] This was the first organization in exile devoted entirely to promoting a clandestine insurrectional and anti-Fascist movement in Italy and the first to use modern equipment for action and propaganda (after several failed attempts, the escape from Lipari became possible through the use of a motorboat).[54] The first anti-Fascists affiliated with Giustizia e Libertà belonged to the early political emigration (between 1922 and 1927), and apart from the "heretical socialist" Rosselli, most were liberals and republicans (the latter, given their Mazzinian background, had a propensity for conspiratorial action). To this group—whose first act was to organize the flight from Lipari—Rosselli brought "his impetuous nature," and above all his patrimony, without which the organization could not have survived.

Like Rosselli's liberal socialism, Giustizia e Libertà was based on voluntarism (the "moral factor"), freedom, and pluralism. As Garosci

[49] Ibid., p. 141.

[50] Carlo Rosselli, "Fuga in quattro tempi" (*Almanacco socialista*, 1931), now in *Opere scelte* 1:514–15.

[51] Francesco F. Nitti, *Escape: The Personal Narrative of a Political Prisoner Who Was Rescued from Lipari* (New York: Putnam, 1930). The flight was narrated also by Emilio Lussu, "A Thousand to One" and "The Flight from Lipari," in *Atlantic Monthly* (June and July 1930): 721–32, 31–42.

[52] In the course of the many police searches Rosselli's family suffered in Lipari, the manuscript "migrated for some periods into a piano and the rabbit hutch in the garden." See Marion Cave Rosselli, "Lettera della moglie," in Carlo Rosselli, *Socialismo liberale*, first Italian edition (Rome: Edizioni U, 1945), p. 4.

[53] Carlo Rosselli, "Capirci" (*Giustizia e Libertà*, December 21, 1934), now in *Scritti politici*, p. 308.

[54] Also memorable was the airplane flight over Milan in May 1930 that dropped a cascade of leaflets denouncing the regime and urging political revolt.

pointed out, the fact that it had few resources gave the movement "an impulse otherwise improbable." Giustizia e Libertà did not have a hierarchy and did not become an organization composed of "functionaries." Because its members were not employed by it, they were independent and spiritually motivated.[55] Another original element was that Giustizia e Libertà was formed outside of the existing parties already active in exile. Free from any party's discipline, the members, though committed to different political ideas, were devoted to the welfare of Giustizia e Libertà and avoided the restless discussions and divisions that often transformed clandestine groups into sectarian and internally discordant organizations. Giustizia e Libertà intended to be a national (in the sense of nonpartisan) organization, the inspiration for a second Risorgimento, this time able to unify and involve all social classes in the struggle for liberty and justice. Its propaganda materials were written for, and distributed to, "soldiers, priests, students, workers," "white-collar employees," small industrialists, and farmers. "All these publications show a great variety of cultural interests, a profound capacity to understand the various political tendencies, which had not been seen since Gobetti's *rivoluzione liberale*."[56] "People came to the movement," wrote Rosselli in 1937, "from all parties: there were socialists, Communists, democrats, republicans, Sardinian autonomists, pupils of Gobetti, Gramsci, and Salvemini, intellectuals without party. The very young came to the rebellion on their own path, passing through a spiritual solitude imposed by the tyranny."[57] Among them I mention Carlo Levi, Luigi Salvatorelli, Vittorio Foa, Norberto Bobbio, the literary critic Leone Ginsburg, the musical critic Massimo Mila, the writer Cesare Pavese (all of them active in Turin),[58] Nicola Chiaromonte, the jurist Silvio Trentin, and Gaetano Salvemini (already in exile).

Internal dissension occurred, however, especially between members of the exiled branch on one hand and the domestic branch on the other. Eager to go beyond "action for the sake of action," Carlo Levi from Turin was one of the first to express the need for a political program. The transition to this political phase started in 1931. On this occasion Rosselli emerged as a natural leader who aided the political alliance with the Socialist party and finally succeeded in writing the *Revolutionary Program of "Giustizia e Libertà"* (1932) along with, among others, Gaetano Salvemini, Carlo Levi, and Emilio Lussu, the leader of Sardinian autonomism.

[55] Garosci, *Vita di Carlo Rosselli* 1:175.

[56] Ibid., pp. 181–83.

[57] Carlo Rosselli, "Giustizia e Libertà" (*Giustizia e Libertà*, May 14, 1937), now in *Scritti politici*, p. 397.

[58] For useful information on these anti-Fascists and their activities, see Stille, *Benevolence and Betrayal*, in particular the chapter titled "The Foas of Turin."

The basic principles of the program, which was devoted to shaping the new, post-Fascist Italian society, were parliamentary democracy, large regional autonomies (almost a federal system), and workshop democracy (councils and unions).[59] Regarding the economic and social sector, the proposal's aim was to combine different solutions, like the nationalization of the most vital services, cooperation, and free enterprise: civil society was conceived as a sort of federation of federations.[60] The program, Rosselli wrote, "was based on the concepts of autonomy and councils inherited by the *L'Ordine Nuovo* and by *La Rivoluzione Liberale*," that is, by Gramsci and Gobetti.[61] The program, as well as the book, was strongly criticized by the anti-Fascist parties, especially because it sounded too moderate, too timid, in envisaging the "new Italy." The socialists complained that Giustizia e Libertà did not recognize the working class as the only, or the major, political and social protagonist, the Communists that it conceived only of a democratic revolution. To Trotsky, whom Rosselli met in 1934, he tried in vain to explain that "our revolutionary liberalism has nothing to do with bourgeois liberalism, that the struggle against a Fascist dictatorship compels even the Communists to put the passwords liberty and democracy first."[62]

In 1932 the movement started to publish its own journal, *Quaderni di "Giustizia e Libertà"* (Papers of "Justice and Freedom"), which expressed the inner pluralism of the movement.[63] It was Rosselli, however, who put his stamp on the journal with his polemic against the dogmatism and sectarianism that were widespread among the anti-Fascists and his

[59] Carlo Rosselli, "Chiarimenti al Programma" (*Quaderni di "Giustizia e Libertà,"* January 1932) now in id., *Opere scelte*, vol. 2, *Scritti dell'esilio*, ed. Costanzo Casucci, t. 1, "*Giustizia e Libertà" e la Concentrazione antifascista, 1929–1934* (Turin: Einaudi, 1988), pp. 35–49.

[60] Carlo Rosselli, "Discussione sul federalismo e l'autonomia" (*Giustizia e Libertà*, December 27, 1935), now in id., *Opere scelte*, vol. 2, *Scritti dell'esilio*, ed. Costanzo Casucci, t. 2, *Dallo scioglimento della Concentrazione antifascista alla guerra di Spagna, 1934–1937* (Turin: Einaudi, 1992), pp. 261–65.

[61] Rosselli, "Giustizia e Libertà," p. 399. Giustizia e Libertà's socialism was "autonomist, federalist, and liberal" (Fedele, *E verrà un'altra Italia*, p. 195).

[62] Trotsky's negative judgment of Giustizia e Libertà derived mainly from a comparison with the Bolsheviks. In answer to Trotsky's criticisms, Rosselli reconstructed the origin of the liberal socialist ideal: "I talked to him of the Italian movements, of the journal *Rivoluzione Liberale* that since the 1920s defended the Russian revolution by exalting its liberal values and fought in favor of an intransigent class struggle led by workers avant-garde. . . . I presented him with data, our battle, which had endured since 1920, our program" (Carlo Rosselli, "Incontro con Trotski" [*Giustizia e Libertà*, May 25, 1934], quoted in Tranfaglia, *Carlo Rosselli*, p. 11 and n. 1).

[63] The *Quaderni* came out as a quarterly between January 1932 and January 1935. It was a journal of political culture devoted to an intellectual debate. Along with it there was *Giustizia e libertà*, a weekly political bulletin that lasted until after Rosselli was killed.

desire to escape the old ideological labels: "Instead of aiming at a 'renaissance' [of the political values of pre-Fascist Italy], Giustizia e Libertà must venture to give life within itself to the movements of tomorrow." He refused to identify himself and the movement with any party: after the collapse of fascism the new reality would bring forth new problems and new parties. To subordinate the future to any existing political groups—all of them an expression of a reality deeply marked by fascism—would be a mistake.[64] This conclusion, so intelligent and yet so difficult for the anti-Fascist parties to grasp, was inspired by his deep awareness of the peculiar condition of exiles, "almost always very bad judges" both of the politics of the country in which they live and those of their own.[65]

In one of his last articles Rosselli wrote:

> What will Giustizia e Libertà leave us? First of all it will leave the need for a substantial renewal of the political struggle of the workers. Then an uninterrupted tradition of action and initiative; a lucid and disenchanted interpretation of fascism, not simply as a phenomenon of class reaction, but as a debacle of the whole society. It will leave an intimate relationship with the culture and history of our own country, not in the sense of a vulgar patriotism, but as the adhesion to that national reality from which the Italian revolution against fascism will derive its creative originality. It will leave the acute consciousness of several problems that can be considered the problems of modern Italy (the formation of a new elite; the redemption of the south; the alliance between city and country; federalism) and above all a crucial preoccupation with liberty, a preoccupation not abstract and formal, but based on an active, positive, and emancipating idea of liberty and justice.[66]

Giustizia e Libertà's project to create a clandestine insurrectional movement in Italy failed after a few years. At the beginning of 1930 several activists were captured in various Italian cities. In May 1935 the whole Turinese group (the most active one) was arrested. Giustizia e Libertà, however, survived the persecutions, and even after the war, when the movement no longer existed, its ideals persisted in various intellectuals who, in spite of different experiences and allegiances, never ceased searching for a cooperative modus vivendi between liberalism and socialism. This was the case with the historians Franco Venturi, Enzo Tagliacozzo, and Max Salvadori, the writer Nicola Chiaro-

---

[64] Carlo Rosselli, "Realtà di oggi e prospettive di domani: In tema di successione" (*Giustizia e Libertà*, January 3, 1936), now in *Scritti politici*, pp. 327–28.

[65] Carlo Rosselli, "Pericoli dell'esilio" (*Giustizia e Libertà*, November 11, 1934), now in *Opere scelte*, vol. 2, t. 2, pp. 69–70.

[66] Rosselli, "Giustizia e Libertà," pp. 402–3.

monte, the union leader Vittorio Foa, and the legal and political theorist Norberto Bobbio.

But Giustizia e Libertà also survived abroad. It had branches in France, Germany, the United States, and England. In the United States, Salvemini found supporters in many universities, particularly in New York, Cambridge, Poughkeepsie, Providence, Los Angeles, and San Francisco. Among the American sympathizers of Giustizia e Libertà Max Salvadori mentions Bruce Bliven of *The New Republic*; Hamilton Fish Armstrong of *Foreign Affairs*; Frieda Kirchway of *The Nation*; Alvin Johnson of the New School for Social Research; Roger Baldwin, founder of the American Civil Liberties Union; the Supreme Court judge Felix Frankfurter; Norman Thomas; Lewis Mumford; Raymond Graham Swing; and Dorothy Thompson.[67] In 1937, immediately after the assassination of the Rosselli brothers, Salvemini became the inspirer of the Friends of Carlo and Nello Rosselli, a society devoted to publishing books on politics and social justice. Among the subscribers we find, in addition to the ones I have mentioned, John Dewey, Charles Beard, Charles Burlingham, Dorothy Canfield Fisher, Robert Hutchins, William A. Neilson and Frank Taussig.[68]

In 1936 Rosselli left Paris to fight in Spain. Along with the Spanish anarchists, Giustizia e Libertà had formed the Catalonian battalion. This would be the last of Rosselli's enterprises. Back in France, in Bagnoles de l'Orne—where he went with his family to recover from phlebitis before returning to Spain—he and his brother Nello (who was never active in the anti-Fascist movement) were assassinated by Mussolini's hired killers, in collaboration with the Pétainistes.[69] It was June 9, 1937, several weeks after Gramsci's death in prison.[70] Carlo Rosselli was thirty-seven years old. The assassination aroused strong emotions

[67] Max Salvadori, "Giellisti e loro amici negli Stati Uniti durante la Seconda guerra mondiale," in *Giustizia e Libertà nella lotta antifascista*, pp. 274–75.

[68] The first book of the collection was Gaetano Salvemini, *Carlo and Nello Rosselli: A Memoir*, with a preface by Ernest Backers (London: For Intellectual Liberty, 1937).

[69] Carlo was killed instantly by two stabs to the throat; Nello, struck by a less expert hand, died after seventeen stabs; Gaetano Salvemini, "Carlo e Nello Rosselli," *Il Ponte* 7 (1951): 455. In September 1944, the high court appointed to prosecute Fascist crimes declared the personal responsibility of Galeazzo Ciano and Benito Mussolini in ordering the Rossellis' assassination. In 1949, although the French cagoulards were sentenced, the Italians who participated in the assassination were absolved by a court in democratic Italy. See Garosci, *Vita di Carlo Rosselli* 2:514, and *Storia dei fuoriusciti* (Bari: Laterza, 1953), p. 281.

[70] A few weeks before, Rosselli had read a speech on Gramsci at the commemoration organized in Paris on Gramsci's behalf in which he compared two kinds of mankind: one represented by Mussolini and the other by Gramsci: "The one was external, noisy, irrational, an extemporizer, a demagogue, an adventurer . . . the other one inward, reserved, rational, severe, an enemy of the rhetoric and all sorts of easiness" ("Due climi politici: Due tipi d'umanità," in *Opere scelte*, vol. 2, t. 2, p. 542).

in Paris, where an immense crowd gathered at the cemetery of Père-Lachaise.[71]

The last of Rosselli's political actions was the famous slogan he uttered on radio Barcelona in 1936: Today in Spain, tomorrow in Italy (Oggi in Spagna, domani in Italia).[72] This phrase captured the essence of the new anti-Fascist generation reshaped by years of inner travail and divisions regarding the role it should play in the defeat of fascism.

The problem of whether to take part in an anti-Fascist war was a lacerating issue for members of the Italian Left. It was extremely difficult for them to abandon the pacifism that had been one of the strongest socialist commitments since World War I. But it was also difficult to decide to participate in a war against Italy (the Italian government was openly intervening against the Spanish republic). As Claudio Pavone wrote in his book on the Italian civil war, this ambiguity and uncertainty were felt especially by the Italian socialists, who in 1914 had assumed a much less antinationalist position than the other European socialist parties.[73]

The problem was dramatic. Rosselli had understood this immediately and clearly when Hitler came to power. In 1933, in *Quaderni di "Giustizia e Libertà,"* he wrote an article entitled "La guerra che torna" (The war is back): "It is sad to have to talk of war without thinking of the past. . . . The struggle between fascism and antifascism is going before the judgment of God. . . . War is coming, will come . . . Mussolini can proclaim even now his anathema against the betrayers of the Fascist fatherland."[74]

Once the war started, Giustizia e Libertà faced the problem of choosing between the nation and the ideals of freedom and justice with the same lucidity. None of the members hesitated in wishing the defeat of Italy, "even if 100 percent of the Italians were Italian by ethnic origin," wrote Altiero Spinelli, the spiritual father of the European Community.[75] At stake were "the institutions in which we placed our trust in a tolerable future." When we thought of these institutions, said Vittorio Foa, "we did not hesitate even a moment to desire the defeat of our country."[76] Certainly it was hard to reach this decision. "But [this de-

---

[71] Two hundred thousand people took part in or watched the funeral procession. The ashes of the Rosselli brothers were brought back to Florence in 1951.

[72] He then developed the argument in the article "Sul corso della guerra" (*Giustizia e Libertà*, January 15, 1937), now in *Scritti politici*, pp. 354–56.

[73] Claudio Pavone, *Una guerra civile: Saggio storico sulla moralità della Resistenza* (Turin: Bollati Boringhieri, 1991), p. 65.

[74] Carlo Rosselli, "La guerra che torna" (*Quaderni di "Giustizia e Libertà,"* November 1933), now in *Scritti politici*, pp. 273–74, 281–82.

[75] Pavone, *Una guerra civile*, p. 69.

[76] Ibid., p. 68.

sire] had its price, because a man does not end up desiring the ruin of all that is immediately closest to him without having thought long and hard, and without having faced the hostility and contempt of a multitude of his own fellows."[77]

The exceptional nature of a situation is shown by the drama of the choice it imposes. But, perhaps, as Pavone remarks, it is precisely in this exceptionality that the importance of values emerges. In that exceptional moment the loyalty to an ideal had to come before the sentiment of national or communal membership. Thus, in one who placed such importance on this sentiment, betrayal of this kind could better serve the ultimate cause. As Rosselli understood, *la patria* is not the same for everyone: to declare war on the Fascist fatherland was a way to profess one's faith in a free and more just patria. By betraying their nation, the anti-Fascists expressed the will to save and regenerate it— each according to his or her ideals of patria. There were as many patrie as there were ideals, and for this reason, in their dramatic choice, there was not, strictly speaking, a conflict between faithfulness to their people and faithfulness to their ideals. Sometimes, even in much less exceptional situations, closeness and distance are reversed, and that which seems to be a sign of ideological distance may in fact be a sign of closeness to one's people. What lies near us, what is empirically here, may be farther away than ideals apparently as abstract as those of liberty and justice.

Beyond the Ideological Walls

This book is fine enough to have succeeded in slipping
through the somewhat coarse fingers of immediate
comprehension and success, but I am convinced that in its
title there is a great deal of future.
(*Henri Pollès, 1937*)

Liberal Socialism is a book of theory with a practical aim.[78] It is composed of two parts; in the first Rosselli criticizes Marxism and revisionism, and in the second he sketches a liberal-democratic version of socialism.

[77] From the Party of Action's newsletter, *La Libertà*, September 8, 1943, the day of the Italian armistice with the Allies, quoted in ibid., p. 69.

[78] Norberto Bobbio, Introduction to Carlo Rosselli, *Socialismo liberale* (Turin: Einaudi, 1979), p. vii (this introduction has been an indispensable source for me).

Liberal Socialism is a fundamental work for historical as well as theoretical reasons. Historically, it inspired the movement Giustizia e Libertà, whose founders became the most respected political and intellectual leaders of postwar democratic Italy. *Liberal Socialism* is also an
essential document for understanding the debates among Italian anti-
Fascists and should be read, alongside Gramsci's *Prison Notebooks*, as a
key to understanding the reasons for fascism's defeat of the democratic
and socialist movement and for its pointing the way to a possible
rebirth.

Theoretically, it is important for its analysis of fascism and further for
its investigation of the history of Marxism and its innovative interpretation of the ideology and practice of socialism. Rosselli's analysis
provides an illuminating account of the ideological triumph of Marxism (in its determinist version) in the late nineteenth century and
shows the intellectual weakness of the revisionists' efforts to elaborate
new versions of Marx's doctrine.

Rosselli did not intend to add another interpretation of Marx's texts.
In this sense, *Liberal Socialism* does not belong to the crowded family of
revisionist literature but is a part of the complex phenomenon of the
crisis of Marxism that took place at the beginning of the century.[79] The
reader will immediately perceive the author's annoyance with the restless discussions on Marx's thought, which Rosselli considers theoretically useless and politically harmful. Those who are familiar with
never-ending and pedantic disquisitions on the holy texts will find
here a source of refreshment and a stimulus to intellectual freedom,
while the experts will perhaps discover some theoretical inaccuracy
behind Rosselli's critical furor. *Liberal Socialism*, however, is not an
academic book. It is the militant testimony of a young man who felt the
strong desire to escape the cage of sectarianism, "an explicit confession
of an intellectual crisis that I know to be widespread among the new
generation of socialists" (p. 5). It is valuable for both those who prize
intellectual freedom and those who value political commitment to a
moral idea. Without this moral idea, Rosselli writes, any political
project—even democracy—"is reduced to nothing more than a melancholy dream of bureaucrats" (p. 107).

Rosselli felt the need to separate socialism from Marxism in order to
put socialism in agreement with itself, with its liberal spirit. In pursuit
of this goal, he made two basic assertions: Marxism is a unified system,
and Marx is a classic of political thought. From the first point he drew
the conclusion that Marxism cannot be amended; from the second, that

---

[79] Regarding the crisis of Marxism in Italy, see Emilio Agazzi, *Il giovane Croce e il
marxismo* (Turin: Einaudi, 1962).

one can find some plausible ideas in Marx's works without being Marxist, indeed, that one can be Marxist without being socialist, and that one can be—*must* be—socialist without being Marxist.

Rosselli considers Marxism a Weltanschauung in which system and method are strictly combined, a system according to which history follows necessary laws. The mode of production lays down the rhythm of history and represents the real subject of history. The dialectical method is consistent with the category of necessity that entirely dominates human activity. No doubt Engels's positivism had much of the responsibility for promoting a reductionistic interpretation of Marx, but Engels did not betray the systematic spirit of Marx's thought.

Rosselli defines Marxism as a nonhumanism. Indeed, "the central problem of Marxism . . . lies in the role it assigns to the human element, to the factor of will" (p. 11). Marx's man is not free, and for this reason his socialism is the expression of economic necessity, not of belief. "Psychologically speaking, the Marxian man is no more than the *homo oeconomicus* of Bentham"; his reactions "are not spontaneous and autonomous but are caused by changes in the relations of production and thus in social relations" (p. 12). Marx focused only on the social transformation and postponed to a future society the possibility for human beings to realize themselves completely and freely, as if human beings could separate economic relations from other aspects of their lives. "Problems of consciousness, of autonomy, of the formation of free personalities, do not exist for Marx. They are all postponed to the new day following the social transformation. Nothing could be more utopian and antiliberal than this abrupt and messianic shift of position, this switch from a realm where inexorable necessity dominates to one where sovereign liberty reigns" (pp. 106–107).

Class struggle appears to be the result of a conscious effort. In reality, the will of the proletarians is not among the causes of revolution. In Marx's vision of history, moreover, there is little room for political propaganda, which in fact Marx considered a mistake, particularly if based on the idea of justice. Class consciousness has to mature by itself, as the outcome of social factors. It cannot be encouraged or stimulated.

Rosselli recognizes the existence of a discrepancy between Marx the scientist and Marx the political agitator. He sees only one voluntaristic moment in Marx's thought: in the doubt Marx had on the convenience of promoting revolutionary action once the social system reached its critical stage. But once one accepts a sphere of liberty, no matter how qualified, then the concept of historical necessity fails and the alternative arises. Historical necessity and politics are antithetical because politics needs moral freedom and implies possibility. If one wants to preserve the socialist ideal and a political commitment to it, one must abandon Marxism.

Rosselli's attitude toward liberalism is different. Liberalism is not a system but a method and a spiritual (or mental) attitude. As a political method, Rosselli identifies liberalism with the "democratic method," the method of pursuing a political goal through free discussion by replacing force and imposed consent with dialogue and the search for consent. "On the political level," writes Rosselli, "it can be defined as a complex of rules of the game that all the parties in contention commit themselves to respect, rules intended to ensure the peaceful co-existence of citizens, social classes, and states; to restrain competition, which is inevitable and indeed desirable, within tolerable limits; to permit the various parties to succeed to power in turn; to guide the forces of innovation that will arise from time to time into legal channels" (p. 94).

The democratic method is a pact of civility through which citizens and groups defend and develop their ideas—their diversity—without losing the attributes of their common humanity. *Political* liberalism, concludes Rosselli, is nothing more than loyalty to a framework that presupposes an antagonistic and pluralistic society, and guarantees the breadth of human liberty in all its spheres, because it does not subordinate the historical process to a given end. The liberal individual is a combatant, and liberalism more than a philosophy is the mental condition of modernity; it implies a conflictual attitude in both the inner and private life and the cultural and public life. "Wherever two illiberal forces fight each other, there liberalism lies. . . . All the active and revolutionary forces of history are, by definition, liberal."[80] Liberal were the Bolsheviks in 1917; liberal had been the Third Estate in the eighteenth century. "The truth is that liberalism is by definition historicist and relativistic; it sees history as a perpetual flux, an eternal becoming and overcoming" (p. 87). The liberal spirit cannot be imprisoned in any system whatsoever, and contrary to Marxism, it rests precisely on the separation between method and system. From this important standpoint Rosselli goes on to two conclusions: the dissociation of liberalism from the ideology of the free market, and the interpretation of socialism as part of the "dynamic idea of liberty."

In *Liberal Socialism* Rosselli does not discuss free market ideas to which, however, he had dedicated several articles in the early 1920s. Besides, the book is addressed primarily to socialists, its aim being the reformation of their culture and strategy.

---

[80] Carlo Rosselli, "Liberalismo rivoluzionario" (*Quaderni di "Giustizia e Libertà,"* January 1932), now in *Opere scelte*, vol. 2, t. 1, pp. 50–51.

The attempt to separate liberalism from the ideology of the free market had been one of the main ambitions of the "new liberalism" since the turn of the century. In England, the most prominent protagonist of this renovation was L. T. Hobhouse; in Italy the major contribution came from Benedetto Croce, who, during the 1920s debate with Luigi Einaudi, made clear the distinction between ethical-political liberalism and economic liberalism. According to Einaudi, the free market was the foundation of liberal institutions. Croce maintained the contrary, that it was theoretically inconsistent to recognize the primacy of economic over ethical liberalism. The ideology of the free market (which Croce called *liberismo*) and liberalism had a common ideal root, but because of its ethical dimension, liberalism could not be content with only those goods able to satisfy the "individualistic libido" and could not see wealth simply as "the accumulation of the means to that goal." Moreover, liberalism had to evaluate economic goods and wealth not for themselves, but as means to "human elevation." A liberal should judge a policy not insofar as it matches the free market premise, but because it matches the liberal premise, looking for what is "qualitatively valuable" and not "quantitatively valuable." This amounted to saying that free-market politics were not always and everywhere consistent with liberalism. Bearing in mind Hobhouse's *Liberalism*, Croce did not fear even the liberal socialist "paradox": "Hence, when we face the problem of civil and moral respect, the dispute again becomes between good and bad, better and less good or worse; in accord with the most sincere and vivid liberal consciousness, one can support measures and laws that the theorists of an abstract economics classify as socialist."[81]

When in *Liberal Socialism* Rosselli placed Marxism close to Benthamism, he probably had Croce in mind, particularly his idea that *liberismo* was in some way a mirror image of Marxist socialism; both of them considered political liberty in terms of its tactical value; both assumed the existence of an invisible hand; and both finally aimed at a systematic conclusion. In the case of liberismo, this tendency was particularly harmful because it created a dogmatic climate intrinsically contradic-

[81] Benedetto Croce, "Liberismo e liberalismo" (1927), now in Benedetto Croce and Luigi Einaudi, *Liberismo e liberalismo*, ed. Paolo Solari (Milan and Naples: Ricciardi, 1957), pp. 11–15. In the same collection of essays see also another important article by Croce, "La concezione liberale come concezione della vita" (1927), and the comments by Einaudi, "Liberismo e liberalismo" (1931), pp. 3–10, 121–33. Croce's opinion on liberismo was already well known even before 1927. See his *Elementi di Politica* (Bari: Laterza, 1925), where Croce collected three essays on the same subject published in 1924. An English account of Croce's distinction is in Benedetto Croce, *My Philosophy and Other Essays on the Moral and Political Problems of Our Times*, selected by Raymond Klibansky and trans. Edgar F. Carritt (London: Allen & Unwin, 1949), pp. 29–30.

tory to the liberal method. On the other side, the mistake of the "modern utilitarians" (that is, the Marxists), wrote Rosselli, was that of having identified liberty with bourgeois liberties, without considering that even though those historical conquests were the expressions of a particular class, they nevertheless had the moral and political force to become universal. Indeed, after the French Revolution the working class had defended those liberties precisely to emancipate itself from social and political subordination.

So we have Rosselli's definition of Marxism and liberalism. But what about socialism? Rosselli's socialism is neither a system like Marxism nor a method like liberalism. It is supposed to give substance to the liberal method: "Liberalism is the ideal force of inspiration, and socialism is the practical force of realization" (p. 87).

Socialism expresses an ideal, an end that is, however, only possible but not necessary. As an end, it is not already inscribed within the historical order, and in this sense it is only possible. But the fact that socialism has nothing to do with scientific demonstration does not mean that it is irrational. When Rosselli spoke of faith he did not imply any kind of irrational attitude. His belief in socialism is based on reflection on history, on empirical observation of the real conditions of individual lives, on consideration of the social movements that took and are taking place, on individuals' needs, claims, and aspirations. "I am a socialist by reason of culture, and by reaction, but also—I say this loudly so that those deterministic and shrunken Marxists may hear me—by *faith* and *sentiment*. I do not believe that socialism will come from the fatalistic evolution of things, apart from the human will. To those who use this language I repeat with Sorel (here all my voluntarism rests): *socialism will be, but it could also not be.*"[82]

We cannot describe the ideal society because there is in fact no ideal society. More than a policy, socialism must therefore be interpreted as a moral ideal and a commitment with which one can ameliorate and amend, the society within which one lives, a project to be pursued through the "liberal method." This work never ends, however, because, Rosselli writes, the goal lives in our present actions as an answer, or reaction, to some particular historical and social circumstances, which are unique for each generation and place. This I take to be the meaning of Eduard Bernstein's motto "The socialist movement means everything, the end means nothing," which recurs frequently in *Liberal Socialism*.

It is hard indeed to imagine that somebody could sometime in the future detect the realization of a socialist society. For this reason,

[82] Rosselli, "Liberalismo socialista" (1924), p. 127.

Rosselli writes that "socialism is not socialization; it is not the proletariat in power; it is not even material equality" (p. 78). It is not a static
model of society but a limiting ideal, which, once it is assumed as an outlook on our political actions, "is realized in the small portion of it that
succeeds in penetrating our lives." Whereas Marxism is antithetical to
liberalism, socialism is not, because more than "an external state to be realized," it "is, for the individual, a plan for living to be actuated" (p. 82).

In presenting his liberal socialism Rosselli is deliberately generic. His
aim is to provide moral criteria, leaving to each of us the responsibility
of using our creative imagination to work out answers to the problems
of our time and societies. The definition of socialism we find in *Liberal
Socialism* is the following:

> Socialism, grasped in its essential aspect, is the progressive actualization
> of the idea of liberty and justice among men: an innate idea that lies more
> or less buried under the sediment of centuries in the marrow of every
> human being. It is the progressive effort to ensure an equal chance of
> living the only life worthy of the name to all humans, setting them free
> from the enslavement to the material world and material needs that today
> still dominate the greater number, allowing them the possibility freely to
> develop their personalities in a continuous struggle . . . against the cor-
> ruptions of a civilization too much the prey of the demons of success and
> money." (p. 78)

In other words, socialism is the realization of liberalism, even if Rosselli
is aware that liberalism has only started this process—indeed, the
condition of inequality, still common to the majority, transforms the
liberty enjoyed by the minority into a privilege.

If socialism is a regulative idea, a belief, it presupposes a philosophy
of history or a teleology. What distinguishes it from the Marxist philosophy of history? Actually, the difference exists and is very deep, because for Rosselli the moral factor is inscribed within a skeptical perspective. Not only do we have no assurance concerning the direction of
the historical process, but it is probable that what each of us desires or
aims for will never be. If it will be, it will be only because we have
wanted it, because we made it happen. According to Rosselli, this
radically humanistic vision of history is more in tune with the liberal
method, which transmits to us an idea of history in which conflicts,
antagonisms, and provisional agreements between different forces,
ideas, interests, and values play a central role. The modern tradition
fostered the idea that the human world is an entirely human construc-
tion. The "liberal spirit"—on which Rosselli insisted so much and
which he desired to see spread within the socialist movement—is
nothing more than a skeptical and searching spirit. Human activity—

especially politics—takes place without protective nets and meta-historical models. In this sense, along with Georges Sorel, Rosselli repeats that "socialism will be, but it could also not be."

The immediate and spontaneous objection to this profession of faith both skeptical and voluntaristic is foreseeable: how can a skeptic have faith? Rosselli succeeds in demonstrating that there is no contradiction if we make the preliminary and decisive distinction between science and morality. Skepticism corrodes all those systems based on the idea that social dynamics can be understood and modified according to scientific laws. Scientific theories of society do not give a full account of the human condition, and for this reason they are nonhumanistic. Moreover, they are harmful to human action. Doubt is addressed against philosophy when philosophical theories seek to sustain moral and political action, to find the true answer for everything. Political action, especially socialism, does not need to embrace a Weltanschauung; rather, when intellectual energy concentrates on philosopical disputes, it is a loss for politics: "A little bit more faith and a little bit less science."[83]

On this subject Rosselli and Henri De Man spoke the same language. In the last pages of his *Au delà du marxisme*, the Belgian socialist stressed the independence of political action from social science again and again. Sociology (and Marxism as part of it) could never serve social and political actions except by helping the actors to understand the conditions of their acts. But the understanding did not figure as the motive or inspiration of the acts. "Social science can never do anything more than show us the place where we must apply the lever of our will in order to get the best effect; it cannot arouse this will to action, or give it reasons for action." By arranging social facts in a causal system, Marxism did nothing more than embody in the causes the motives regarded by its author as having the highest value . . . but then went on to camouflage them as if they were objective and immanent laws. This led De Man to conclude that "socialism is a *passion*, not a *cognition*," and that "one who is fighting for the establishment of a better society does not need scientific proof that the coming of this system is inevitable. It suffices that his conscience should tell him to work for its coming."[84]

Doubt can be a great stimulus to action, because it requires us not to leave anything unattempted. If it is not history (or God) that plays the game, if nobody can know in advance what the outcome of the game

---

[83] Carlo Rosselli, "Aggiunte e chiose al 'bilancio marxista' " (1923), in *Opere scelte* 1:103.

[84] Henri De Man, *Au delà du marxisme* (1927), English version from the second German edition (1927) with the title *The Psychology of Socialism*, trans. Eden and Cedar Paul (London: Allen & Unwin, 1928), pp. 490, 497.

will be, then everything is possible and no human energy is wasted. The critical demon compels us to take thought for our present lives, to take a position, not to subtract ourselves from our responsibilities, to try to count for something. Skepticism implies that history is a perennial conflict of acquiring and correcting opinions and induces us to respect our political enemies; indeed, if nobody has the truth, all opinions must be respected. As Albert O. Hirschman wrote, speaking of this generation of Italian anti-Fascist "free-thinkers": "It was almost as though they set out to prove Hamlet wrong: they were intent on showing that doubt could *motivate* action instead of undermining and enervating it."[85] They invoked doubt to suspend judgment about social truth and allow political action.

Rosselli's socialism is a humanism. For him "there is only one final goal in sight: the single person, the concrete individual, the primary and fundamental cell. Or rather, society comes first, but only to the extent that by this name we designate an aggregate of individualities and concentrate on the majority. For, as an organization, society is a means to an end, an instrument in the service of mankind, not of metaphysical entities like the land of one's birth or communism. There exist no purposes of society that are not at the same time purposes of the individual as a moral personality" (p. 79).

Rosselli justifies the divorce of Marxism from socialism with historical and theoretical arguments. The analysis of the collapse of liberal institutions before fascism persuaded him that orthodox socialists bore the major responsibility. Devoted as they were to Marx's authority, their fatalism led them to surrender before Fascist violence, waiting for a future that would inevitably come. But the split between theory and practice, ideology and concrete culture, was already a reality before the First World War. While the "professors" were discussing the fatal collapse of capitalism, the people involved in the social movements were acting to achieve practical goals and using the rules of the democratic dialogue to obtain political and social rights. Indeed, the first confutation of the Marxist system came from the movement itself when it started negotiating. Politics gave the coup de grace to high theory, pushing aside every logical obstacle.

Rosselli's thesis that the easy victory of fascism was the consequence of Italian socialists' commitment to Marxism is questionable. Nevertheless, like Gramsci's notebooks, *Liberal Socialism* is an attempt to reconcile the theory and practice of socialism. Both Gramsci and Rosselli felt the need to overcome the abstract universalism of class theory. Unlike

---

[85] Albert O. Hirschman, "Io, detective dell'economia fascista," *Il Corriere della sera*, November 13, 1987.

Gramsci, Rosselli did not go beyond the formulation of a project. But many important ideas are apparent in the first pages of the eighth chapter, where he clearly recognizes that the Left needs to break the monopoly of patriotism held by the nationalists. "As the different socialist movements in the different European countries grow more specific and individual, we must guard against seeing this as symptomatic of the failure of the universalistic ideal of socialism. On the contrary, it must be seen as a sign of the shift from the abstract to the real" (p. 122).

Rosselli and Gramsci tried to overcome abstract internationalism by inscribing socialism in the Italian tradition, the latter by interpreting Marxism as a radical historicism (following the legacy of Antonio Labriola and Benedetto Croce), the former by activating a dialogue between liberalism and socialism (going back to the liberal-anarchic and republican roots of the Risorgimento). Whereas Gramsci intended to create an alternative cultural and political hegemony, Rosselli assigned socialism the goal of extending democracy as much as possible and wherever possible. The former envisaged a preferably homogeneous and organic society, the latter a more antagonistic and conflictual one.

If Marxism and socialism ceased to be identical, this was also because Marx began to be considered a classic of political thought, which meant that accepting some of Marx's ideas did not entail being a Marxist. Rosselli accepted the method of class struggle as an example of political conflict among opposite interests but clearly knew that even non-Marxists and anti-Marxists could have accepted these Marxian ideas. Vilfredo Pareto, for instance, used the theory of class struggle precisely to oppose the socialist movement. Croce, too, whose interpretation of historical materialism was extremely important for Rosselli, accepted some Marxist ideas without being either Marxist or socialist.

In a seminal essay on Marx's philosophy written in 1896, Croce declared that historical materialism "is not a philosophy of history."[86] Marxism was a critical and "realistic reflection" upon history insofar as it overthrew the systems built up by metaphysics and destroyed the old philosophy. Marx did so at the very moment he refused to reduce history to a sequence of "general concepts" and introduced concrete facts. He liberated human activity from religion of all kinds (whether transcendental or rationalistic) and distanced himself from the vulgar materialism that "substituted an omnipresent Matter for an omnipresent Idea."[87] By translating Marxism into a methodological guide or, as

[86] Benedetto Croce, "Concerning the Scientific Form of Historical Materialism" (1896), in id., *Historical Materialism and the Economics of Karl Marx*, ed. Michael Curtis (New Brunswick and London: Transaction Books, 1981), p. 3.
[87] Ibid., p. 9.

he said, a "realistic historicism," Croce reached a conclusion that necessarily had a tremendous impact on Rosselli and other revisionists (Sorel among them).[88] The conclusion was that there is no relation between historical materialism and socialism. "If historical materialism is stripped of every survival of finality and the benignity of providence, it can offer no apology for either socialism or any other practical guidance for life."[89]

In Marx's system the discrepancy between science and ethics emerges even more clearly when we reflect on the political role of the ideologies. One of the critiques raised by traditional socialists and anarchists against liberalism was that liberalism was "an aristocratic idea unable to rouse popular passions." But according to Rosselli all theories are aristocratic, even Marxism: the distance between Marx and a naive Communist militant is not shorter than the one in the Middle Ages between a doctor of the Roman Catholic Church and a Crusader. What bestows an aristocratic or a democratic character to a political theory "is not its capacity of being understood, but its capacity of becoming useful, of awakening elementary enthusiasms by projecting its own rays on a vast horizon." Marxism awakens the spirit not with its theory of surplus value or of the inversion of praxis, "but with class struggle and the apocalypse of the *Manifesto*; that is, with the call for justice."[90]

Rosselli's motto, that one can be a Marxist without being a socialist, was a logical conclusion drawn from Croce, according to whom a serious scholar cannot but accept Marx's "realistic historicism," even if he is not a socialist. "In substance," echoes Rosselli, "the whole of historical materialism, once interdependence is substituted for determinism, boils down in practical terms to a lesson in historical realism" (p. 60). But to adhere to a system is a fact of intellect, not of conscious-

---

[88] This was also the case with Salvemini, who recognized that Marxism—not as a philosophical and economic doctrine but as a "canon of historical interpretation"—had an enormous impact on the culture of his time: "In my view, Marx is a great historian more than an economist or a philosopher" (Salvemini to Piero Gobetti, August 27, 1922, quoted in *Le riviste di Piero Gobetti*, p. xxviii).

[89] Croce, "Concerning the Scientific Form of Historical Materialism," p. 22. Croce's conclusion was an elaboration of Antonio Labriola's ideas. Labriola (for information on him see n. 2 of ch. 1), who used to submit all his writings to Engels, wrote in 1895 that "Marxism is and remains a *doctrine*. Parties can draw neither their names nor their justification from a doctrine" (Antonio Labriola, "In memoria del Manifesto dei Comunisti" [1895], in id., *La concezione materialistica della storia*, ed. Eugenio Garin [Bari: Laterza, 1971], p. 41 n. 2). The English edition, with the title "In Memory of the Communist Manifesto," was published in Antonio Labriola, *Essays on the Materialistic Conception of History*, trans. Charles H. Kerr (Chicago: Kerr, 1908), p. 68 n. 2.

[90] Rosselli, "Liberalismo rivoluzionario," p. 51.

ness. It does not need internal travail; nor does it require a moral commitment. Croce's conclusion offered Rosselli the final argument: in the Marxist interpretation of history one cannot pretend to find "the ethical or sentimental motives, moral judgments and the enthusiasm of faith" that socialism needs to be a "guidance for political action." The moral element is extraneous to Marxism and "must be added" from the outside.[91]

If Marxism were a science, its predictions would be susceptible of proof. Rosselli isolated two facts able to falsify Marxism: it is not true that in capitalist societies the masses are moving toward a general impoverishment and proletarianization; it is not true that socialist revolution comes only when capitalist society has reached its complete maturity. Following Eduard Bernstein, Rosselli underlined the fact that industrial workers were everywhere in the minority and that through the evolution of capitalist societies differentiation was more marked than class uniformity. Moreover, socialist political movements made for a general improvement in economic, moral, and juridical terms.[92]

Contrary to Marx's theory, violence had been the mother of history in the Russian revolution, not simply its midwife. The 1917 revolution was a defeat for Marxist socialism because tragically it showed that the problems created by the revolution were so serious that one ought to ask oneself if the proletarians of Russia were conscious at the time of the sacrifices they were about to make. After Russia's experience, writes Rosselli, the socialists can no longer promise paradise: "Heaven is forbidden for the revolutionary generation."

Rosselli not only rejects Leninism, but rejects violence as the negation of politics, even if it is necessary in those exceptional cases, as under fascism, when civility and toleration are suspended. He makes a claim for the educational function of political participation within the practice of democracy. According to him the superiority of liberal socialism rests on the fact that it presupposes an "intellectual and moral human capacity," which is superfluous in all the other sorts of socialism. "Whereas State socialism is always possible in whatever degree of evolution reached by the workers, a socialism that—on the contrary—must be based on 'self-governing workshops' is possible only when the workers . . . have already acquired the moral and intellectual capacity."[93]

Rosselli acknowledged the revisionists' contribution to the discussions on the relationship between theory and practice and the neces-

[91] Croce, "Concerning the Scientific Form."

[92] Eduard Bernstein, *Evolutionary Socialism: A Criticism and Affirmation*, trans. Edith C. Harvey (1961; reprint, New York: Schocken Books, 1967; 1st German edition 1899), pp. 95–96, 106.

[93] Carlo Rosselli, "Il movimento operaio" (1924), in *Opere scelte* 1:73.

sity of dismantling fatalism in order to recover politics. But he thought that one should go beyond revisionism. To boost his opinion Rosselli wrote a brief, stimulating history of Marxist socialism that recalls that of Christianity, from the committed minority communities of the first believers to the establishment of church orthodoxy, and finally to the Reformation. He distinguishes three phases: the religious, the critical, and the overcoming of Marxism.

The first is the phase represented by the *Communist Manifesto*: the triumph of Marxism was made possible by the sense of certainty that it transmitted to socialists. The militants found support for their struggles in the rational character of their faith. In keeping with a romantic illusion, Marxism attemped to unite justice and science. Its language was the prophecy of its persecuted apostles; its faith was a creative faith in which utopia and science were unified. "In the *Manifesto* Marx speaks the language of nemesis" (p. 19). Nothing could have been more dramatic than a fatalistic vision of the new society emerging from the remains of the old one. In that stage fatalism and propaganda came along, and "Marx, like Joshua before the walls of Jericho, was proclaiming that victory was imminent" (p. 19).

The liberal practice, however, gradually conquered the citadel and eroded its formidable unity. Instead of the apocalypse of a social revolution, the workers' movements attained political liberties and social legislation. The Marxist priests "found themselves forced to reconcile the irreconcilable: . . . the messianic simplicity of their teleology with concrete syndicalist demands" (p. 20). Like a liberating wind, "bourgeois freedoms" blew systematic certainty away. Theory and practice did not match anymore and the sphere of practice imposed itself with an anxiety to find a new theoretical guide. Thus the revisionist period began. Eduard Bernstein in Germany, Georges Sorel and Jean Jaurès in France, and Georges Sorel and Rodolfo Mondolfo in Italy had something in common, "the effort to make room in the Marxist system for . . . will" (p. 23). For the first time Marxism showed an inner complexity and even its distance from Marx. Marxism exposed itself to the consequence of the dissociation between faith and science. Heresy grew up, undermining Marx's indisputable authority.

To correct the determinism of Marxism, the revisionists tried to overcome necessity and to insert some kind of voluntarism. Each of them presented a personal interpretation of Marx, so that revisionism was anything but a unitary movement. Nevertheless, each wanted to enrich Marxism by recognizing the importance of human volition in history. Because of its dogmatic character, however, Marxism is unable to withstand critical revision. This is the reason, in fact, that the revisionists—despite their intentions—destroyed Marxism, or more precisely, destroyed the distinctive character of Marxism—that is, the scientific demonstration of the final socialist solution.

From Marxism to revisionism and from revisionism to liberal socialism: this was the path of contemporary socialism that Rosselli traced. The ideal progenitor of liberal socialism was Bernstein, because he claimed that socialism is above all an ideal. But he was a progenitor *malgrè lui*, because Bernstein was under the illusion that he was readdressing Marxism, without seeing that, like any systematic doctrine, it could not be amended. Revisionism suffered the destiny of all heterodoxies: intending to fortify its foundations, it demolished the entire edifice. "The real problem for socialists does not therefore consist in denying Marx but in extricating themselves from him" (p. 72).

Revisionism's limitation, for Rosselli, is that it was too timid, a prisoner of orthodoxy, more Marxist than Marxism. In addition, it was harmful to the socialist movement, which, if it had carried out its democratic transformation completely, would have had the strength to defend and enlarge democratic institutions. The path of revisionism was a mirror image of Marx's path: the "revisionists followed Marx's trail in reverse, and from socialist science they returned to faith, to the position, that is, of the pre-Marxist schools" (pp. 57–58). But at the moment they refused to recognize their substantial unfaithfulness to Marx and presented themselves as true Marxists, they increased dogmatism and scholasticism. "Marx would be the first to deride the ridiculous claim of his epigones" (p. 72) when they tried to make him a liberal. In its paradoxicality, Rosselli's conclusion has a stringent logic: "I hold that it is sterile to try to tie philosophical positions too closely to practical programs. But if one does wish to establish this tie for the theory of historical materialism, the revisionist interpretation of it leads not to socialism but to full liberalism—a more concrete and realistic liberalism that looks to the substance of the social movement" (pp. 58–59). The conclusion of revisionism thus is liberal socialism, which is not a heresy, because it openly states that it goes beyond Marxism.

When he discussed the failure of the Italian Marxist reformation, Rosselli confronted the figure of Rodolfo Mondolfo, a de facto revisionist who, however, never recognized himself as such. Mondolfo faced the problems of the relationship between theory and practice in Marxism with Giovanni Gentile's and Georges Sorel's elaborations in mind. In particular, he developed the theory of the "inversion of praxis" explained by Gentile in his *La filosofia di Marx* (1899).

"Praxis," wrote Gentile, "which has as its principle the subject and as its end the object, inverts itself by moving in turn from the object (as its principle) to the subject (as its end)."[94] Gentile's inversion of praxis encouraged a subjectivistic interpretation of Marx's dialectic. By bringing Marx closer to Hegel, Gentile offered an idealistic reading of historical materialism in such a way that history appeared as a complete human creation (a reading that Gramsci would have appreciated). By starting from Marx's reading of Feuerbach, Gentile pursued two strategies: he presented Marx's thought as a definite overcoming of vulgar materialism; but in that moment of vindicating Marx's allegiance to Hegel, Gentile also made it clear that Marx's idealism was less coherent than Hegel's. "Actually, Gentile depicted Marx as a Hegelian precisely in order to conclude that he was an unfaithful pupil of Hegel, a bad Hegel."[95] Gentile studied Marx according to the idea that all true philosophy was idealistic or else it was not philosophy at all. Following his own strategy, he came to the same conclusion as Croce, that is, that Marxism was not a philosophy. But Croce's and Gentile's project to dismiss Marxism (and socialism) raised such a fertile debate among both philosophers and socialists as to give the impression that Marxism was all but dead.

Through the interpretation of the "philosophy of the praxis" Mondolfo aimed to confute both determinists and voluntarists. He granted Sorel's reasons against determinism but criticized his exaltation of liberty as totally arbitrary and antihistorical, since it was subjected to the manipulatory creation of myth. This, according to Mondolfo, was the case with Lenin's voluntarism, which, because it intended definitely and suddenly to cut off all ties with the past, led to dictatorship: "Once all the existing old branches are cut off, new buds will rise from the very roots." When, therefore, should the revolution stop? When and how does one decide that negative will must become constructive will? Dictatorship is the only available solution: by a decree, one forces the will to cease its renewing fury and tamely to preserve the new order. Under its voluntarism, Leninism hid the most orthodox determinism.[96]

In spite of his efforts, Mondolfo's solution sounded like alchemy. In fact, when he tried to criticize the determinists he insisted on the subjective moment; when he wanted to criticize the voluntarists he stressed determinant historical conditions. Moreover, the balance between human will and the laws of history never reached an equilibrium. Indeed, Mondolfo conceived of socialism as a phenomenon contained within things (history), whereas the subject (social class) was

---

[94] Giovanni Gentile, *La filosofia di Marx: Studi critici* (Florence: Sansoni, 1974), p. 85.

[95] Bobbio, Introduction to Mondolfo, *Umanesimo di Marx*, p. xxii.

[96] Rodolfo Mondolfo, "Il socialismo e il movimento storico presente," in id., *Sulle orme di Marx* (1919; reprint, Bologna: Cappelli, 1920), pp. 7–8.

chosen by the laws of production. He converted Marxism from a Lamarckian determinism to an immanentist historicism but did not renounce the category of necessity. He conceived of the relationship between history and praxis, environment and human will, as a dialectical one, but synthesis was the work of history. Indeed, subjects reached their maturity within the social order they were supposed to wreck, but they did not have the right to the last word: the masses had to become an "aware and *effective cooperator* in the making of the new society."[97] In spite of his attempt to mediate between history and individual will, Mondolfo was still convinced that socialism had a "historical function," not merely an ethical one: "It is not enough to say that the socialist ideal also has an ethical value, that it is universalistic; this is important but not sufficient." Its final aim was not raising the moral energies of the masses, but seeking to join with the rhythm of history. Socialism thus could not renounce the need for a philosophy.[98]

Rosselli did not find Mondolfo's strategy convincing, and instead of spending all his energy in shoring up Marxist philosophy, he took Mondolfo's arguments to their extreme conclusions.[99] Rosselli did to Marxism what Mondolfo had done to Leninism. He claimed that Marxism is not a humanism, precisely because it cannot renounce the category of necessity, and he stressed that socialism is a belief. If Bernstein was his main source in his defense of the connection between liberal tradition and the ideals of socialism,[100] from Sorel and De Man Rosselli derived the inspiration for his humanistic socialism. He greatly appreciated Henri De Man's *Au delà du marxisme*, which was published in German in 1926 and was translated into French in 1927.[101] In this regard, both De Man and Rosselli experienced emancipation from Marxism as a spiritual liberation: "Our concern," wrote De Man, "is not with the dead Marx, but with living socialism."[102] However, even before writing *Socialismo liberale*, Rosselli had reached the conclusion that adherence to socialism was a question of consciousness and commitment to a moral ideal, not a necessary outcome.[103]

Sorel had an important influence on Rosselli ever since the latter had been working on his dissertations. As the reader will see, *Liberal Social-*

---

[97] Ibid., p. 8.

[98] Rodolfo Mondolfo, "Socialismo e filosofia", in *Sulle orme di Marx*, pp. 23–24.

[99] Rosselli engaged in a polemical exchange with Mondolfo in the journal *La Critica Sociale* in 1923. See Rosselli, "Aggiunte e chiose al 'Bilancio marxista,'" pp. 83–106; Mondolfo, "Contributo ad un chiarimento di idee" (1924), in *Umanesimo di Marx*, pp. 234–41.

[100] Bernstein, *Evolutionary Socialism*, in particular pp. 139–65.

[101] The German edition came out with the title *Zur Psychologie des Sozialismus*.

[102] De Man, *The Psychology of Socialism*, p. 16.

[103] See, for instance, his article "Liberalismo socialista," pp. 107–28.

ism contains many implicit references to the early writings of Sorel, beginning with a quotation, in the preface, from Ernest Renan's *Histoire du peuple d'Israel*, a book and an author particularly loved by Sorel. To better understand *Liberal Socialism*, one should at least keep in mind three of Sorel's works, "L'éthique du socialisme" (1899), the *Critical Essays on Marxism*, whose first edition appeared in Italian in 1902, and *Réflexions sur la violence* (1906). But with Sorel's voluntarism, as with Leninism, Rosselli had no hesitation in rejecting its myth of violence and its antidemocratic spirit. Sorel's contribution was above all a negative one: he offered Rosselli good arguments against fatalism and Marxist orthodoxy. Rosselli was aware that Sorel in his early essays intended to revise Marxism more than to overcome it. Sorel went from revisionism to an appreciation of both Leninism and fascism but never overcame Marxism and never succeeded in appreciating democracy.

As Bobbio wrote, "The liberal socialist formula was not an abstract elucubration, especially because it was born of a reflection on the dramatic events" suffered by Italian society.[104] Chapters 3, 7, and 8 testify to the fact that Rosselli's concern with liberal socialism was at one with his concern for the rebirth of Italian democratic institutions. As he writes, fascism made it clear that the problem of Italy was one of liberty. Socialism could either become an expression of liberty or would have no future—it did not deserve to have a future. "When Marxists demand liberty they do so not for its intrinsic value, but only because they think it favors the self-awareness of the proletariat, and in fact capitalist development" (p. 108). Their instrumental vision of political liberty would not help restore free institutions, which collapsed precisely because they were never rooted in the consciousness and customs of the Italians. Even before fascism the Marxists were unable to appreciate the evolution of democracy (for instance, they never gave priority to universal suffrage), and for this reason they did not understand that along with "bourgeois liberties" fascism was sweeping away liberty itself. But because politics implies antagonism and struggle, it presupposes moral and political freedom. In this sense, totalitarianism is not a politics. "Fascism," writes Rosselli, "has in some sense been the autobiography of a nation that shrugs at the political contest, that worships unanimity and shrinks from heresy, that dreams of the triumph of facility, trust, and enthusiasm" (p. 108). Rosselli borrowed the quotation from Gobetti to distance himself not only from the Marxists but also from the liberals, in particular Croce, who interpreted fascism as a parenthesis, a momentary pause within the glorious history of free-

---

[104] Bobbio, Introduction to Rosselli, *Socialismo liberale*, p. xxx. See n. 28 here.

dom.[105] Liberal socialism had to act against this attitude by inspiring a deep sense of human dignity and responsibility. It had to fulfill what Piero Gobetti called a "liberal revolution."

A Permanent War of Position

It is all very well to fantasize of a society at once free and just, in which liberty rights and social rights will be globally and totally implemented. . . . Even if each of them [liberalism and socialism] claims to make the synthesis . . . what we may expect is not an ultimate synthesis but, at most, a compromise (that is, a synthesis indeed, but provisional).
(*Norberto Bobbio, 1967*)

Socialismo liberale did not enjoy good fortune. When it appeared in French in 1930 and in Italian in 1945, it did not have many readers, and the few who read it did not appreciate it. Its critical and provocative character did not fit the Manichaean sectarianism of the time and was immediately met with the hostility of both the liberals and the Marxists, in particular Benedetto Croce and Palmiro Togliatti.

Croce, who sincerely admired Rosselli for his bravery and consistency, insistently pointed out the hybrid quality of Rosselli's program.[106] According to him, Rosselli yielded to the temptation of "easy conclusions, falling into the logical mistake of juxtaposing" liberalism with socialism for the purpose of creating a "synthetic formula." Croce compared it to a hircocervus, a fabulous creature half-goat and half-stag, an absurd and aesthetically unpleasant combination that purported to attach the rough, rude, and shaggy body of socialism to the long and agile legs of liberalism. This critique may indeed have been true for the later socialist-liberals, such as Guido Calogero, who did in fact attempt a

[105] In 1922 Gobetti had written: "One can speak of Minister Mussolini as of a run-of-the-mill matter. But fascism has been something more. It has been the autobiography of the nation. A nation that believes in class collaboration, that gives up political struggle for laziness, is a nation of no account" ("Elogio della ghigliottina," p. 292). For an analysis of fascism elaborated by Rosselli and his followers, see Fedele, *E verrà un'altra Italia*, pp. 33–38.

[106] Benedetto Croce, *L'idea liberale. Contro le confusioni e gli ibridismi* (Bari: Laterza, 1944), pp. 16–20, and *Nuove pagine sparse* (Naples: Ricciardi, 1929), t. 2, pp. 195–96. Croce had had the chance to meet Rosselli in Paris several times and to be present at the discussions that accompanied the birth of Giustizia e Libertà.

theoretical synthesis between freedom and justice.[107] But such was not the case with Rosselli, who quite explicitly did not identify liberalism with socialism and did not want socialism to replace liberalism.

Because of its devotion to the idea of justice, socialism intends to reduce privileges and extend liberties. In this sense, it is, historically, an evolution of liberalism. According to Rosselli, liberalism alone was not able to carry out its promises because its primary beneficiaries were no longer a progressive class; they were content with their own liberties, which had became privileges because they were not shared equally among all the members of the society. The legitimacy of liberal socialism rests on the conviction that the socialist ideal has the moral force to continue the road opened by liberal movement. Indeed, it represents the need for liberty of the oppressed minorities, as liberalism did in the previous century. "A liberalism that remains confined to the virgin and sovereign mind of some philosopher and historian, or historian-philosopher [here the allusion to Croce is evident], a liberalism that does not graft itself onto a concrete mass movement, that does not seek to conquer the forces that express—perhaps unconsciously—a liberal function in society, is a pure abstraction."[108]

Togliatti's critique was much harsher while it was unfair. In a Third International style, the general secretary of the Italian Communist party portrayed Rosselli as an ignorant, presumptuous petit bourgeois who tried to adapt the "constitutive elements of Fascist ideology" to socialism and affirmed the absolute value of democratic institutions. It is curious to note that Togliatti criticized Rosselli precisely because he had invited the socialists to pay attention to the peculiarities of their national societies, an argument that, a few years later Togliatti himself would use to distance his own party from Soviet hegemony.[109]

Rosselli was aware of the oddness of the formula "liberal socialism," "a strange sound to many who are accustomed to current political terminology." In his time, the word *liberalism* was "used to smuggle so many different kinds of merchandise and has been so much the preserve of the bourgeoisie in the past, that today a socialist has difficulty bringing himself to use it." But Rosselli did not want to propose

---

[107] See, for instance, Guido Calogero, "Intorno al concetto di giustizia" (1941), in *Difesa del liberalsocialismo*, pp. 3–25 (see also n. 42 above). Croce's critique of Calogero's liberal socialism was first developed in "Libertà 'morale' e libertà 'politica,'" *Quaderni della 'Critica,'* no. 1 (March 1945): 109–10. An English account is in Croce, *My Philosophy*, pp. 97–108.

[108] Rosselli, "Liberalismo socialista" (1924), pp. 116–17. On liberalism's dilemma before democratic politics and the debate between Croce and the liberal socialists, see Richard Bellamy, *Liberalism and Modern Society* (University Park: Pennsylvania State University Press, 1992), pp. 152–54.

[109] Palmiro Togliatti, "Sul movimento di Giustizia e Libertà" (1931), in id., *Opere*, ed. Ernesto Ragionieri (Rome: Editori Riuniti, 1973), vol. 3, t. 2, pp. 411–22.

either a "new party terminology" or a theoretical synthesis. Instead, he wanted "to bring the socialist movement back to its first principles, to its historical and psychological origins, and to demonstrate that social-ism, in the last analysis, is a philosophy of liberty" (p. 84).

After sixty years, these words sound all but outdated. Yet *Socialismo liberale* remains a powerful text that compels us to rethink both the notion and the role of liberalism and socialism. In the face of the crisis of socialist ideology and the unsatisfactory performance of democratic institutions, Rosselli's book might suggest useful theoretical and politi-cal clarifications to contemporary actors. At any rate, its context has something in common with our own.

Rosselli wrote and lived before the cold war, whereas we have left it behind us. While he never experienced that ideological rivalry, we have finally got free of it, after decades of forced anachronism *Social-ismo liberale* may be able to speak to us again. It has, one might say, acquired modernity with the passage of time.

Finally, like us, Rosselli faced the crisis of the Left and, more gener-ally, of democracy. The crisis of the 1930s was certainly more dramatic than ours but no less deep. On one side the decay of Marxism had left socialism without a theoretical framework and, moreover, unnerved and disillusioned; the various quarrelsome voices of revisionism were indeed incapable of speaking to those who were fighting for their very survival. On the other side, liberalism was internally divided between a dry libertarian economism and a moral resistance to a regime that was enjoying a large popular consensus. The old was dead and the new was unable to come to light, Gramsci wrote forcefully.

In such circumstances Rosselli was able to find the moral energy to penetrate that wall of dense fog. He was able to extract from the histori-cal experiences of previous centuries the spirit and meaning of both liberalism and socialism and to challenge the consciousness and pas-sions of his contemporaries by asking them to commit themselves to that spirit and renounce the search for the certainty of truth. There was a good deal of voluntarism and perhaps a grain of the pleasure of action in his message. But it was needed.

As far as we are concerned, the Cold War did not end for nothing. Proposals for widening areas of political activity, for dissociating social-ism from Marxist dogmatism and conceiving of it as a constitutive part of the democratic tradition, are today the only way of keeping the socialist ideal alive. But no less than Rosselli's, our cultural milieu is also characterized by a tendency to reproduce conceptual barriers of non possumus: if you take freedom you have to drop equality, because—as Karl Popper wrote in his autobiography—to combine the two is "no more than a beautiful dream," whereas "freedom is more important than equality" and "the attempt to realize equality endangers freedom."[110] But if values are not reconcilable, nonetheless they cohabit in our lives, and in this sense they cannot live apart from one another. The liberal-socialist intellectual strategy was to "sabotage" the certainty of the ideas and beliefs of its time by showing that they were anything but "natural" or "conceptually clear" and ultimately that it was possible to change course "without stopping, perplexed, before the fatal crossroads" of freedom and justice.[111]

To present socialism as a medium for promoting democracy may sound a little strange to the American reader. Nonetheless, this was the path of development in Europe. Indeed, for those liberals who grew up before World War I it was anything but easy and natural to convert to democracy. No less than liberal socialism, liberal democracy was for them a hybrid creature. In some illustrious cases, as, for instance, Benedetto Croce's, democratic contaminations of liberalism were never accepted, although Croce maintained an honorable moral opposition to fascism. In other cases, liberals turned to democracy after their experiences in social and political movements or their commitment to concrete problems of social justice.

To better understand how unnatural the process of democratization was, we may recall Tocqueville's description of European political life. "The political existence of the majority of the nations of Europe commenced in the superior ranks of society and was gradually and imperfectly communicated to the different members of the social body."[112] As with Plotinus's Idea, political power and participation radiated down from a lofty people to a broad bottom. This diffusion was neither a necessity nor a concession, nor was it a peaceful evolution, as T. H. Marshall suggested, but the result of hard and long political work in which the socialist movement played an important role.

The history of liberty, the "dynamic idea of liberty," as Rosselli says, had, has, and will have many different protagonists. It cannot be the prerogative of a select class. For him the constriction of social reality into a class was a sign of lack of liberty. Tomorrow, he wrote in 1934, when these people are free, they will develop their numberless energies, composing and dissolving numberless groups and loyalties. "Where then is liberalism alive, where is it being implemented?" According to Rosselli, the spirit and legacy of liberalism is "in *all* the active, revolutionary (in the full sense of the word) forces of history"

---

[110] Karl Popper, *Unended Quest: An Intellectual Autobiography* (La Salle, Ill.: Open Court, 1976), pp. 36, 33.

[111] Calogero, "Ricordi del movimento liberalsocialista," pp. 198–99.

[112] Alexis de Tocqueville, *Democracy in America* (New York: A. A. Knopf, 1948), vol. 1, ch. 2, p. 40.

that "exercise an innovative function" and "open up ever new domains and new horizons for liberty" (p. 89). What these forces will be cannot be decided in advance, because of the rise of ever new subjects and claims. This permits the conclusion that liberal socialism is a permanent critique of existing reality, made by those who still do not benefit completely from the democratic condition even if they are members of democratic societies. The subordinated of yesterday may be the privileged of tomorrow. The human being, he wrote in 1932, does not end in the bourgeois or in the proletarian; his long-lasting historical experience made him an extremely complex being. An individual is at once conservative and revolutionary, dogmatic and liberal. The bourgeois, almost always conservative in the economic sphere, is more liberal than the proletarian in questions concerning culture and customs. In the case of the proletarian, as well as in the case of the bourgeois, his or her influence is beneficial within particular spheres, and one must take advantage of it where it is beneficial.[113]

In Rosselli's age the major protagonists of "the dynamic idea of liberty" were the workers. This led him and his fellows to claim that socialism made possible the transition from liberalism to democracy.

As Guido De Ruggiero wrote in 1925 in his *Storia del liberalismo europeo*, nineteenth-century socialism "created a profound perturbation in the liberal mind," which was prompted to rethink itself, its foundations, its aspirations, and its limits.[114] Socialism was a positive challenge that enriched the liberal tradition and helped the transition toward democracy. Compared with the previous utopias of ideal cities, the novelty of nineteenth-century socialism consisted in the fact that it became a true school of democracy for those people—the majority—who have always been kept out of civil and political life, who did not have voice to denounce justice but only hope for charity, and who at the very moment they received charity were deprived of full citizenship status. They needed to invent the language of social rights, as they did.

Workers' and women's organizations within the unions, cooperatives, mutual associations, and political parties were important schools of democracy because they combined freedom and responsibility, claims for rights and consciousness of duties. For these people, such associations had the same role that the religious communities of the dissenters had for the bourgeois and the merchants of the seventeenth and eighteenth centuries. Through them other more numerous protagonists learned to become autonomous political and moral subjects,

---

[113] Rosselli, "Liberalismo rivoluzionario," p. 52.

[114] Guido De Ruggiero, *The History of European Liberalism*, trans. Robin George Collingwood (1927; reprint, Boston: Beacon Press, 1959), p. 381.

conscious and responsible citizens, intellectuals able to fit the means to the ends, to reflect on their condition and on the potentialities of liberal institutions, representatives who learned to apply democratic rules, administrators who became expert in the exercise of local government.

By lifting these people out of the narrowness of their immediate concerns, socialist ideals opened a new perspective of action beyond that imposed by the material needs of survival and allowed them to think in more general terms, to look beyond their individual lives and partisan interests, to see themselves as citizens. In this sense socialism was a "specification of democracy" and, moreover, an "exigency" like that expressed by liberalism in its constitutive era. Indeed, socialism helped promote the art of discussion and resistance, of defending one's opinions through persuasion, of dissenting, of tempering passionate rebellion with programs for gradual change and reformation, of dealing with others as equals, of not submitting to authority. The socialist movement pushed the liberal message further and pressed liberalism toward its necessary democratic evolution.[115]

Which rights could those who did not start from a condition of ownership claim? Civil rights and then, to defend them, political and social rights. In fact, wrote Bobbio, once political rights were extended to everyone, to poor people or illiterate people, it was inevitable that they would ask through their representatives for jobs, public schools, medical care, and housing. If before the democratic evolution of the liberal state these demands never came, it was because those who were exercising political liberties did not need them.[116]

The language of social rights (which include health, housing, education, and employment) conveys a strong sense of dignity because it does away with all kinds of relationships based on a noblesse oblige benevolence. Charity is a way of emphasizing the status of those who give and those who receive and preserves a culture of dependence. Social rights are instruments that promote autonomy and self-reliance because they entail the implementation of services enjoyable by all people not because they are poor or unlucky, but because they are citizens. Public schools should not be second-rate schools for those who cannot pay for private ones, but schools for all citizens. The word *public*, here is synonymous not with a philanthropic activity performed by the government instead of, or along with, private individuals, but with goods whose enjoyment should not be left to a market decision, because such enjoyment constitutes a basic premise for enjoying essen-

---

[115] Ibid., pp. 391–94.

[116] Norberto Bobbio, *The Future of Democracy: A Defence of the Rules of the Game* ed. by Richard Bellamy (Cambridge: Polity Press, 1987; 1st. Italian ed. 1984), p. 112.

tial civil and political liberties. Whenever we speak of social rights, of a "welfare state," we should primarily mean a public system of services, not a policy of subsidy or relief.

Unless they are in perfect worlds, our democracies cannot avoid, indeed they positively need to include, social rights in their legislations if they do not want to remain or become inhospitable to many of their citizens or inhabitants. The two other options could be a society deeply divided, unjust and violent, or a paternalistic society (perhaps not less violent), like the one the old liberals of the last century envisaged. In either case it will be a society that lacks equal liberties and for that reason will be a bad democracy.

All this amounts to saying that social rights are not an aberration of the liberal state but a political conquest that transformed the liberal state into a democratic one. Indeed, in a predemocratic or nondemocratic state, cases of state intervention are really expressions of paternalism, because they are not answers to claims coming from below but concessions or gifts made by the rulers, sometimes in the name of their benevolence, more frequently to secure social peace or pursue a militarist policy. Mussolini's government had formidable social legislation for families, but its aim was to protect existing family roles—to make happy wives and mothers—not to enable women to have autonomous lives. To judge a social policy we need to consider if it comes with civil and political liberties and what its goals are, whether it supports and promotes self-dependence or constructs golden cages.

It is a common belief that the individualistic perspective cannot be consistent with socialist discourse, even of a liberal kind. The individual is the rationale of liberal-democratic institutions, of a rights-based society: the word *citizen* indicates the *political* status of the individual as a *moral* responsible subject. Moral individualism is the theoretical basis of democracy. As Rosselli wrote, "Justice, morality, right, and liberty are realized only to the extent that they are realized in separate individualities." (p. 79).

This premise does not imply a philosophy (or rather an ontology) that sees the individual as an abstract self or, as political philosophers say in our day, an uprooted and "unencumbered" self, a monad without memory and history. This is all the more true in the case of the Italian political and philosophical tradition. As we have seen, one of the permanent characteristics of this tradition, in its liberal and socialist expressions, was the critique of every sort of abstract universalism. This was true in the case of Gobetti, Gramsci, and Rosselli, but also of their more or less direct heirs. As the liberal Gobetti wrote in 1922, general ideas are regulative ideas rather than ironclad principles or pure and abstract concepts; for this reason they have to be conceived of and interpreted according to the peculiar social and historical circumstances in which they are modeled. We all have a shadow, but each of us has her or his shadow. Bobbio himself, who continues the path opened by *Socialismo liberale* and believes in a productive tension between a politics of civil rights and one of social rights, in spite of presenting himself as an analytical philosopher and a liberal, has never theorized about the existence of an "unencumbered" self.[117]

According to the tradition of Italian liberal socialism the theory of natural rights is to be perceived as an effective ideology, having a "pragmatic" more than a theoretical value.[118] The "abstract universality" of natural rights was a useful instrument created by the philosophers to support, through rational arguments, a political and social battle. "Human beings de facto were not born either free or equal," in spite of the declaration of 1789; both conditions had to be conquered and implemented. In this sense, universality is an achievement, not a starting point, a regulative idea, not a given. To keep this idea alive and effective we have to work untiringly.[119] As one can see, even if rights are more a matter of defense and implementation than of justification—more of political action than theory—this perspective is more in tune with the historicist argument—the argument from consent—than with arguments based on "an objective and constant datum such as human nature" or on the idea that rights are "self-evident truths." Thus rights are not a corpus given once and for all, but a process always open and exposed to both evolution and involution; in this process human activity (politics) plays a central role; and finally, rights are a matter not of possession but of intersubjectivity; they are a network through which human beings settle on a modus vivendi able to regulate their relationships as subjects who *practice* liberties rather than owning them.[120]

[117] I am referring here to Chantal Mouffe's interpretation of Bobbio's individualism: "Toward a Liberal Socialism?" *Dissent* (Winter 1993): 84–85.

[118] This perspective echoes that of Pareto. "The objections that might be raised against any assertion of natural law," wrote Pareto, "are met in the following way: 'Why must I subscribe to your opinion?' 'Because it is in accord with reason.' 'But I am using reason too, and my idea is different from yours.' 'Yes, but my reason is *right* reason.' 'How comes it that you who are blessed with this right reason are so few?' 'We are not few: our opinion enjoys universal consensus.' 'And yet there are some who think differently.' 'I should have said the consensus of the good and the wise.' 'Very well! It was you then, the good and the wise, who invented this natural law?' 'No, we got it from Nature, from God'" (*Trattato di Sociologia Generale*, English ed. Arthur Livingston, trans. Andrew Bongiorno with the title *The Mind and Society*, 2 vols. [New York: Harcourt, Brace, 1935], vol. 1, p. 245).

[119] Norberto Bobbio, "Sul fondamento dei diritti dell'uomo" (1964), in id., *L'età dei diritti* (Turin: Einaudi, 1990), p. 22.

[120] Ibid., pp. 19–20. "From a theoretical point of view I have always sustained, and new arguments are corroborating my opinion, that human rights, however fundamen-

Civility, though, is not harmony. Parliaments have replaced battle-fields, not suppressed the conflict. The historical perspective not only represents a confutation of ontological individualism, but presupposes the idea that political and social conflicts are the basis of all kinds of discourses on rights: "Religious liberty was an effect of the religious wars; civil liberties of the struggles between the parliaments and the absolute sovereigns; political liberty and social liberties the results of the birth, growth, and maturity of wage-earning workers, peasants with little or no land, or the poor."[121]

By starting from a universalist framework, it has been possible to put differences on the table, to claim other kinds of guarantees. The history of our societies can be read as the gradual transition from the abstract to the concrete, from a *self* intrinsically free of any burden and eager to secure a system of negative liberties to guarantee his freedom of choice to a *person* who, by enjoying those liberties, comes to realize that her very concrete condition asks for other liberties. Little by little, new subjects enter the scene, bringing into politics their differences, starting from what they are, interpreting the individual according to their individuality, marking the evolution of rights with their own lives.

This transition coincided with the recognition of people as beings situated in a specific social and historical context. From the perspective of negative liberty no one can have more liberty than anyone else, no one can claim special treatment. But universality and equality meet their first obstacle when we shift from civil rights to social ones. In this case it is differences that ask for recognition. "Equality and difference have a different weight when considered in relation to civil or social rights."[122] This means that liberty without legal restraints becomes privilege. In the case of social rights, these restraints should take into account that in societies based on a market economy money can become a strong force, able to jeopardize the effective possibilities or capacities of individuals to exercise their civil and political liberties.

One of the most eloquent testimonies of this shift from the abstract to the concrete is the evolution of rights that followed the United Nations declaration of universal rights. These charters explicitly state that instead of dealing with an abstract self, we deal with persons who are women and men, children and elders, immigrants and native citizens,

---

tal, are historical rights, that is, they were born in particular circumstances characterized by struggles in defense of new liberties against old powers, and came gradually, not all together and not once and for all" (Ibid., p. xiii).

[121] Ibid., pp. xiii–xiv. This could be the answer to Mouffe's critique, according to which Bobbio "does not provide us with a new rationale for representative democracy, one that would take account of the role played by interest groups" (p. 85).

[122] Bobbio, "Diritti dell'uomo e società" (1988), in *L'età dei diritti*, p. 72.

healthy and sick, and so on. All these differences "do not allow equal treatment and equal protection." Here rights are requested in the name of differences, not in the name of universality or equality, and differences ask for legislative interventions so that human dignity and autonomy—that is, universality itself—can be safeguarded.[123] Social policies are justifiable only insofar as they are capable of preventing economic differences from becoming excuses for moral and political inequalities and succeed in redressing the balance between liberty and equality. What they want to defend is not human similarities but human differences. They do not want to "suppress varieties of individual genius and character," wrote R. H. Tawney in 1931, but to allow these varieties to "find their full expression and due appreciation."[124] Like equality, liberty is a *plural idea* (Rosselli used to speak of "joint liberties") and asks to be considered according to the concrete situations and spaces in which human life expresses itself.[125]

On the question of social justice, Rosselli's legacy is particularly important because it does not simply involve a quest for state intervention. The liberal-socialist experience cannot be understood without considering that it was formed of a radical revision of the main cultural product of nineteenth-century European history: the positivist myth of replacing political government with technocratic administration, in conformity with the idea that only impartiality and rationality would liberate society from the domination of man over man. The social utopias of modernity depicted the good society as one in which all human beings feel and live according to the value and duty of productivity. They envisioned a society of producers—of social men—not of citizens. In the 1920s this perspective prevailed, overriding the ideological divisions among liberals, Fabians, and Marxists, all of whom liked to imagine the ideal social order as "a well-oiled machine" in which, wrote Bukharin, "there will be no need for special ministers of State, for police and prisons, for laws and decrees—nothing of the sort."[126]
To appreciate the original character of liberal socialism, we have to

[123] Ibid, pp. 69–73.

[124] Richard H. Tawney, *Equality* (London: Allen & Unwin, 1931), p. 49.

[125] The expression "joint liberties" was borrowed by Gobetti, who, commenting on Rosselli's article "Liberalismo socialista," wrote in 1924: "Our liberalism is also socialist once one accepts the evaluation of Marxism and socialism that we have done on many occasions. It is enough to accept the principle that all liberties are joint"; Gobetti's comment is now published as a footnote to Rosselli, "Liberalismo socialista" (1924), p. 107.

[126] Nikolai I. Bukharin and Eugene A. Preobrazhensky, *The ABC of Communism: A Popular Explanation of the Program of the Communist Party of Russia*, trans. Eden and Cedar Paul with an Introduction by Sidney Heitman (Ann Arbor: paperback, 1966), p. 74.

consider that it developed during the Fascist regime and while the Soviet Union was perfecting its own statism. The search for a new vision of socialism was, for the liberal socialists, the consequence of their revulsion at the incorporation of civil society into the state. Thus they felt strongly that it was indispensable for the social sector to remain autonomous, articulated, and pluralistic, because its multiplicity was "a providential safeguard against the power of the state and social groups." Rosselli complained of the increasing power of the state during the previous century, when it started expropriating from civil society all of its "numberless forms of association, as rich in their content as they were free and limited in extension. Before that, instead of a despotic and centralized state, there was a social federalism"; afterward, when "personal and free property became an anonymous and monopolistic capital" that "conquered the state," the state "devoured society."[127]

Liberal socialism stresses not the limits of democracy, but its potentials and promises. To take democratic promises seriously means to aim for an extension of democracy in all spheres of society, in economic and social life as well as in politics. Rosselli perceived remarkably well the centralizing and bureaucratic vocation of some versions of socialism (he knew Fabianism), which appeared to him exceptionally good at planning social services but much too insensitive toward the role that human commitment and active participation could play. During his journeys in Britain he was impressed by the life of the miners in the villages of South Wales: "Here I had, as never before, a clear and strong vision and faith in the irresistible ascent of a people who aspire to a full autonomy even in the government of industry."[128] This was the main reason he appreciated guild socialism, whose federalist utopia intended to break the power of the state and allow people to "look after the affairs of their own communities, as much as possible."[129]

Rosselli did not elaborate on the theory of an "integral federalism"; nevertheless he had a clear perception of the evolution of bureaucratic economies and techniques and understood that the core of modern socialism should be civil society. He fought in the name of diversity and

---

[127] Rosselli, "Contro lo Stato" (in *Giustizia e Libertà*, September 21, 1934), now in *Scritti politici*, p. 296. As in the case of G.D.H. Cole and R. H. Tawney, in Rosselli too the critique of the modern condition gained force from the comparison with the premodern era. In particular, Rosselli exalted the free Italian republics of the Middle Ages: "The prototype of antistatist federal society existed between the thirteenth and fifteenth centuries: they were the *comuni*, the free and equal unions represented by the cities, the corporations, the universities, the fraternities, the mutualist societies" (pp. 296–97).

[128] Rosselli, "Battaglia storica," p. 77.

[129] Rosselli, "Il movimento operaio," p. 73.

concrete differences against the ideology of the masses. In that context civil society was taken to mean pluralism, individual responsibility, the democratic ethos, and political antagonism. In our time, this can be read as an invitation to consider critically the main product of modern European democracy, the welfare state, with its propensity to produce juridical and bureaucratic hypertrophy, to induce us to believe in "the innocence and objectivity of the apparently neutral instruments of administrative power,"[130] and to replace politics with distributive techniques and citizens and parliaments with experts and public officials.

As in Rosselli's day, today we too need to tame the interventionist state. The problem, however (at least in those countries where the welfare state exists), is not that of dismantling it in order to go back to charity or private philanthropy, but that of reforming it by applying to the welfare state the two major strategies classic liberalism elaborated to limit state power: *distribution* (or decentralization) of its functions and *control*. These strategies, in turn, will be most effective when the space occupied by civil society is filled with numerous vibrant and articulated associations, through which citizens participate equally in the political dialogue that advances claims and shapes democratic institutions. "Civil associations contribute to the effectiveness and stability of democratic government" because they entail "equal rights and obligations for all" citizens, who are "bound together by horizontal relations of reciprocity and cooperation, not by vertical relations of authority and dependency . . . not as patrons and clients nor as governors and petitioners."[131]

Unlike civil rights, social rights ask for the state's direct and active intervention. But whereas the state must have the monopoly of force, this is not necessary in the case of social rights. Here the state may share with civil society the responsibility of managing and implementing social services (this is already happening even in countries where the social state is a long-standing reality). Nevertheless, even in the case of social rights, the state cannot be an association among others, because it must provide general criteria for the distribution of social services, so that every citizen can count equally. The decision about "which criteria" to apply belongs in the political arena, because it is the outcome of political and social conflict between groups or parties, not of a general theory. Indeed, it is an exquisitely political question, not one concerning the truth.

[130] Jurgen Habermas, *Die Nachholende Revoluzion* (1990), quoted from the Italian edition, *La rivoluzione recuperante* (Milan: Feltrinelli, 1990), pp. 196–97.

[131] Robert D. Putnam, *Making Democracy Work: Civic Traditions in Modern Italy* (Princeton: Princeton University Press, 1993), pp. 88–89.

Social and political conflicts may lead to partial and temporary compromises that work for a while in particular circumstances. Social justice lies in these impermanent solutions, which are, however, always at risk and partial. To make them more stable or broader depends on us, on our capacity to keep political commitment alive.

It is vital that the tension between liberty and equality remain. Political conflict is not avoidable; moreover, it is desirable because it is the channel through which citizens come to prize the common good, which is "common" not because it has one and the same meaning for all, but because it is open to be modeled and reinterpreted according to the various (and not conflict-free) voices that make of it a good for all.

And it is possible that social justice satisfies the principles of freedom whenever one succeeds in grasping the difference between a system of recognized liberties and the value this system has for all the individuals and groups that live in a given society. In the first case we are free because we have the right to choose among different possibilities of action, in the second we are free because we have the power to act, to implement these choices. Among the various modern and secular political traditions, socialism was the first to denounce the moral arbitrariness of the unequal value of sanctioned liberties in relation to the inequalities in social conditions.[132] "If the choice is between an intermediate grade of liberty that applies to the whole collectivity and an unbounded liberty furnished to a few at the expense of the many, an intermediate liberty is better, a hundred times better" (pp. 86–87).

If we cannot solve the tension between liberty and justice, nevertheless, because we live in democratic societies we are driven to imagine, and work for, a better society, a better democracy, precisely because democracy is a political system that compels us to look at politics not from the top but from below, that is, from the point of view of the citizen.[133] Democracy is another starting point from which to make a different history, not the end of history. "In substance," wrote Rosselli in 1921, "democracy, contrary to oligarchy, represents not a fixed point, but only a tendency, a tendency, moreover, unattainable."[134]

As we have seen, Rosselli frequently used Bernstein's expression "the movement means all, the end means nothing" in order to stress the voluntaristic and skeptical character of socialism. At first glance,

[132] See Salvatore Veca, *Etica e politica. I dilemmi del pluralismo: Democrazia reale e democrazia possibile* (Milan: Garzanti, 1989), ch. 9.

[133] Starting from this perspective, Giovanna Zincone analyzes the evolution of social rights in Western European societies in *Da sudditi a cittadini* (Bologna: Il Mulino, 1992).

[134] From an unpublished comment on Roberto Michels, *La Sociologia del partito politico nella democrazia moderna* (1912), quoted in Tranfaglia, *Carlo Rosselli*, p. 91.

this formula may seem ephemeral, if not empty. But this may change if we reflect on Rosselli's outline of the evolution of Marxist socialism.

As its first step the socialist movement needed, and created, a new kind of discourse, in which language had to sacrifice its richness and nuances in order to gain strength: this was the purpose and meaning of the *Communist Manifesto*. Then political action started to flow, little by little it grew more complex, to the point where the previous language ceased to be helpful. The movement needed strategies, reflections on possible aims and viable means. Then the first conquests came: workplace regulations, pensions, health insurance, universal suffrage, public schools. The final goal became more and more distant, theoretical, and hypothetical, while small and short-term goals became more and more relevant. It was as if once the stone was hurled, every point along the arc of its trajectory became a goal in itself. Finally, that mythical and prophetic language lost its power and became almost a hindrance. Only a few philosophers and leaders still used it. The gospel gave rise to commentaries, the commentaries to glosses, the glosses to footnotes, until finally the gospel lost its spirituality and the apostles became clergymen. The distance between theory and practice increased to the point where someone finally realized that theory had to be changed. A possible solution suggested itself: instead of persisting in the idea of reinterpreting the path toward the final goal, we might start to reflect on the goal itself, in particular on its place. If the goal is the perfect society, then it will always be beyond our present reach, and in the end it will be nowhere, a burden that leaves individuals feeling that they are advancing toward something that continually evades them.

Rosselli invites us to think of socialism no longer as the model to be implemented (the society par excellence) but as a status or a condition, a concrete arrangement that can improve even a little the conditions of our life and those of our fellow humans. This is already the final goal. We are not walking toward a better world; we are here, glued to the present, with a selective memory of our past and only a short view of what lies before us.

To mold a society according to a rational principle is always possible, but only at the cost of disregarding actual people and their lives—which are the only ones that exist. For this reason Rosselli writes that "socialism is not socialization, it is not the proletariat in power, it is not even material equality," but a regulative idea, spoken in the very language of our concrete society which, once it is assumed as a viewpoint on our political actions, "is realized in the small portion of it that succeeds in penetrating our lives."

Some may say that this sounds too idealistic and contingent, too skeptical and voluntaristic. But having a good public school or implementing social legislation for families has value per se, not because it prepares for the perfect society. It has value per se because it allows us, here and now, to live more in tune with our fellow citizens. If every step has a value in itself, not as a function of something else, then we will again have a goal that is able to invigorate our public discourse, one that will be no less effective and powerful than the old one that was spoken in the language of nemesis. We will have not *a* goal but *many* goals, as many as are the spaces of our lives in which we succeed in recognizing that our lives perhaps are, or can be, better now than they were before. This time our actions will have an *absolute* value, not an *instrumental* one. Every point of the space covered by our actions has its own importance, and the results of our deeds will count, even the negative ones, because a defeat can damage us much more now than when we cling to a vision of the final battle. In a permanent war of position, every individual, deed, and result is relevant. And for a liberal socialist there is no other war than a war of position.

One may object on the grounds that by insisting on the contingent moment we miss the ideal, the project, the something able to give significance and energy to our small and contingent battles.[135] But, as I said, the opposite is true. Indeed, an ideal embalmed in a society already modeled, yet always unattainable, erodes the will much more dramatically. It does so because it accustoms us to transgress and make deviations, to compromise and adjust ourselves to the empirical reality that, because it has no value in itself, deserves not to be respected, but only exploited for the good of the Ideal. This tendency will continue until the Ideal evaporates completely and the movement is nothing more than a question of bureaucratic management, incapable of speaking to anybody but its own experts. "It is so easy," wrote De Man, "to love the good in the cloudy regions of the remote future. As Dostoevskij says: 'In the abstract love of mankind, what we love is almost always nothing but ourselves.'"[136]

This story is anything but out-of-date. In recent times, those who embraced politics as a means of implementing the ideal society experienced the same dichotomy between words and deeds. The crisis of the Western European Left emerged at the moment it began to feel that its catchwords were simply words and the goal simply a fiction. Then

---

[135] During a conversation on the Italian anti-Fascists, Albert O. Hirschman suggested to me a line by Yeats where this nostalgia for a synthesis of firmness of opinions and passion is captured: "The best lack all conviction, while the worst / Are full of passionate intensity" (W. B. Yeats, "The Second Coming," in *The Collected Poems* [New York: Macmillan, 1959], p. 185).

[136] De Man, *The Psychology of Socialism*, p. 473.

even its small achievements lost their value. What is the meaning of a good public school or day-care center, an efficient library, and better care for the aged if they start to be seen as nothing more than purely empirical results? This was the tendency that led the Left to focus only on state management, to abandon its tradition of political activism and social critique. The disappearance of the ultimate goal transformed socialist ideals into a conservative defense of the welfare state and of the interests of particular and protected groups.

The call for contingency implies that the ideal rests within things, within all those particular circumstances able to make some difference in our lives. Each action is important because of the real contingency that characterizes it. The good society "is realized in the small portion of it that succeeds in penetrating our lives," in every point of space. If it is incorporated into the many little ideals we manage to implement, the ideal has great value and our responsibility will increase alongside our moral energy and the effectiveness of our actions. If we are asked to sacrifice for the socialist society, we have good reason to resist. But if we are asked to do something for our fellow citizens here and now, we may accept the invitation.

Rosselli was right when he opposed possibility to necessity, contingency to finalism, voluntarism to mechanism. He was actually making a case for political activity and moral commitment. A skeptical attitude toward the final goal can be a great stimulus to action, because it requires us not to leave anything unattempted. What we are meant to do is to keep alive the faith in equal and plural liberties, human dignity, and solidarity for all our fellow citizens, among the many other goals each of us happens to have. We must ask ourselves if it is concretely possible to pursue our life plans in a city where suffering and injustice reign. It is a matter not of identifying the individual's goals with society's goals, but of insisting that we do not endanger our moral autonomy if, among our other goals, we also include justice.

Between revolution and acceptance of the status quo there is sufficient space for political commitment, as there is between omniscient theoretical solutions aiming to eradicate injustice and acquiescence to injustice: "Socialism, considered the aspiration of people to affirm themselves in the history, . . . is a perennial becoming. There is not a day in which this process can be said to be accomplished. It is an immense ideal of life and action which induces us continually to surpass a position we have reached by facing the new challenges and problems emerging day by day."[137]

[137] Rosselli, "Liberalismo socialista" (1924), pp. 123–24.

LIBERAL SOCIALISM

Carlo Rosselli

EDITORIAL NOTE

T HE TEXT of the present essay, which appeared in its original version only in volume 1 of the author's collected works (*Opere scelte di Carlo Rosselli* [Turin: Einaudi 1973]), has had a rather complicated editorial history.[1] Carlo Rosselli composed it during his banishment on the island of Lipari in 1928–1929; from there his wife, Marion, smuggled the manuscript abroad. When Rosselli fled from Lipari and reached Paris in the summer of 1929, he seems to have set about revising the manuscript. It was not, however, published in Italian at that time but appeared instead in a French translation by Stefan Priacel (Paris: Librairie Valois, 1930).

After Italy was liberated, a "first Italian edition" appeared, with a letter from Rosselli's wife and an appendix on the polemic between Rosselli and Rabano Mauro, the pseudonym of Claudio Treves (Rome, Florence, and Milan: Edizioni U, 1945).[2] At the time this edition was being prepared the Italian manuscript of *Socialismo liberale* was unavailable, having been left behind in France together with other papers during the German invasion in 1940. Thus the text had to be translated back into Italian from the French version, a task carried out by Leone Bortolone with revisions by Aldo Garosci.[3]

[1] This Editorial Note by Carlo Rosselli's son appeared in the first Italian edition to be based on the Italian manuscript of *Socialismo liberale* in 1973 and was reprinted with an introduction by Norberto Bobbio (Turin: Einaudi 1979), from which this English translation has been made. To the manuscript of *Socialismo liberale* John Rosselli added an appendix entitled "My Reckoning with Marxism" (*I miei conti col marxismo*). As John Rosselli himself recognized in the last sentence of his Editorial Note (which I have omitted), the "very different style" of this appendix suggests that it may have been "a rough draft for a preface that was later discarded" by the author himself when the book was published in French in 1930. For these reasons I have decided to omit it here.

[2] Claudio Treves (1869–1933) was born to a Jewish family in Turin, where he studied law. As a student he became politically active among trade union and socialist circles. He was one of the founders of the Italian Socialist party, deeply involved in the Second International and particularly interested in the critique and emendation of the Italian Civil Law Code. Treves was among the socialists exiled in Paris and was close to Rosselli; he was also among the critics of *Liberal Socialism*, which he accused of throwing out socialism by rejecting Marxism. In the first Italian edition of *Socialismo liberale* (1945), the editor Aldo Garosci published an "open letter" in which Rosselli answered Treves's critique.

[3] Aldo Garosci (b. 1907) was born in Piedmont. While he was a student in Turin he joined the clandestine movement Giustizia e Libertà. Having escaped arrest, he went into exile in France, where he became one of the closest collaborators of Carlo Rosselli, with whom he fought in Spain. When the Nazis occupied Paris, Garosci emigrated and finally reached the United States, where he joined the Mazzini Society. In the United

When the family regained possession of the papers that had been left in France, they decided to deposit a number of them, including the manuscript of *Socialismo liberale*, in the National Library in Florence (see the note by Aldo Garosci in the April 1949 issue of *Il Ponte* and the further particulars furnished by Gaetano Salvemini in the July 1949 issue of the same journal). The present edition is based on this manuscript.

The manuscript appears to constitute a second draft; probably it was prepared in Paris on the basis of the original manuscript composed on Lipari. In fact, there are two versions of chapter 6 among Rosselli's papers, one of which is written in a tiny, dense hand suitable to be smuggled and seems in all likelihood to belong to the Lipari manuscript, while the second is uniform with the rest of the extant manuscript and includes various revisions. I have based the text of chapter 6 also on the second draft.

There are variants to be noted between this manuscript and the French translation of 1930: alterations, omitted passages, and additions, including two of a certain consistency. It is highly likely that these variants represent the intention of Carlo Rosselli rather than that of his translator. But since I cannot ascertain this, I have chosen to include in the text both the passages of the manuscript that are not found in the translation (distinguished by angle brackets: ⟨ ⟩) and those that are found in the translation but not in the manuscript (distinguished by square brackets: [ ]). For the latter, in the absence of a manuscript, I have used the 1945 retranslation into Italian.

In establishing the text, I have silently corrected trivial errors of orthography, punctuation, and agreement between adjectives and nouns, and so on. The subtitles are those found in the manuscript.*

John Rosselli

States he wrote a biography of Carlo Rosselli (see the Bibliographical Note). In January 1944 he was parachuted near Rome, where he joined the Party of Action's partisans. After the war he taught history at the University of Turin.

* The footnotes both of John Rosselli's Editorial Note and Carlo Rosselli's book are my addition.—ED.

PREFACE

THIS BOOK has a brief history, which accounts for its principal shortcomings and its lack of notes and a bibliography. I wrote it in secret a few months before my escape from the island of Lipari, to which I had been deported by the Fascists. It has therefore been affected by the peculiar state of tension in which I composed it, for I was compelled to use every sort of subterfuge to keep it from being confiscated during the frequent searches that were carried out: for a long time an old piano was its hiding place.

Rather than a fully elaborated book, the present work is intended to be an explicit confession of an intellectual crisis that I know to be widespread among the new generation of socialists.

This crisis is still part of the crisis of Marxism, but it has reached an infinitely more acute stage than the one it was at thirty years ago, when the well-known work of Bernstein appeared.[1] By now the crisis involves the basic foundations of Marxist doctrine, not just its practical

---

[1] Eduard Bernstein (1850–1932) was born in Berlin to a Jewish family. His political commitment started in 1871 through a reading of the works of August Bebel and Wilhelm Liebknecht (see n. 1 of ch. 2), the leaders of the anti-Lassalian German socialists, devoted to Marx and Engels and critical of the state socialism and pro-Prussian nationalism of Lassalle (see n. 2 of ch. 5). Involvement in the party was for him (as for others at that time in Europe) a true schooling, a stimulus to enrich his culture. He started studying and delivering lectures all over the country and actively participated in the process of unification of the two parties finally reached in 1875 at the Gotha Congress. Because of Bismarck's antisocialist laws, in 1878 Bernstein went into exile in Zurich, then the second most important center of the International after London. In 1883 he became the director of the *Sozialdemokrat*, the party newspaper. Meanwhile, Bismarck started a new social policy and gradually introduced health insurance (1883), accident insurance (1884–1885), and old age insurance (1889). The aim of this policy was to delegitimize the socialists, who, in fact, could not avoid a split between a left and a right wing. Bernstein lined up with the Left (Engels and Bebel), opposed class reconciliation, and distinguished between socialist politics and anti-Manchesterian politics (or professorial socialism). The trade war between Switzerland and Germany changed Swiss attitudes toward the German expatriates; in 1888 Bernstein settled in London. Bernstein, along with Kautsky, became the leader of a party deeply altered after ten year of Bismarckism: in theory intransigent and orthodox Marxist, in practice involved in reformist politics. The London experience changed Bernstein. He became an enthusiastic admirer of the Fabians and participated in the intellectual movement against positivism that started in the early 1890s all over Europe. Bernstein's Marxist revisionism expressed itself through a series of articles entitled "Probleme des Sozialismus," which appeared in Karl Kautsky's *Neue Zeit* between 1896 and 1898. In 1899 he published what became the manifesto of revisionism: *Die Voraussetzungen des Sozialismus und die Aufgaben der Sozialdemokratie*, the book to which Carlo Rosselli is referring here.

applications. Marxist philosophy, Marxist morality, and even the Marxist conception of politics leave us profoundly unsatisfied, and we are driven to set out along a new road, toward vaster horizons.

I have expressed my views with absolute frankness, for I am convinced that only a courageous reexamination of its moral and intellectual premises can give back to socialism the freshness and capacity for growth that have been missing for much too long.

In the part of the book devoted to reconstruction, my aim has been to offer a picture, albeit a foreshortened one, of a revived brand of socialism: I call it the liberal socialist position. From the historical point of view this formula might seem to contain a contradiction, inasmuch as socialism arose in reaction to the liberalism—especially the economic variety—that characterized bourgeois thought at the outset of the nineteenth century. But we have traveled a long way between then and now and accumulated a great deal of experience. The two opposing positions have gradually been drawing closer to one another. Liberalism has gradually become cognizant of the social problem and no longer appears automatically bound to the principles of classical, Manchesterian economics. Socialism is stripping itself, though not easily, of its utopianism and acquiring a new awareness of the problems of liberty and autonomy.

Is liberalism becoming socialist, or is socialism becoming liberal?

The answer is, both at the same time. Each contains an exalted but narrow vision of life, and the tendency is for both of them to interpenetrate and complement one another.

Greek rationalism and the messianism of Israel.

The first contains a love of liberty, a respect for autonomies, a harmonious and detached conception of life.

In the second the sense of justice is entirely down-to-earth; there is a myth of equality, and a spiritual torment that forbids all indulgence.

In the preface to his *Histoire du peuple d'Israel*, Renan, a great admirer of Greek civilization, observes that "liberalism (Greek) will no longer have the monopoly of the government of the world. England and America will long preserve the vestiges of biblical influence; and with us in France, the socialists[—who are, unknown to themselves, the disciples of the prophets—will always bring the practical politicians to terms."[2]

But is it even possible to describe a politics as rational if it does not put the idea of justice ahead of everything else?

C. R.]

---

[2] Ernest Renan, *History of the People of Israel* (Boston: Little, Brown, 1905; 1st French ed. 1887–1893), vol. 1, p. ix.

ONE

THE MARXIST SYSTEM

MARX'S proud intention was to furnish a scientific basis for socialism, to transform socialism into a science, into the social science par excellence: hence his disdain for his predecessors and his refusal of all moralizing. In *Socialism: From Utopian to Scientific*, Engels writes that with the two great discoveries of the materialistic conception of history and the secret of production through surplus value, "socialism became a science. The next thing was to work out all its details and relations."[1]

Marx no longer required of the socialist acts of faith and romantic devotion; indeed he distrusted chivalrous idealists. He required of the socialist the sound use of cool reason, the courage to see historical reality for what it was. Socialism was a matter of objective fact, of the intimate mechanism of capitalist society; it did not lie in the hearts of men. It had to come about, it could not fail to come about, and it would come about as the consequence not of an imaginary human free will, but of the transcendental forces that dominate men and their relations—the forces of production, in their incessant development and progress. Scientific socialism, as a very authoritative interpreter of Marxism, Antonio Labriola, used to say, announces the advent of Communist production not as a postulate, or an object of free choice, but as the result of the immanent process of history.[2]

[1] Friedrich Engels, *Socialism: From Utopian to Scientific* (1st ed. in French, 1880), now in Marx and Engels, *Collected Works* (New York: International Publishers), vol. 24, p. 305.

[2] Antonio Labriola (1843–1904) was born in Cassino and studied at the University of Naples, where the major figure was Bertrando Spaventa, the leader of German idealism in Italy. Because of serious economic difficulties, he worked at various jobs before getting a professorship at the University of Rome. In his youth Labriola wrote important essays on Spinoza, Socrates, and Vico and gradually passed from Hegelianism to Marxism. The first document of his approach to socialism was the lecture "Del Socialismo," which he delivered at the University of Rome in 1889. He then enrolled in the Italian Socialist party and began a rich correspondence with Engels, Kautsky, Liebknecht, Adler, Bebel, Ellenbogen, and Lafargue. Between 1895 and 1899, both in French and Italian, Labriola published several important essays on Marx's philosophy: "In memoria del Manifesto dei Comunisti," (1895), "Del materialismo storico, delucidazione preliminare" (1896), and "Discorrendo di socialismo e di filosofia" (1897). He was deeply critical of the revisionists and the theorists of the so-called crisis of Marxism, particularly Croce, Sorel, Bernstein, and Masaryk. Labriola was one of the first great European interpreters of Marx's and Engels's thought. During his lifetime he was almost an isolated thinker in

The principles of this Marxist science are so universally known that here it is enough to refer to them summarily: Marx assumes that economic need is fundamental for humans. For the progressive satisfaction of this need, humans are *forced* to resort to methods and relations of production that are independent of their will. The forces of production are the determining factor in the historical process. All the phenomena of social, political, and spiritual life have a derivative, relative, and historical character, since they are the product of the mode and the relations of production.

The historical process is the result of an immanent dialectical law, the rhythm of existence; in other words, it unfolds by virtue of, and through, a perennial conflict, which becomes dramatic at critical moments, between the expansive forces of production and the conservative forces symbolized by preexisting social relations. The passage from one phase of production to the next will come about through intrinsic, iron necessity, through the operation of historical laws that correlate with the various systems of production.

Class struggle is the expression of this contrast between the forces of production and ossified forms of social life. All of history resolves itself into an endless series of class struggles. This struggle always ends with the victory of the exigencies of production, that is, with the political victory of the class that, albeit unconsciously, embodies these exigencies.

The capitalist system of production is also torn by an insuperable inner contradiction between the character of the system of production, which is ever more collective, and the character of the system of appropriation of the means of production and exchange, which is ever more individual and monopolistic. Bourgeois relations of production, trade, and property, which are necessary for the bourgeois class to exist and dominate, clash ever more strongly with the imperatives of life and development present in the forces of production.

This contradiction, through the operation of the dynamic law that governs capitalist development, will lead necessarily to the negation of the bourgeois regime (the category of value generates that of surplus value, which in turn generates the concentration of capital, the progressive impoverishment of the proletariat, the disappearance of the middle class, overproduction, and crisis).

The manifestation of this contrast is the ever more pitched battle between the proletariat and the bourgeoisie. It will of necessity end—

Italy because of his irreducible antipositivism. His interpretation of Marxism as a philosophy of praxis found more sympathetic readers among the intellectuals of the new generation, such as Giovanni Gentile, Antonio Gramsci, Piero Gobetti, and Rodolfo Mondolfo (see n. 4 of this chapter, n. 10 of ch. 3, and n. 24 of the Introduction).

unless a social catastrophe supervenes—with the victory of the proletariat as it takes on the burden of the expansive thrust of the forces of production. The proletariat will conquer political power through violence and will abolish the bourgeois mode of appropriation, since it goes against the necessities of increasingly collectivized production; it will socialize the means of production and exchange. The state will disappear along with all class distinctions. Out of the ruins of bourgeois society there will arise a society of the free and the equal, in which the prodigious development of production, no longer blocked by the monopolistic system of social relations, will furnish to each the possibility of satisfying fully his material needs and will liberate humanity from enslavement to material forces.

This is in essence the constant belief of Marx, as proclaimed in the *Communist Manifesto* (1847), reaffirmed in lapidary phrases in the preface to the *Critique of Political Economy* (1859), developed and illustrated in *Capital* (1867), and confirmed until the end of his life. Marx's thought is thoroughly deterministic, and in this respect the efforts of Sorel,[3] Labriola, and Mondolfo[4] to prop up an interpretation of it that leaves

[3] Georges Sorel (1847–1922) was born in Cherbourg, France, and studied at the École Polytechnique in Paris. As an engineer he joined the Bureau of Bridges and Highways, a state company. In reaction to his uninspiring job (which, however, he never quit), he developed a deep concern for "heroic" virtues. His socialism was inspired more by Proudhon than by Marx and his attraction for heroism by Ernest Renan's reflections on progress, industrialism, and decadence. This background explains the centrality Sorel gave to both productive life and will. Sorel's socialism passed from an orthodox Marxism to an antiorthodox one; this transition took place during the 1890s and reflected the increasing separation, all over Europe, between a dry Marxist academicism and the political problems imposed by social legislation and parliamentary action, between revolution and reformism. Between 1894 and 1897 Sorel was the editor of two important journals, *Ere Nouvelle* and *Devenir Sociale*. During the disputes between Bernstein and Kautsky, Sorel sided with the former, becoming one of the leading European figures of the so-called crisis of Marxism. His rupture with socialist politics came in 1901, in tandem with his changed opinion on the Dreyfus case (he had been pro-Dreyfus until 1899). He started to see the socialists of his time as supporters of statism and became increasingly critical of their parliamentary involvement, until he rejected the party as the leading structure of the proletariat. He started to see the syndicate as the only political force, because of its inner connection with the sphere of production, the proper place of the working class. Sorel then theorized the "general strike" as the "absolute" and creative revolutionary act par excellence: he assigned to the intellectuals the role of provoking the strike by evoking heroic myths and symbols. His exaltation of violence found supporters among the rightists too, especially Charles Maurras (the leader of *Action Française*) and then Mussolini, and led him to exalt the Bolshevik revolution. The main characteristics of Sorel's thought were antidemocratism and a deep contempt for the "arrogant and cynical bourgeois democracies." Among his writings are *Le Procès de Socrate* (1889), "L'Avenir socialiste des syndicats" (1898), "L'éthique du socialisme" (1899), *Réflexions sul la violence* (1906 and 1908), and *Les Illusions du progrès* (1906).

[4] Rodolfo Mondolfo (1877–1976) was born in the Marche region, to a Jewish family. He

room for the autonomous function of men in history have always come to grief. Either the Marxist system is deterministic, or else it is not—as an organic system of thought, I mean. On every occasion on which Marx consciously set out to restate his meaning, to say exactly how far his theses went, he did so in language that leaves no purchase for doubt. I shall not dwell on the famous section of the preface to the *Critique of Political Economy*, written in 1859 and well known to even the humblest devotees of Marxist studies. It will be enough to recall that in the preface to *Capital*, Marx observes that modern society can neither bypass nor cancel by decree a single phase of its *natural* development; at most it can shorten the period of gestation and delivery. These phases are governed by natural laws and tendencies that are fulfilled by iron necessity. Marx returns with careful deliberation to the necessary, indeed fatal, character of the evolution of the productive forces, and of the entire historical process, in the famous passage from the last chapter of volume 1 of *Capital*, which ends with the phrase: "But capitalist production itself begets its own negation with *the inexorability of a law of nature.*"[5] In these concluding lines of *Capital* Marx feels compelled to refer to the corresponding pages of the *Manifesto* in order to demonstrate his own perfect coherence, and thus puts, at a distance of twenty years, a definitive gloss on his earlier work.

Six years later, responding to a long and brilliant review of his work, Marx explicitly endorses the words of his penetrating Russian critic: "Marx treats the social movement as a process of natural history, governed by laws not only independent of human will, consciousness, and intelligence, but rather, on the contrary, determining that will, consciousness, and intelligence."[6] Bernstein would certainly protest

studied at the University of Florence and taught at the Universities of Bologna and Padua. As a historian of philosophy he wrote important books on ancient Greek philosophy, Spinoza, and the French Enlightenment. Contrary to the deterministic tendency of Marxism, Mondolfo interpreted historical materialism as a historicism, insisting on the human factors of consciousness and will. Attempting to provide theoretical foundations for a reformist socialism, he engaged in a polemic with all proponents of contemporary forms of Marxism, such as determinism, maximalism, revolutionary syndicalism, and finally Leninism. In his attempt to accommodate the philosophy of socialism in the Italian political tradition, Mondolfo tried to combine Marx and Mazzini. This project made a strong impression on Gobetti and Carlo and Nello Rosselli. In 1939, because of racial laws, Mondolfo went into exile in Argentina, where he taught at the Universities of Córdoba and Tucumán between 1940 and 1952. Among his writings are *Dalla Dichiarazione dei diritti al Manifesto dei comunisti* (1906), *Tra il diritto di natura e il comunismo* (1909), *Il materialismo storico in Federico Engels* (1912), and *Sulle orme di Marx* (1919).

[5] Karl Marx, *Capital: A Critique of Political Economy*, trans. Samuel Moore and Edward Aveling from the 3d German edition by Friedrich Engels (New York: Modern Library, 1906), p. 837 (Rosselli's italics).

[6] In the Author's Preface to the second edition of *Capital* (1873), Marx used A. Sieber's

vehemently at this synthetic interpretation. But Marx, who is the only competent judge in this matter, not only did not object to it, but adopted it with satisfaction, praising the author for his perspicacity.

Countless citations from Marx could be adduced in support of this deterministic interpretation, but the spirit that pervades his work, the approach he takes to all the problems he confronts, carry even more weight than his individual words. The thrust of his polemic against the utopians and the bourgeois ideologues may, as Engels maintained in old age, have driven Marx to accentuate the deterministic aspects of his system, but it would never have led him to reverse its basic meaning.

Certainly, the value of Marxist determinism is entirely conventional and relative. When Marx states that the material forces of production are the determining factor in the historical process, he knowingly fastens on just one link in the deterministic chain. But this does not mean that he ignores the preceding links: Marx repeatedly insisted on the influence of natural and environmental factors, and in particular on that of race. But he takes them as given, as constants. What interests him are the variations of social phenomena in the context of this environment, which he assumes to be fixed, and the law of these variations. For example, the natural and anthropological characteristics of the territory of Britain can safely be assumed not to have changed in the period 1760–1830. If one then asks what the far-reaching changes that took place in English social relations, and in the fundamental historical events of the period generally, are to be attributed to, Marx replies without hesitation: to the transformation of the mode of production. The enormous influence exerted on him, and on all the writers of the period, by the industrial revolution, in which the machine and the factory system were truly seen to play the role of demiurges, is well known. But it is also well known that Marx never dared to produce explicit arguments to support his general thesis about history. It resulted from an arbitrary extension, by analogy, of the conclusions at which he had arrived in his powerful analysis of the birth of the capitalist system.

Now the central problem of Marxism as the doctrine of the proletarian revolution lies in the role it assigns to the human element, to the factor of will.

In his youth, under the influence of Feuerbach, Marx had defended the purely human character of history: it was not to be handed over to the rule of transcendental forces. But this defense, robust and full at the outset, is gradually drained of content and significance as his doctrine

---

words to answer those critics who had accused him of treating economics "metaphysically" (*Capital*, p. 23).

takes shape, until it is reduced to a merely polemical and formal residue. In the Marxist system we are dealing with a human species that is sui generis composed of men who by definition are not free, who strive under the pressure of need, who are forced to have recourse to methods of production that are independent of their will and to participate in the social relations thus dictated. They have only one claim to have any operative role in the historical process, which is that they are an integral part of the productive process. Other aspects are derivative and secondary, a function of the development of the productive forces. They will acquire genuine worth and functional autonomy only in a Communist society, because then and only then will they be liberated from enslavement to material forces. Psychologically speaking, the Marxian man is no more than the *homo oeconomicus* of Bentham. His psychological state is a constant factor, like race or climate. The reactions that this homo oeconomicus displays are not spontaneous and autonomous but are caused by changes in the relations of production and thus in social relations. It is precisely because he assumes this to be a psychological given that Marx takes for granted that the proletarians will revolt as soon as the state of subjection in which they are living and the causes of this subjection have been revealed to them. But it is clear that the determining cause of this interior revolution resides not in them, but in the external mechanism of capitalistic production.

The inner focus of Marxism is entirely on this concept of the historical necessity of the advent of the socialist society by virtue of an objective and fatal process in which *things* are transformed. (Individual subjectivities will also change, but along a necessary path laid down by the psychological "constant.") If this concept is removed, or attenuated, the result is that the entire system will collapse. If Marx had really assigned an autonomous influence in the unfolding of the historical process to human will; if, as the revisionists pretend, he had affirmed that the relation between the material forces of production and social consciousness is one of interdependence, and not of cause and effect, how would he have been able to state with such categorical certainty the law governing capitalist development? ⟨To do so he would have had to possess an equivalent categorical certainty about the laws ruling the inner life and psychological mechanism of mankind. But where would he have found a certainty of this kind?

Experimental psychology is a young science, and even today we are far from possessing categorical certainties in its domain. Marx for his part never showed much interest in problems of individual and collective psychology.⟩ It would be absurd if Marx had dedicated his whole life to studying one side of the problem—the one that relates to the external world—while totally ignoring the other side, the one that relates to the world of consciousness.

Clearly the introduction of the factor of "human will" into the historical process means that any sociological prognosis one might care to make automatically loses all scientific value. The fact is that one either has to accept a sphere of liberty, no matter how qualified, in the life of the spirit, in the mode of being of consciousness, or deny it. If one accepts it, the concept of historical necessity fails, and the alternative arises. One introduces an element of doubt, in other words, that is entirely alien to the Marxist system. Or else one denies this sphere of liberty; in other words, one maintains that human will, in given circumstances, must go in a determined direction, in which case the manifestation of human will is reduced to the rank of an effect, no longer that of a contributing cause. In either case, the attempt to reconcile the Marxist system with a nondeterministic interpretation fails.

There are various further indirect proofs of determinism implicit in the Marxist system. If Marx had assigned an independent and determining influence to human will, how would we explain his scorn for all those who grounded the claims of the proletariat on morality and right? If the will is to play a role, all the stimuli that combine to turn it in the desired direction have to be powerfully encouraged. But we see that he considers any socialist propaganda that appeals to a principle of justice profoundly aberrant and dangerous.

Marx is always fearful that in the cut and thrust of debate he might somehow reveal the historicist origins of his thought. He is always careful to warn us that his point of view is "less [apt] than any other" to make the individual responsible for the relations from which, socially, he derives, "whatever he does to get free of them." The immanent laws of capitalist production impose themselves on capitalists as "coercive external laws." Their will is irrelevant. Indeed, it is well that they should not try to rebel against the role that the dialectic of history assigns them. They would waste their time and delay the following stages.

The proletariat, for its part, cannot accuse capitalism of moral or juridical failings. Morality and right are historical categories, pure offshoots of the relative economic structures. The capitalists are perfectly in tune with the morality and the right that are proper to the capitalist era. If they exploit the proletarians by paying them only a fraction of the value they produce, they do no more than obey the "immanent laws" of exchange in the capitalist regime. In order to conform to the economic, juridical, and moral principles of capitalism, the capitalist has only to furnish the wage earner the means—in cash—to live and reproduce himself. If he behaved differently, he would not be fulfilling his social function as a "fanatical agent of accumulation." The worker cannot protest. If he is losing the surplus of value that human labor, and human labor alone, has the virtue of producing, he is doing so because of an ineluctable historical necessity. Profit, in this historical phase, is just as natural as the introduction of machines, the division of labor, the factory system, the wage earner, the world market, crises. . . . The bourgeois, Marx writes, are perfectly correct to maintain that the present distribution is "just," because in fact "it is the only 'just' division on the basis of the present form of production."

Those who referred to *Capital* as the most rigorous justification of capitalism had good reason to do so!

Labriola remarks that the *Communist Manifesto* is utterly prosaic; it contains no rhetoric, no protests.[7] Communism is now a science. It does not bemoan pauperism in order to eliminate it. It does not shed tears for nothing. The sorrow of living is transformed on its own into a spontaneous force of revendication. Ethics and idealism now consist in putting scientific thought at the service of the proletariat.

In truth, Marx is so strongly convinced of the inevitable realization of Communist society through the operation of the law of capitalist development, that, like a scientist conducting an experiment, he is principally concerned with eliminating from the social game all factors that might disturb or inhibit the full development of that law. Above all he wants to eliminate sentimental and moralistic residues. All the tactical guidelines, the whole practical program that Marx advises socialist parties to adopt, answer to this fundamental purpose: to accelerate and facilitate the process of capitalist development. His discourse on free trade supplies a typical example.

Only one strong objection to the deterministic interpretation of Marxism can be advanced: the theory of class struggle. How can one explain Marx's effort to awaken class consciousness in the proletarians, his revolutionary rhetoric, if the role assigned to men in the historical process is purely passive?

Here it is necessary to distinguish between the general formulation of the theory of class struggle, which in no sense contradicts the deterministic trend of his thought, and the particular way he applied it to the case of the struggle between the proletariat and the bourgeoisie. In general terms, Marx confines himself to stating that class struggle is the *necessary* result of the conflict that exists in things themselves, the

---

[7] Antonio Labriola, *In Memoria del Manifesto dei Comunisti* (1895), now in id., *La concezione materialistica della storia*, ed. Eugenio Garin (Bari: Laterza, 1971), p. 45. English edition with the title *Essays on a Materialistic Conception of History*, translated from the French edition by Charles H. Kerr (Chicago: Kerr, 1908), p. 72.

human face of the dialectic immanent in things. He notes that the formal and external revolution in social relations arrives only when a revolution has already taken place at the core, in the mode and technique of production. For Marx the psychological reaction is a posteriori, it follows economic fact as shadow follows light; and economic fact, let us remember, is the result not of a free will but of an instinctive, enslaved will, dominated by need. This may be a very simplistic and vulgar conception of psychology, but undoubtedly it lies at the root of the Marxist construct. Marx himself attaches so little importance to it that he never addresses the matter directly.

It cannot be denied, however, that in applying the general theory to the particular case of the struggle between the proletariat and the bourgeoisie, and especially when writing as a propagandist, Marx sometimes abandoned the deterministic position. But he comes back to it when he is expounding his system of thought in a more measured and inclusive fashion. When he departs from determinism, this is not only the result of an inner conflict between two parts of his nature, that of the scientist and that of the agitator, but also a consequence of the doubt he felt about the resolution of the conflict that was just beginning to take shape. Where the past was concerned, he could safely affirm that the clash had always ended with the triumph of the class that, interpreting the needs of production, fulfilled a revolutionary function; but where the future was in question, his historical sense prevented him from offering such ironclad guarantees. So he attached to his prediction of the standard outcome a subsidiary hypothesis: that the struggle might end with the exhaustion of the two combatants, perhaps through a lack of historical awareness on the part of the proletariat. This element of doubt had the effect of legitimating the use of propaganda, efforts to organize, and insurrectional action; it is due to very complex causes, and it actually constitutes the only voluntaristic moment in his system. We might note as well that this final voluntaristic moment is, psychologically, the product of Marx's axiomatic belief that the death knell of capitalism, in England at least, was about to sound—that within the body of the old society, which was ever more incapable of solving the main problems of social life, there had matured the objective elements that alone could ensure the viability of a Communist society.

The fundamental impetus of the revolutionary process, even as the drama reaches the final act, truly lies not in propaganda or in the progressive awakening of proletarian consciousness, but in the dramatic collision of the contradictory elements that capitalism contains. It is catastrophism, that is, the phenomenon of universal proletarianization, of the spread of poverty, of the concentration of capital in a few hands, of the ever more uncontrollable crises, that provokes, excites, and exasperates the proletarian rebellion and endows its prophet with a messianic certainty. Propaganda has the task of accelerating the process and eliminating obstacles; it never plays a causal role. It is the crowning effect of a complex of causes that are prior to and independent of it, and without them it would be left impotent and sterile. The space that Marx gives to the element of will is thus very limited indeed; it is more a formal seal than a shaping force. ⟨I repeat: the Marxist system is either deterministic or it is not—at any rate as an organic system of thought.⟩

TWO

FROM MARXISM TO REVISIONISM

[The Marxist Religion]

THOUGH THE LIBRARY of socialist literature contains thousands of volumes, it does not include a serious ideological history of contemporary socialism—in other words, a history of Marxism and its revisionist currents down to the actual phase of criticism and overcoming.

Pure Marxists have never placed any importance on such a history, *et pour cause*; but we cannot reprove the orthodox for not having given us the history of heresy. They are stuck fast, like an oyster to a reef, and under the delusion that they alone possess the absolute, integral, intangible truth, they gaze fixedly at the "underlying economic structure" while stubbornly denying that there is anything to revise in the corpus of Marxist doctrine. But the odd thing is that the revisionists have not made the effort to provide a history of this kind either, despite their typically heretical anxiety to deny their heresy by claiming a strict descent from Marxism.

And yet such a history would be a singularly ironic and suggestive one, especially if it were done according to Marxist historiographical criteria, since this would force Marxism, *as the doctrine of the socialist revolution*, to devour itself, rehabilitating the revisionism it has so often reviled. The fact is that if we admit for a moment that ideological positions reflect the stage of development reached by the forces of production and the relations of class, the consequence is that, after the profound economic transformations that have taken place from Marx's time to our day, his doctrine of the proletarian revolution also calls for a substantial revision—unless we take the view that Marxist relativism applies to everything else, economics, law, art, politics, and morality, but not to Marxist doctrine itself.

In the history of Marxism, three stages can be distinguished: the religious stage, the critical stage, and the current stage, in which it is clearly being overcome. In the first, which can be said to end around 1900, the Marxist system in its entirety received the enthusiastic, almost unanimous allegiance of the Continental socialist elite. For the likes of Bebel, Kautsky, Liebknecht, Guesde, Lafargue, and Plekhanov,[1] the connection between socialism and Marxism soon turned into complete identity. Marxism appeared to them to be a monolithic whole, a new vision of the world and of life, the specific philosophy of the socialist revolution. There was no question of interpretation, only of application. The movement, still young and militant and swayed by messianic preachers, set itself apart by a proud, intransigent declaration of faith meant to signal its detachment from and superiority to all the other social and socialist schools. Despite its overpowering realism, the new doctrine exerted an almost religious hold. To be Marxist was like belonging to a different breed, a chosen people for whom the veil of life's mystery had been torn away. Humankind was still wrapped in a mist of false ideology produced by false shepherds to serve class interests, unaware of its own existence and its own future. Only the Marxist saw clearly into the past and the present and had the ability, because of his realization of the laws of development of capitalist society, to work rationally for the advent of a new age. Marxism was like a new consciousness, totally critical, lucid, and rational; it trusted with mathematical certainty in the rightness and the inevitable victory of the socialist ideal. Marxism triumphed not so much because of the intrinsic contribution it made to the understanding of the capitalist world as because of the certainty it succeeded in instilling in its followers of the rational nature of their faith and because of its appeal to the positivist method then so much in vogue.

Everything in Marx, and in his works, conspired to the same end: the extreme difficulty of penetrating his writings; the absence of a systematic précis; his learning, which was both encyclopedic and aristocratic; his style, which was apodictic and abstruse; the mystery surrounding his life; his long exile; and above all the awareness he had, to an unprecedented degree, of his own greatness and the irrefutable verity of his teachings. It is enough to reread the *Manifesto*, one of the most powerful pamphlets in history, to understand the reasons for its immense influence. It is hard to resist him, indeed for a simple soul who first comes to realize the state of subjection in which he is living it is impossible. No believer in the power of the will, no man of action, ever succeeded in arousing more rebelliousness and more fanatical dedication than this irritable bookworm did with his twenty famous pages. He traps you with his seductive dialectic, and when he has you in his grip, he makes your brain shiver with pronouncements worthy of the

---

[1] August Friedrich Bebel (1840–1913), Karl Kautsky (1854–1938), Wilhelm Liebknecht (1826–1900), Mathieu-Basile (Jules) Guesde (1845–1922), Paul Lafargue (1842–1911), and Georgy V. Plekhanov (1857–1918) were the leaders of European socialism who remained devoted to Marxism and, in different degrees, depositaries of what was called Marxism.

god of vengeance. The *Manifesto*, which was the only conduit between him and the masses, possesses all the marks of revelation to an eminent degree. The premises are laid down with apodictic finality, the chain of reasoning is formidable and compelling. The work has a brutal and agitated sincerity, with faith disguised as science, and science transformed into a polemical engine; life and the rhythm of society are viewed in cyclopic focus. In the *Manifesto* Marx speaks the language of nemesis. Nothing could be more dramatic than his deliberately frigid analysis of the capitalist system of exploitation, which terminates with his vision of the inevitable catastrophe, from which alone the new society of free and equal men, the socialist society, can emerge. A romantic dream in the name of reason! Justice allied with science— indeed science that is justice itself! What a power of attraction! How can one resist it, and why should one?

But we have to admit that Marxist canons of propaganda and tactics were admirably suited to the immediate task faced by the first socialist vanguards, which was that of awakening the great sleeper—the proletariat—and giving it the first rudimentary awareness of itself, its power, and its right not to live enslaved and famished. What did Marx's fatalistic determinism matter, or his erroneous apocalyptic vision, or the angry aspersions he cast on eternal moral values, which he called the token of "petits bourgeois" socialists and the source of their impotence? What did these things matter when Marx, like Joshua before the walls of Jericho, was proclaiming that victory was imminent?

What a sense of inner peace and certainty his prophetic language imparted to the first persecuted apostles! Strike at us but hear us, they could say to bourgeois society. Hear us because we possess the secret of your moral life. We do not rise up against you in total, blank negation; rather we recognize, as no one has ever done before, your grandiose, indispensable historical function. Indeed, we wish you to conduct your experiment to its conclusion and to complete the cycle that the god of production has assigned to you. This is necessary for our own victory. But remember that soon after, following the gigantic convulsion that will signal your death throes, we will be your only legitimate heirs. You yourself will supply us with the human material for our battle, the proletariat, along with all the other conditions that will make your end inevitable. You will dig your own grave by magnifying to an infinite degree the contradictions that are already quietly eating at you. You yourself will accumulate the wealth, the productive power, the technical capacity, that will permit what is today a utopia to become reality. Rebellion is useless; all efforts to escape from the ineluctable laws of capitalistic development are in vain. We speak the language of Fate, and Fate in our century goes by the name of Science.

With extraordinary rapidity, through an elementary psychological mechanism, these putative new truths were transformed into dogmas to which all categorically subscribed, in the belief that Marx's genius had delivered an irrefutable demonstration of them in his famous books. The masses adopted the most transitory and antiscientific, but terribly suggestive, portion of Marx's thought (the rigid opposition between the classes, the catastrophic vision, the apocalypticism) and made of them so many articles of faith, which it was a gross transgression to call in question. The few who took it on themselves to retrace all the steps in Marx's very elaborate proof either fell victim to it, becoming the captives of a system that they were not strong enough to refute and too timid to criticize, or else rebelled and thus automatically cut themselves off from the movement. Ferocious persecution by the bourgeoisie made it certain that the orthodox were on the right track and thus validated the articles of the new Marxist creed. On the barricades and in the jails faith grew stronger and principles more inflexible, and hope waxed that the marvelous dream was about to come true.

And instead . . . instead it was different, as the more cautious and farsighted had warned it would be. Instead of a social revolution and expropriation taking place, the workers' movement was born, and with it political liberties, social legislation, and mass political parties.

The Workers' Movement

The reform praxis, or rather the anti-Marxist praxis, of the socialist workers' movement took hold in all countries in an almost muted fashion, more as the result of force majeure and the lesson of experience than of conscious choice, and often counter to the intent of the theoreticians. The latter have always felt a certain mistrust of the syndicalist movement, beginning with Marx himself, who almost ignored its existence. In the Marxist system the area of useful action assigned to the *sindacato* (trade union) is very restricted, and it is valued only as a factor in politics. In all of Europe, with the exclusion of England, where a party arose as the political expression of the trade unions, friction developed from the outset between the parties and the sindacati—to the apparent detriment of the syndicalist movement, which the leadership wanted to harness to the parties, but in reality to the complete detriment of the parties, who found themselves forced to reconcile the irreconcilable: the theoretical with the practical, the messianic simplicity of their teleology with concrete syndicalist demands, the revolutionary tactics and purposeful intransigence of the class struggle with the day-to-day phenomena of bargaining and collaboration on the part of the sindacati. In the name of their ultimate goals, the socialist parties found themselves constrained to intervene in favor of modest sections of the work force or to support detailed demands, compromising their revolutionary purity for one mess of pottage after another. But they had no choice. As the dikes of reaction fell, the proletarian tide could not be contained and had risen inexorably, overflowing new territory, battering down theoretical walls, washing aside every logical obstacle, all the cries of non possumus, the excommunications, and the thunderbolts from Mount Sinai uttered in the *Manifesto*. Either they jettisoned their formulaic credo and went along with this groundswell, or else they were capsized. Even the most intransigent Marxists wisely grappled onto the first horn of the dilemma, though verbal equivocation might conceal the surrender that had taken place.

The syndicalist movement basically never adhered to the Marxist program, much less to its spirit and its *forma mentis*. Of all the theses of Marxism, the only one it retained, with due modifications, was the principle of class struggle and the self-emancipation of the proletariat, and this was undoubtedly a fundamental tactical and pedagogical principle, to whose elaboration Marx had contributed more than any other writer. But it certainly cannot be considered the exclusive property of the Marxist school (Marx stole the formula outright from Blanqui), if for no other reason than that it was always the instinctive rule of the workers' organizations. For the rest, the syndicalists have implicitly denied all the beliefs of the Marxists, asserting the possibility and the desirability of a gradual transformation of bourgeois society through the use of the ballot box, contract negotiations, agitation—in sum by having recourse to the democratic method. Though employing the force of numbers and the weight of its interests, the syndicalist movement has been careful not to deride, as Marxism taught it to do, the old substrate of belief in natural law and morality; and it has appealed effectively to innate personal rights and a higher principle of justice. Far from legitimating on historical grounds the power and function of the bourgeoisie, far from bowing before the necessity, however transient, for the labor force to obey the laws of the market under the capitalist regime, the syndicalists have contested their validity for ethical reasons and set about eroding them in contract negotiations. They have replaced Marx's dramatic and pessimistic vision of the social process with an optimistic, constructive one that rejects the simplifications and the linear contradictions in which Marxism delighted. Powerful syndicalist organizations have replaced the tiny revolutionary clans lurking in the shadows and awaiting the final crisis; they have stridden forth in broad daylight, directed by men with their heads on their shoulders and the ability to get things done, men who have given the coup de grace to the romantic figures of the conspirator and the revolutionary and who, since they come from the ranks of the workers themselves, dismiss any abstract contemplation of the social revolution and any excessive idealization of proletarian virtue. Spokesmen for the masses, representatives of average values, hopes, and needs, rather than standard-bearers of small, exceptional groups, they fight for concrete and immediate ends like increased pay, a shorter working day, a wider suffrage, and the democratization of the factory regime, and in so doing they sometimes go too far in the direction of pragmatism. They no longer wait for a political party to order them to revolt but instead demand sustained action in parliament and in public bodies to promote an environment of complete liberty and the passage of legislation protecting labor. Growing awareness of the limits of syndical action, contact with economic reality, the habit of dealing with contradiction and responsibility, the magnitude of the results gradually achieved, which create an unforeseen, albeit limited, sense of solidarity with the world around them—everything combines to snuff out facile illusions within the workers' movement concerning the possibility, and above all the desirability, of a sudden and violent upheaval. The proletariat, following the rise of the syndicalist and cooperative movement and the conquest of political liberties, feels ever more clearly that in truth it no longer has everything to gain and nothing to lose from a social catastrophe. Especially in the more advanced countries, it knows that it is guaranteed a level of well-being, and a complex of institutions and rights that it will preserve only by keeping the social organism from suffering violent shocks, and above all by maintaining the level of productivity and the rhythm of progress unchanged.

This, in a word, means standing the Marxist creed on its head; extremists call it the reformist "degeneration" of the sindacati. But as this "degeneration" has lasted more than half a century and grows more pronounced with every passing year, it is one with which even the most puritanical are bound to come to terms.

This pronounced change of course in the practical realm was matched by another in ideology. The monolith of Marxist doctrine, having withstood unscathed the fury of persecution, soon revealed deep fissures in an atmosphere of untrammeled criticism. Revisionism, a critical review of the whole new and imposing state of affairs, came into being.

Revisionism

Revisionism should be viewed less as a systematic attempt at a critique and consolidation of Marxism by a unified group of writers than as a

protest, variously articulated and motivated, by the new socialist generation against the dull conformism of pure Marxists, who are unable
to adapt their theory to the new praxis of the workers or to conceive of a
socialism not strictly bound to the materialist position in philosophy.
Among Bernstein, Sorel, Jaurès,[2] Croce,[3] Labriola, and Mondolfo, to
mention only the best known of them, there is a bond that is more
psychological than tangible, a product of the ongoing debate. They
were driven by a common urge, but the conclusions concerning the
essence and significance of Marxist teaching at which they arrived
were often divergent and even contradictory. Each of these writers
advanced his own personal interpretation and often fathered a "trend"
or a "school," like Bernstein in Germany and Sorel in France and Italy.
Still, despite this disharmony, they had something in common that
linked them and that permits us to speak of them as a unitary movement. The whole of revisionism, both of the Right and of the Left, can
in fact be summed up as the effort to make room in the Marxist system
for the will and the optimism of the workers' movement. Even the

---

[2] Jean Jaurès (1859–1914) was professor of literature at the University of Toulouse and
the most prominent figure of French reformist socialism. Deeply engaged in the reopen-
ing of Dreyfus trial, he never embraced the scientific socialism professed by his alterego
within the French Socialist party, Jules Guesde. He was killed in 1914, perhaps as a
consequence of his opposition to the war. Among his writings are *La Pensée nouvelle*
(1895), *Études socialistes* (1902), and *L'Armée nouvelle* (1910).

[3] Benedetto Croce (1866–1952) was born in the Abruzzi region and studied in Naples,
where he then lived, except for a few years spent in Rome after having lost his parents in
the earthquake of 1883. In Rome he met Antonio Labriola, who introduced him to
Marxism. Along with Giovanni Gentile (see n. 10 of ch. 3), his companion in the battle
against positivism, Croce edited the philosophical journal *La Critica*, which he founded
in Naples in 1903. In 1925 he signed (or subscribed to) the *Manifesto* against fascism which
had a tremendous impact among the new generation of anti-Fascists. Croce developed
his idealism through a critique of historical materialism and by meditating on the role of
economics in spiritual life. His conclusion was that life is a synthesis of a plurality of
spheres: utility (economics), beauty (aesthetics), good (morals), and truth (logic). This
plurality was not horizontal, though, because of the superiority of the last category,
concerning which Croce—following Hegel—also distinguished between intellect (based
on abstract and general concepts) and reason (as synthetic understanding), including the
former (which is peculiar to natural sciences) within the category of utility and not of
truth. The spheres were not static and given hypostases but were in perpetual conflict.
On this conflict human life was based. From this Croce came to the conclusion that
history is the history of freedom and that freedom is the last religion (the secular religion)
of humanity. Liberalism was for him life itself, the most complete and mature way of life,
an ethical liberalism that he always kept clearly distinct from both economic and political
liberalism. Here lies the source of his polemic against both the theorists of free market
and the democrats. Croce's production is huge and embraced the range of the human-
ities. For our purpose we may mention at least *La storia ridotta sotto il concetto generale
dell'arte* (1893), *Materialismo storico ed economia marxistica* (1899), *Filosofia della pratica* (1909),
Storia d'Italia dal 1871 al 1915 (1928), *Etica e Politica* (1931), and *La storia come pensiero e come
azione* (1939).

revolutionaries are driven by the same need: to break with the concept of historical necessity that Marx had asserted so forcefully, or else reduce it to a formula sufficiently elastic to accommodate the needs of Blanquist voluntarism. Leninism itself, with all its respect for the letter of Marxism, did no more than develop in an autonomous and original manner all the voluntaristic aspects of the system, which is to say its doctrine relating to periods of transition and the functions of dictatorship and terror.

The revisionists themselves were not always conscious of how far their critique went. Indeed, it has to be said that in the beginning their purposes had been more than modest, merely a question of correcting a few one-sided postulates, of combating notions about tactics that were a little too absolute, and above all of reducing belief in catastrophe to relative and secondary importance. No one dreamed of attacking the foundations of the system to which they all made obeisance. Bernstein never thought of taking a stand against Marx. The revision was intended to stay inside the bounds of the system and cautiously proceed, with the aid of countless quotations from Marx, to replace the angular and rugged Marx of orthodox tradition with a more complex and human Marx.

It is not the case that they accomplished what they did through pure dialectical virtuosity and a priori reasoning. They were powerfully aided, and up to a point justified, by the extraordinarily complex personality of Karl Marx himself, whose own process of development they had the merit of calling attention to. Marx is not totally identifiable with Marxism, and indeed he confutes it on many points. In Marx's whole life, and hence by derivation in his writings, there is a fundamental contrast between sentiment and reason, science and faith. There is in him a spirit eternally youthful and rebellious, the spirit of a moralist, apostle, and fighter that seems to make fun of the gelid scientist. Following the classic pattern of every intellectual to whom action is precluded, repressed energies surface in the theoretical domain and contaminate it. Despite his condemnation of any kind of ethical leap or rush of faith, Marx never succeeded in hiding, even in the most arid and abstruse reasoning of *Capital*, the religious glow of the faith he had held before he began to build his system.

By regressing from the system back to its author and reconstructing the phases through which his thought had advanced, by cleverly insisting on his youthful experiences and influences and then interpreting the dry theorems of Marxism in light of these more complex factors, it was not hard for the revisionists to demonstrate that the reigning version was simplistic and one-sided. They weighed every word with care, recalled every precedent, all his states of mind and all

the attendant circumstances, and in the end they complicated the debate in an unbelievable manner; even where Marx had used incisive
language and uttered peremptory declarations, they introduced the
germ of doubt.

But . . . he who lives by the sword dies by the sword.

Marxism is a dogmatic construct; it cannot tolerate the germ of
doubt. Revisionism, despite all its precautions, attenuations, and reservations, was unable to dodge the fate of all the other heresies, which
begin with scruples of a marginal kind and end in total subversion.
What counts in these cases is not the aim but the method, and
the method employed by the revisionists was singularly destructive.
Within a short time their divergence had turned into a parting of the
ways. Progressing unstoppably from pragmatic and tactical questions
to more general ones, they finally reached the point where they im-
pugned the theory of historical materialism itself, the hinge on which
the whole system turned. In vain the revisionists attempted to camouflage the depth of the breach they had made by refusing to draw up a
final balance sheet and continuing to proclaim their underlying conformity. It was orthodox Marxists, and especially bourgeois onlookers,
who drew up the balance instead and found that bankruptcy was near.
To gain an idea of how serious the slippage was, it is enough to examine summarily the position that the two most typical exponents of the
revisionist movement, Bernstein and Sorel, were taking around 1900.

Bernstein began his famous work *Die Voraussetzungen des Sozialismus*[4] by stating that he shared the philosophical premises of Marxism;
he defended its profoundly scientific nature. His aim, he said, was to
"clarify" it and "widen" its scope, setting the principles of the new
socialist science on an unshakable foundation. In this Marxist science
he distinguished a *pure*, untouchable part—historical materialism—
from the part that was applied science: the latter was, on the contrary,
susceptible of modification without harm being done to principles.
When, however, he set about determining what this pure part was, the
trouble began. Under the pretext that Marx had sometimes been be-
trayed by the expressions he chose and that like all innovators he had
expounded his new theory in too ironclad a manner, Bernstein adulter-
ated it to the point of making it unrecognizable. For example, he affirmed that he is "bound in addition to the development and influence
of the productive forces and conditions of production to make full
allowance for the ideas of law and morality, the historical and religious
traditions of every epoch, the influence of geographical and other cir-

---

[4] First German edition 1899; English edition with the title *Evolutionary Socialism: A
Criticism and Affirmation.*

cumstances of nature, to which also"—note the finesse with which he slips this in—"the *nature* of man himself and his *spiritual* disposition belong."[5] He further maintained that in modern society the capacity to guide economic development is increasing all the time, simply because we have a better understanding of development, with the result that individuals and groups are able to shield an ever larger portion of their existence from the influence of a necessity over which they have no control. Bernstein concluded by asserting that in the realm of ideology, one no less real than that of economics, modern society is richer in comparison with previous societies precisely because the causal nexus between technical and economic development and the development of social trends is becoming increasingly indirect.

These observations are axiomatic and are tacitly accepted by all contemporary socialists, but they are truths that absolutely cannot be deduced from Marxist premises. Nor is that all. Although he professes to be in essence a 100 percent pure Marxist, Bernstein in this book recommends nothing less than getting rid of . . . the idea of historical necessity: an idea, he says, that creates the illusion that the world is marching toward a predestined regime. He naturally takes this stand on the basis of the famous notes on Feuerbach that Marx drafted in his youth, a text with which all revisionism begins and ends.

Bernstein's ingenuousness strained credulity when he made a show of believing that all he was offering were some "supplements." "The fundamental idea of the theory," he wrote, "does not thereby lose in uniformity, but the theory of itself gains in scientific character." The only problem at this point, he wrote in conclusion, is that "the result of the working of different forces can only be reckoned upon with certainty when all the forces are exactly known and placed in the calculation according to their full value."[6] Goodness gracious, this was exactly the problem that Marx boasted of having categorically resolved.

Sorel (I refer to Sorel in his gradualist phase, before he adopted syndicalism) was even more unsparing and radical. He actually denied the existence of a Marxist "system" and made fun of those who believed in "scientific" socialism. He rejected the deterministic interpretation of the materialist doctrine of history, did not accept the theory that the proletarian class was homogeneous (indeed, he denied that there were two classes and that they were necessarily in conflict), and insisted on the part race, historical conditions, and intellectual development played. He refused to believe in the incorrigible anarchy of

---

[5] Eduard Bernstein, *Evolutionary Socialism*, trans. Edith C. Harvey, with an introduction by Sidney Hook (New York: Schocken Books, 1961), p. 12 (Rosselli's italics).
[6] Ibid., pp. 16, 10.

capitalism, denied the belief in catastrophe, judged the theory of value erroneous, defended the primary importance of moral problems, drew attention to the utopistic traces in Marx's predictions, and judged Marx highly deficient as a historian both methodologically and historically. He even cast doubt on the originality of the Master. . . .

He too assumed that it was possible to make these criticisms in the name of Marx himself, or at least in the name of the spirit of his doctrine, which fatuous scholars had failed to grasp. It was contrary to the "spirit" of Marx to want to posit for all time what the influence of the forces of production in history was to be—the more so because Marxism does nothing to explain the development of technology, the story of which is filled with contingency and chance. Even if we did possess such principles, they would not be of great use, because we would then have to discover the further principles in virtue of which the forces of production make their appearance. We should not forget, he warned, that the forces of production are generated by men.

For Sorel the value of historical materialism was of a purely pragmatic, tactical kind: since it was intended to be a philosophy of action, it deliberately exaggerated the importance of objective things so as to keep revolutionaries from making false moves. Marx, Sorel says, wished to advise revolutionaries to be prudent. For reasons of tactics and psychology, in other words, for the purpose of making the most impact, he gave them "the form of an absolute law that governs history." This is an ingenious explanation, no doubt, which Marx would have done well to give us himself so that we might at least have been spared an entire library of exegesis. All honor to Sorel, but it has to be said that it is not very convincing. The truth is that this absurd "explanation," like the many others in which revisionist literature abounds, documents with clarity the increasingly grave state of embarrassment and disquiet in which the new generation found itself as it faced the problem of accepting unreservedly the Marxist legacy.

[We ought not to overlook, in addition to the criticism of the philosophers and the sociologists, that of the economists, from Böhm-Bawerk to Pareto. They bear witness to the numerous errors, sophistries, and contradictions of *Capital* and to the important part Rodbertus played in elaborating the most famous theories of Marx.[7] The definition of value as a function of labor alone was thrown in doubt; the incurable contradiction inherent in the fundamental Marxist thesis (that is, that vari-

---

[7] Eugen von Böhm-Bawerk (1851–1914) was an economist and a protagonist of the so-called Austrian School; Vilfredo Pareto (1848–1923) played an important role in the renovation of disciplines such as political theory, sociology, and economics; and Johann K. Rodbertus (1805–1875) was a German economist who based his theory on a rigid organicism and whose writings were widely read among socialists.

able capital produces surplus value on its own) was proved; and the belief that wages were tied to the minimum necessary for subsistence was denied. In appearance, the criticism of the economists, who were described summarily as bourgeois, produced no reaction except scorn and irony among "scientific" socialists. In fact, following these criticisms, which were taken up by Bernstein, no serious socialist any longer dared to propound the economic theories of Marx.

The criticism had been so devastating that in his *Preface to the Poverty of Philosophy* Engels went to the length of admitting that the principle of surplus value was not essential to the scientific conception of socialism, given that Marx had based the Communist claim on the inevitable collapse of the system of capitalist production.[8] The new school of marginal utility, ignored by Marx though it had come into existence long before he died, had won over the majority of socialist economists. Engels, however, ended by admitting that it was equally possible to construct socialism on the theory of the final degree of utility. He merely added that this would be socialism of a vulgar kind.]

What was left standing of the Marxist system after this wave of criticism?

The unity of the system was shattered. Historical materialism was transformed into a historiographical theory, as eclectic as it was generic, which enveloped everything and nailed down nothing; its usefulness in guiding the actual socialist movement was reduced virtually to zero. Revisionism also threw out determinism, postulating that humans in the totality of their being, and not as mere components of the productive process, stood at the center of the historical process. It substituted a bond of complex interdependence for the simple dependence of ideology on economics, or to be more precise, the dependence of social relations on the forces and relations of production, even though it acknowledged the great importance of economic factors, especially in past epochs. It rejected the theory of pure value in the strictly economic domain while defending it as a hypothesis in the ethical and juridical realm. It did not believe that violence and dictatorship must necessarily come to pass, nor that they would help a new world to be born. Armed with statistics, revisionism showed that Marx's famous laws of the concentration of wealth in fewer and fewer hands, of growing impoverishment, of proletarianization, were mistaken. It denied that social relations were becoming more conflictual, indeed it pointed to a shift toward democracy in all countries, a shift in which the bourgeoisie, which was becoming more open to new de-

---

[8] Friedrich Engels, *Marx and Rodbertus*, preface to the first German edition of *The Poverty of Philosophy* by Karl Marx (1884), now in Marx and Engels, *Collected Works* 26:281–82.

mands, was participating. Social democracy, wrote Bernstein in con-clusion, must attend more to immediate tasks than to final goals. Such final goals as the conquest of political power and the expropriation of the capitalists are not final goals at all but simply means for the attain-ment of certain purposes and aspirations. The new formula is this: the movement is everything, and the end is nothing. Bernstein wrote: "Social democracy could have the courage to emancipate itself from a phraseology which is actually outworn if it would make up its mind to appear what it is in reality: a democratic, socialistic party of reform."[9]

Such was the revisionism of the Right. There was also a revisionism of the Left, though it was less profound and original. In sum, Marxism as an organic system of categorical and unique significance was fin-ished. Various political and cultural currents could now legitimately claim a connection to Marx, and the adjective "Marxist" became in-creasingly generic and vague. Determinists and voluntarists, reform-ists and revolutionaries, battled fiercely for the legacy of the Master. The economists leaned more toward strict determinism, the philoso-phers and agitators toward the voluntaristic point of view.

Loria was a Marxist and so was Sorel.[10] Lenin was a Marxist and so was Turati.[11] The political activist who saw the theory of class struggle

[9] Bernstein, *Evolutionary Socialism*, p. 197.

[10] Achille Loria (1857–1943) was born in Mantua, studied law at the University of Bologna and economics at Pavia, and taught at the Universities of Siena, Padua, and Turin. He was the major—and the most ridiculed—representative of positivist socialism and managed to adapt philosophical determinism to all branches of social science. Loria was a follower of Herbert Spencer and tried to combine socialism with social Darwinism according to an optimistic view of gradual and inevitable progress. His essay on Karl Marx (1883), in which he questioned the existence of the second and third volumes of *Das Kapital* and missed completely the theory of surplus value, was strongly criticized by Engels. While he was alive Loria's popularity increased, but he was totally forgotten after his death. In Italy the expression *lorianesimo*, used frequently by Croce and Gramsci, implies emptiness and superficiality.

[11] Filippo Turati (1857–1932) was the founding father of the Italian Socialist party. His name is associated with Anna Kuliscioff, the Russian exile who became his compan-ion and a leader of the Italian feminist movement. Turati studied law at the University of Bologna and entered the political and social debate with the essay "Appunti sulla questione penale" (1882), in which he discussed anthropologist-criminologist Cesare Lombroso's theory of delinquency and located the main cause of criminality in the social order. In his youth he followed the tenets of radical democracy, which were prevalent in Milan (where he was born), thanks to the Mazzinians. In 1889 he founded the Lega Socialista Milanese (Milanese Socialist League), the seed of the Socialist party, which was finally organized in Genoa in 1892. In 1893 he led the Italian delegation at the Congress of the International in Zurich, where he met Engels, and emerged as one of the most important leaders of European socialism. For his militancy and ideas he was persecuted, tried, and jailed. A representative of the moderate wing, between 1904 and 1912 he led the party toward a more intense parliamentary involvement. He was a pacifist, and in

as the essential contribution was a Marxist, and so were the historian and the sociologist who accepted historical materialism denuded of all connection with faith in the coming of socialism. For some it was a conception that shed new light on every aspect of human speculation, giving rise to a philosophy, an economics, a history, a doctrine of right, an esthetics . . . all of them Marxist. For others it was a mere historiographical canon, or else an ensemble of observations and tendentious prophecies unworthy of being raised to the rank of a philosophy. The result was a little tower of Babel, which allowed contradictory theses and currents to pride themselves on the illustrious paternity of Marx and provided fuel for an ever more sterile and inconclusive debate.

For us, the succeeding generation, who traversed a whole critical literature on the way to socialism and Marxism and had a precise notion of the great wealth of experience already accumulated, there is nothing new in this, and it arouses no dismay or sense of crisis. But for the old conformists of the time, who were accustomed to reason exclusively and perpetually within a Marxist framework, it was like a spiritual revolution. They could not bring themselves to revise the intellectual patrimony that had formed the glory of their youth, and even when they agreed in their hearts that some revision, however cautious, was required, they felt restrained, indeed trapped, by the propaganda that had formed them: such propaganda had to be mythic in order to capture the masses in their raw state. Threatened with a landslide, they reacted energetically, led by Kautsky. Bolstered by the ideological, and especially the phraseological, conservatism of the militants who venerated Marx, they accused the revisionists of trying to kill the myth, undermine the final goals, erase all genuine differences between Marxism and bourgeois radicalism, and dampen the enthusiasm and the faith of the masses by postponing indefinitely the possibility of total emancipation. The revisionists, they said, shared the biased analysis of Marxism produced by "bourgeois" writers and thus gave new life to those degenerate varieties of petit bourgeois socialism that Marx had castigated so fiercely.

1914 on behalf of the party he assumed a neutralist position ("nè aderire nè sabotare," neither consent nor sabotage). After the war, Turati elaborated a coherent laborite program but was unable to prevent the radical transformation of the party. In 1921 the Communist wing split, and the year after the reformists were expelled, while the maximalists gained leadership within the party. The rise of fascism found both him and the party totally unprepared, unable to understand the character of the new mass dictatorship, and unwilling to defend themselves against the violence and the destruction of their circles and institutions. In 1926 Rosselli organized Turati's flight to Paris, where he was to die six years later. Rosselli wrote a brief and forceful monograph about him, *Filippo Turati e il socialismo italiano* (1932), now in id., *Scritti politici*, ed. Zeffiro Ciuffoletti and Paolo Bagnoli (Naples: Guida, 1988), pp. 215–73.

The revisionists were bowled over, especially in Germany, the Mecca of Marxism, by the virtually unanimous condemnation of the party congresses, and since they sincerely desired to uphold the unity of the workers' movement (which was what really mattered to them and which they knew would soon take it on itself to vindicate them), they fell back on theoretical positions that were less exposed and submitted in a disciplined fashion to the verdict of the majority. Rather than fight to the last to liberate political socialism from the husk of Marxism, they preferred silence, or they hid their deep reservations within the twists and turns of discussion about pure interpretation.

For their part the pure Marxists, though they controlled the congresses, clearly felt that it was out of the question to excommunicate the workers' movement and the new economic reality on which it was built. Nor did it suit them to leave the younger members to their own devices and let them run the risk of stumbling into total heresy. The purists also felt that reconciliation was de rigueur. Things needed to be welded back together. Though they could never condone the sinful proposition that Marxist doctrine was dated in its fundamentals, there was no need to dig in their heels against new experiences either.

Revisionist and orthodox views were thus artificially aligned. Each side agreed to recognize that Marxism was not a perfectly defined and consummate theory in every particular. There was something fundamental and intangible at its core, which no one undertook to define too clearly but from which practical conclusions that clashed with one another, while not casting doubt on principles, could be derived. Before, they had preached imminent revolution to the masses, along with intransigence and distrust of legal methods and reforming measures, all in Marx's name. Well, now they would preach gradualism and faith in democratic institutions and reforms, all in the name of a Marx who had been revised, padded out, and tamed. The important thing was that they could still invoke Marx and thus save the tradition, keep the extremists from monopolizing his name, and demonstrate to the faithful that nothing substantial had changed, though the letter sometimes had to be sacrificed in order to preserve the immortal spirit.

All this took place in the early years of the new century, through a process so spontaneous and widespread that it evidently corresponded to the underlying raison d'être of the movement itself, which it would be pointless to criticize too harshly here. It is worthwhile, however, to consider briefly the upshot, which was that the fruits of the battle fought by the revisionists were largely left to rot. Just when it seemed that the elite of the new generation was about to shake off Marxist servitude, it turned back and rejoined the mainstream, holding on to a few reservations of a purely formal kind. This was an entirely

exterior and ostensible reconciliation (between theory and reality, between revisionists and the orthodox), one that depended on the con-
tingencies of the situation and the prevalent tendencies—not the resolution of a crisis that ought to have taken place, first and foremost, in
the consciences of those involved. In the revolutionaries it was hypocrisy and blindness that won out; in the reformists it was weakness. The
path of least resistance was chosen, the equivocal path of accommoda-
tion and casuistry. The quarrel took on a scholastic hue, causing un-
happiness and alienation in the best minds and setting a bad example,
or rather no example at all, for the masses. It blocked for many, too
many, years to come the bold ideological clarification that today is a
sine qua non for an intrepid revival of socialism.

THREE

MARXISM AND REVISIONISM IN ITALY

ITALIAN SOCIALISM as a mass movement came into being between 1890 and 1900, with Marx as its guiding star. Before that, there had been attempts at revolt among the most impoverished rural dwellers and a diffuse and tumultuous internationalist propaganda, somewhat anarchist in tendency, in many Italian centers, especially in the south of the country. Only in the north had the workers' movement, though harshly persecuted and misunderstood, managed to make some progress by conducting the first timid experiment in the creation of an autonomous working-class political movement in the form of the workers' party.

Except for its infancy, the ideological history of Italian socialism can be said to develop along the same lines as the socialist movements in countries north of the Alps, especially Germany—with the notable difference that Marxism in Italy was, overall, an artificial implant that never succeeded in penetrating the core of the socialist movement. In the Italian movement there was always a gap between theory and practice, programs and action; and when the two were finally matched, it was found that theory had turned to vapor, while practice tended to issue in a feeble and analytical style of reformism that was vitiated by a paternalistic conception of the state. Heresy first took hold in the real world, in the movement, especially the peasant movement. Only with the new century did it emerge as a theoretical issue in the course of the violent and incessant debates that shattered the unified structure of political socialism.

Italy was ill suited to receiving the graft of Marxist socialism. It had a huge class of rural plebeians who were still tied to the land and ruled by the priests, together with extended oases of artisans and scattered vanguards of proletarians and capitalists. For Italy the problem was not to convert to socialism; it was to launch the process of development toward capitalism and modern life. Its people, corrupted by centuries of subservience, had remained untouched by the entire process of the Risorgimento and hovered close to the threshold of physical and moral existence. The Italian as citizen lacked a rudimentary sense of dignity and liberty, for he was locked in a harsh struggle with nature, just as he lacked a sense of active involvement in the life of the collectivity that grows out of long experience and fruitful opposition. Even the contemporary intellectual elite, though it abounded in original qualities, was spoiled by its predominantly literary education and constrained in many cases by the narrowness and meanness of a provincial setting to live in a stunted fashion. Economics, psychology, tradition—everything in the country was inimical to the full comprehension and fruitful application of Marxist socialism.

For an image of Marxist socialism transplanted to Italy, consider Garibaldi as a proponent of historical materialism! Garibaldi belongs to the last generation of romanticism; he is the epigone of that throng of youth who were linked by their idealism to the epic of the Risorgimento. Garibaldi is the fighter for *every* cause, from Rome to Dijon to Domokos, where socialist volunteers met their deaths. He is the prototype of the largehearted, rebellious, penniless, and utopistic Italian who at age twenty spits on the world and on life because they do not offer him a worthy cause for which to die gloriously.

Historical materialism means Marx, science, wisdom, Germanic discipline, reason armed with all the forces of right, Bentham and Ricardo, Feuerbach and Hegel, classical economics and the utilitarian calculus, determinism and dialectics. Even more than Marx, it relates to the setting of Victorian England, industrialized and powerful, which had supplied Marx with the inductive elements for his construct.

Out of this mixture Italian political socialism was born, with the help of a group of young university students of outstanding character and generous sentiment, who were grouped around a journal, *La Critica Sociale*, that was for thirty years the authoritative disseminator of the Marxist message and certainly one of the finest socialist journals in Europe.[1] They had come to socialism out of a sentimental impulse, offended by the injustices and the wretchedness of Italian life, which was still wrapped in the coils of economic and political feudalism, and by the rapid degradation of the men and the ideals of the Risorgimento. They longed for a light from on high, for a fire to be lit in their souls, for a goal of universal and ethical import. But at the same time, swayed by the science worship and positivism then in fashion and repelled by the superficiality and the demagogy of the leading revolutionaries, they longed to justify themselves in rational terms.

They could not be satisfied with the cramped and empirical vision that had dominated the tiny workers' party, much less with the libertarian utopianism of Bakunin's followers. Mazzini was moldering in his grave, and his abstract moralism was rendered intolerable by the sectarian style of his acolytes and the conditions (tragic in both the physical and moral dimension) in which the greater part of the working class was living; it

---

[1] *La Critica Sociale* (Social Critique) was the magazine of the Italian Socialist party, founded by Filippo Turati in 1891.

could not stand up to their stringent critique, a critique based on concrete reality. The tenuous, noble vein of Malonian socialism,[2] with its honest poverty of themes, its excessive eclecticism, and the vacuousness of its specific features, was certainly not a dish for such refined palates, which desired cultural novelty instead. Marxism, incorporating the most audacious intellectual developments of the century, amply satisfied their thirst. Into the little theater of Italian life it brought the living and subversive echo of European problems and European struggles, spanning, in the realm of ideas at any rate, the pitiable gap that existed in the realm of actuality and wealth between Italy and Europe. To give oneself to Marxism was like diving into the open sea after paddling around in a pool, so rich did its uninhibited realism seem in comparison with all the ideological haze and low-grade patriotism that had gone before. As always happens when ideals are achieved in actuality and so contaminated, the great blaze of the Risorgimento in Italy had been followed by an immense wave of disappointment. National unity was taken for granted by the new generation, whose criticism of the process and its outcome daily grew more strident and who desired other allurements, other ideals, instead. The universal ideal of socialism allowed them to transcend the narrow horizons of Italy and link up in a tangible fashion with the profoundest social, and socialist, experiments then taking place, especially the one in Germany, around which the victorious struggle against the special laws had created a resplendent halo. If we take into account as well a certain, typically Italian, readiness to welcome spiritual merchandise from abroad with special fascination, it will not be difficult to understand the spectacular conversion to Marxism of the best and brightest among the younger generation.

In his *Storia d'Italia*, Benedetto Croce has painted an unforgettable picture of this conversion.[3] He pays high tribute to Marxism, which

[2] Benôit Malon (1841–1893) greatly influenced the first generation of Italian socialists. He was born in Précieux, France, to an extremely poor family. He joined the International in 1865 and started organizing unions among the day laborers in his country. Persecuted by the French government, he emigrated to Switzerland, where he became part of Bakunin's Alliance for Socialist Democracy after having abandoned Marx's International. He was strongly antistatist and collectivist but was also attracted by the philosophy of pessimism, which he adopted from Arthur Schopenhauer's *Aphorisms* and Giacomo Leopardi's poems and which he interpreted as an invitation to humans to unite against the nothingness of life and the cruelty of nature's rules. Because of his participation in the Commune he spent the rest of his life in exile in Geneva. He collaborated actively with the first Italian socialists and radicals by inspiring them with his radical democracy (his relations with Turati and Andrea Costa were particularly important; see n. 8 of this chapter). He founded the international journal *Le Socialisme progressif*. Among Malon's writings are *Exposé des écoles socialistes françaises* (1872), *Histoire du socialisme* (1878), and *La religione e la morale dei socialisti* (1882).

[3] Benedetto Croce, *Storia d'Italia dal 1871 al 1915* (1928), English ed. with the title *A History of Italy, 1871–1915*, trans. Cecilia M. Ady (Oxford: Clarendon Press, 1929), pp. 145–62.

arrived at that epoch to fill the gaping void in Italian thought and ideals and which contributed powerfully to the moral and cultural rebirth of the country. Forty years later, having evolved toward an enlightened conservatism, he readily allows that although he does not accept Marxism today, he is glad to have passed through a Marxist phase, and that if he had not done so, he would feel that his mind was missing something. It is thus easy to understand how the entire new generation converted *d'emblée* (immediately) to Marxism. But while in his case the Marxist experience refined his capacity for criticism and resolved itself into a lesson in historical realism, for the others, militant enthusiasts all, it was sublimated into the ultimate, definitive philosophical experience, yoked to a party program. The key to understanding humanity appeared to have been discovered once and for all, with no more doubts left. Henceforth the only task was to set about applying it in practice, to work along established lines. Step by step, even the best of them grew accustomed to reason on Marxist principles in every case and lost all real autonomy and originality of thought.

When a series of alien methods and concerns was injected into Italy, intimate contact with the reality of the country was gradually lost, and the admittedly slender native socialist tradition, which in Mazzini[4] and Cattaneo[5] had found its leading exponents, was rudely cut off.

[4] Giuseppe Mazzini (1805–1872) was born in Genoa, where he studied philosophy and law. Between 1829 and 1830 he entered a secret Masonic society (la Carboneria) and then devoted his whole life to the cause of an independent Italian republic. Arrested and sentenced to death, he left Italy, to which he returned several times clandestinely, and openly for a short period in 1848 when he led the revolution in Rome and became a leader of its republic. He spent most of his life in London, where he lived with his mother, who was his most intimate friend and whose Jansenist religiosity deeply marked his personality. Along with Alexander Herzen (who was among his many friends in London), Mazzini was the most prominent leader of the democratic nationalism of the nineteenth century. Inspired by the notion of a cosmopolitanism of nations (which has to be read as a polemical answer to the eighteenth-century cosmopolitanism of individuals), in the 1830s he founded two important secret societies, the Young Italy and the Young Europe. Mazzini interpreted the nation as a mystic unity whose aim should be that of replacing the materialistic vision of society as a contractual association of individuals. For this reason he emphasized the discourse of duties over that of rights. Mazzini and his numerous followers were also sensitive to the question of social justice, starting a dialogue with socialism (he found many affinities with the Saint-Simonians) but not with Marxism, which for him was a dreadful perversion of utilitarianism because of its insistence on class interests, especially class struggle, a conflictual vision that could not harmonize with Mazzini's unitarianism. Mazzini's writing and letters (many of them in English and French) are collected in the national edition of his works under the title *Scritti editi ed inediti*, 100 vols.

[5] Carlo Cattaneo (1801–1869) was born in Milan, where he studied law. His disinclination toward political activity did not prevent him from being among the leaders of the 1848 revolution in his city. He founded and led for many years the journal *Il Politecnico*

In the whirl of events and persecutions, the young were overcome by all the demands of an apostolate that had something of the miraculous about it and did not have a chance to examine their new values more deeply. Menaced as they were by the sabers and handcuffs of the forces of order in the redoubled assaults of Crispi and Pelloux (1894, 1898),[6] their imagination naturally plunged toward the outer regions of myth, toward the dream of an apocalyptic transformation in the brief space of a generation. This Marxism can be seen as spurious, and we can call it degenerate if we wish, but that certainly does not mean that there was any increased pliability or laxity about the way it was put into practice. Indeed, much of the movement's propaganda was based on what was in fact the Achilles' heel of the whole system, its belief in catastrophe. What struck observers was not the note of relativism and historicism it sounded, but its messianic aspect, the certainty that an inevitable metamorphosis was on the way. Until about 1898 Turati too adhered to this schematic and ingenuous vision, and when he later attempted to cool down the ardor and dispel the illusions of others, he found himself hammering against a carapace of pseudo-theory and messianic expectation that he himself, in perfect good faith, had helped to create.

The crisis of 1900, after the assassination of King Umberto,[7] put a dramatic end to an exceptional state of tension, which had done much

---

and studied and elaborated on many projects to reform the prison system, welfare, charity, and bureaucracy. He had a pragmatic mind and was an irreducible enemy of any version of spiritualism. Escaping from Milan after the abortive revolution of 1848, Cattaneo spent the rest of his life in Lugano, Switzerland. He refused to go back to Italy when it became an independent country because it was not a federal republic as he would have liked it to be. Elected a deputy in 1867, Cattaneo refused to enter the parliament because he would not swear an oath before the monarchy. His republicanism was different from Mazzini's; it was liberal and based on rights, not only on duties, was free from any sort of mysticism, and was federalist. He coined the phrase "United States of Italy within the United States of Europe." A collection of his most important essays is *Opere scelte*, ed. D. Castelnuovo Frigessi (Turin: Einaudi, 1973), 4 vols.

[6] Francesco Crispi (1818–1901) and Luigi G. Pelloux (1839–1924), heads of the Italian government, were both responsible, the former in 1894 and the latter in 1898, for harshly repressive polities. Crispi (in his youth Garibaldi's companion) adopted Bismarck's policies against the radicals and socialists, whose leaders and supporters he persecuted and jailed. Pelloux ordered the army to intervene against the unarmed population of Milan, which was gathering in the square asking for bread (more than a hundred persons were killed).

[7] Umberto I of Savoy, king of Italy, was killed in Monza (near Milan) on July 29, 1900. The killer was the anarchist Gaetano Bresci, a Florentine who to escape imprisonment emigrated to New Jersey in 1892, where he lived in Paterson. As he said during his trial, because he considered the king mainly responsible for the repressions of 1894 and 1898, he collected money and went back to Italy "with a determined will and a good pistol" to assassinate the tyrant.

to encourage the absolutism of the myth. The boundaries of the possible seemed to expand, as the workers' movement, which until then had been repressed and persecuted, received what amounted to almost an official consecration with the memorable strike at Genoa, and political freedoms appeared to be definitively guaranteed. From 1900 until about 1904 Italy witnessed spreading agitation and strikes; a feverish vitality invaded the country. The dreadful living conditions of the workers improved greatly, a new awareness grew up in social strata that until then had been confined to a brutish state, parliament and city governments opened up to the pressing new forces, and the bourgeoisie showed that it was receptive to the demands of the times. Almost at a stroke, a party that had been banned and obstructed stood at the portals of government ministries. Within a few years Filippo Turati, who had been condemned to prison for fourteen years, found himself being urged to assume power, and Andrea Costa, from being a habitué of the holding cells, was promoted to the status of vice-president of the Chamber of Deputies.[8]

The change of climate occurred so rapidly that it was necessarily very upsetting and brought strong reactions, especially among the young, who felt the ground shift from under them and were naturally reluctant to adopt, without duly making a trial of it, the hasty optimism and legalism *à tout prix* (at all cost) of Turati and the leaders of the workers' movement. A generation that had drawn up its order of battle on premises that were simplistic, intransigent, and revolutionary found itself, through a miraculous combination of circumstances, at the head of the greatest mass movement and faced with the prospect of assuming power. What in England had cost a century of hard and patient fighting, in an atmosphere already marked by the revolutions of the seventeenth century and the reforms of 1832, what in France had been

---

[8] Andrea Costa (1851–1910) was born in Imola (near Bologna) and was one of the most prominent leaders of Italian anarchism and one of the protagonists of the secession of the Italian branch from the International led by Marx and Engels. His political activity was played out in Romagna (the area between Bologna and the Adriatic Sea), where he untiringly organized workers' leagues and was arrested several times. Costa had many connections with the socialist and anarchist leaders of Europe (among them Michail Bakunin, Jules Guesde, and Benôit Malon) and professed a collectivist doctrine and radical democracy. Along with Carlo Cafiero (see n. 4 of ch. 8) he was the inspirer of the first anarchist attempt at insurrection in 1874. In Switzerland, where he fled to escape prosecution, Costa met Anna Kuliscioff, who was his companion until she met Turati. In 1882 he enrolled in the Socialist party, became a deputy, and gradually moderated his radicalism. He never was a Marxist and perceived the party as a federation of autonomous local circles devoted to solving the everyday problems of poverty and oppression. In 1909 Costa was elected vice-president of the Chamber of Deputies, an election of which Rosselli speaks ironically, given the fact that in the past the same Chamber voted to prosecute him for his political ideas.

the fruit of the formidable tidal wave of 1789 and the succeeding revolutionary or moral crises of 1830, 1848, 1871, 1895, and 1900 (in effect, a revolution every generation), and what in Germany was obtained only in 1918 after the enormous disruption caused by the war had been obtained in Italy, or so it was believed, seemingly overnight, with the complicity of a sovereign who declared himself open to the new era and a couple of courageous ministers.

It was probably this speeding up of the tempo, which forced the advance guard to do the work of mopping up, this fatal lack of the psychological and technical maturity necessary to deal with new and positive tasks (for which no one was at fault), that was the main reason for the crisis that, beginning around 1907–1908, began to gnaw ever more deeply at Italian socialism.[9]

Here I will deal with the intellectual crisis.

[Revisionism]

The brief but intense history of Italian revisionism also commences around 1900. Before that there had been notable efforts in this direction, but mostly they came from elements extraneous to the movement that did not have much influence on the common socialist opinion of the period, which still held unquestioningly to the letter of the Marxist system. The Neapolitan philosopher Antonio Labriola took up the cause of historical materialism in two memorable essays. He paid attention primarily to the philosophical aspects of the doctrine, and his writings, rather than revealing, or overcoming, a crisis in Marxism that began to be discussed at this time, were intended to dispel misunderstandings (Loria), crude interpretations (the materialistic one), and deceptive affinities (with Darwin and Spencer). He gave a lesson in aristocratic prudence to the neophytes of Marxism who believed that in the theory of historical materialism they possessed a handy talisman. He warned them that the famous economic substructure, the determinant of all other social phenomena, was not a simple mechanism from which institutions, laws, customs, thought, sentiment, and ideologies emerge as immediate mechanical effects. With great finesse he demon-

---

[9] On many occasions Rosselli says that 1908 was the year in which the debate among the Marxists was concluded, leaving behind a dry theoretical atmosphere among the socialists. At the national congress of 1908, in Florence, the reformist wing gained leadership of the Socialist party against the maximalists. But this victory produced a sort of ideological and emotional emptiness. Rodolfo Mondolfo began his theoretical analysis of Marxism in 1908 precisely with the purpose of filling this ideological lacuna and infusing a new theoretical tension.

strated that the process of derivation and mediation was extremely complicated, often subtle and tortuous, and not always decipherable. Believing himself to be the only firm and logical Marxist in Italy, he did not refrain in his correspondence with Engels from launching shafts at his fellow party members, whom he accused of not penetrating the spirit of the doctrine. This did not prevent him later from becoming one of the harbingers of Italian colonial expansion, transferring the interest that he had taken in the problems of class struggle for a decade to the national plane and justifying it with the claim, widely heard in Germany as well, that colonialism was a necessary phase of capitalist development and thus a premise sine qua non of the advent of socialism. His influence increased greatly after his premature death, and ample traces of his refined— perhaps too refined and sometimes too formal—exegetical contributions can be found in subsequent studies, especially Mondolfo's.

The most profound criticism of Marxism came from philosophers (Croce, Gentile, and Chiappelli)[10] who instead of wearisome debates

[10] Giovanni Gentile (1875–1944) was born in Sicily and studied philosophy at the most prestigious Italian institution of advanced studies, the Scuola Normale Superiore of Pisa. He then taught in Naples, Palermo, and Pisa. Along with Croce—with whom he worked for many years before the advent of fascism—Gentile was the most prominent Italian philosopher of the time. Unlike Croce, he acted from within the academy (marking it deeply) and the state. As Mussolini's minister of education, in the 1920s he completed the reform of the Italian system of education (a reform still partly in place). Gentile's philosophy was an elaboration of right-wing Hegelianism. It was based on the identicalness of history and philosophy in such a way as to resolve the past into the present and coalesce space and time—that is, the whole of reality—in the spiritual act, a pure and absolute expression of thought. In this way, any external limitation on the will was overcome, and the spirit imposed itself as pure and absolute freedom (pure actuality). This allowed Gentile to resolve the dualism between God and the world by reaching a radical immanentism according to which religion was nothing other than a moment of a spiritual evolution to be transcended into philosophy. Gentile applied this absolute idealism (or spiritualism) to all branches of human life, from pedagogy to politics. Concerning politics, Gentile's philosophy was a new version of the theory of the ethical state. The state, as pure and true freedom (not being limited by the interests of individuals and groups), was the highest form of the rational life, into which the individual must be absorbed. The ethical state was neither neutral nor agnostic, but a subject with the mission of implementing the true values of the spirit. Universally identified as the philosopher of the regime, Gentile was killed by the partisans. Among his numerous writings are *La filosofia di Marx* (1899), *La riforma della dialettica hegeliana* (1913), *Teoria generale dello spirito come atto puro* (1916), and *Fascismo e cultura* (1928).

Alessandro Chiappelli (1857–1931) was born in Tuscany and taught history of philosophy at Padua, Florence, and Naples. He wrote important essays on Greek philosophy, particularly Plato, suggesting the hypothesis (later validated) of two editions of the *Theaetetus*. He also participated in political debate and was one of the first representatives of the phenomenon called the socialism of the professors. At the turn of the century, Chiappelli took part in the philosophical debate on neo-Kantism and, as a "metaphysical idealist," started a long polemic against vitalism and irrationalism and wrote on An-

about Marx's texts preferred to study Marx's intellectual connections (Feuerbach, Hegel) and the intrinsic nature of his stance. Benedetto Croce, the master of the new generation and a sympathizer of the nascent movement, undoubtedly remains the most powerful mind to have engaged with the problems of Marxism. Together with Bernstein and Sorel (whom he introduced to Italy), he is a member of the triad that principally contributed to the progressive disgregation of the system. Having stripped historical materialism of every trace of finality and providential design and reduced its import to that of a simple interpretive tool, though a richly suggestive one, he showed that it could not be used to support either socialism or any other practical design for living. To become effectual, Croce maintained, it required a series of ethical and emotional complements, moral judgments and enthusiasms springing from faith; and he rightly criticized the absurd moral relativism professed by the socialists. Croce dismantled the views of Loria, which were much in vogue in socialist circles in Italy, boldly corrected the theory of class struggle in the light of idealistic philosophy (history is the struggle of the classes when classes exist and are conscious of their antagonistic interests), and contributed a series of classic essays to the understanding and the critique of the theory of value, properly denying that it had any scientific status.[11]

The Crocean revision, which its author strangely insisted on viewing as a pure and simple interpretation, anticipated in compressed form almost all subsequent developments in Marxist criticism in Italy and abroad. After 1900 especially it helped to separate many leading figures from the movement, which still officially clung to the Marxist and materialist gospel. Despite this, it had no effect, as logically it ought to have done, on the socialist leadership. The reasons for this were its very boldness, its unsystematic character, and especially its unorthodox source. Indeed, no one seemed to be worried by the reverberations that Croce's powerful thought might have on the young; no one attempted to respond to his suggestive and corrosive critique. He was an idealist . . . that was enough. So it is that his writings, widely known in Italy, have remained unanswered until today, probably because they are unanswerable.

---

glo-American philosophy (Green, Bradley, Bosanquet, Royce, and Caird). After World War I, he became a Fascist, his choice motivated by the need to find a synthesis between liberalism and socialism, state and society. Among his works are *Il socialismo e il pensiero moderno* (1897), *Dalla critica al nuovo idealismo* (1910), *La crisi del pensiero moderno* (1920), and *Distruzione e ricostruzione civile* (1922).

[11] Croce's essays on Marxism were translated into English with the title *Historical Materialism and the Economics of Karl Marx* in 1914 (Allen & Unwin); a new edition by Michael Curtis came out from Transaction Books (New Brunswick and London) in 1981.

The reformist and the revolutionary syndicalist attempts at revisionism were the two major ones undertaken in the years after 1900. Despite the strong divergence in practice between them, both were moved by similar concerns. Both, but especially the second, declared that a profound review, amounting in certain respects to a renunciation, was needed. Both were antideterminist and aimed at a revaluation of moral forces and values. But both were too political, too sectarian, too engaged in bitter fights over what line to follow, too concerned with deriving support for their own practical assumptions from Marxism at any cost.

At an early stage, under the sway of the liberty so recently won and the expanding workers' movement, an attempt was made by the best elements of the old socialist guard (Bissolati, Bonomi, Cabrini; and Turati, but only in part)[12] to carry through a revision in the style of Bernstein, with some hint that the experience of the Labour party too might be taken as a partial model. The aim was to make the movement conform more closely to the reality of the Italian situation. But apart from valuable studies on this or that aspect of doctrine and a laudable preoccupation with practical problems, it has to be said that the revision of Marxism by the Italian reformists, professed in an undertone and accompanied by prudent reservations and distinctions, especially on the part of the political chieftains, not only added nothing substantial to what Bernstein had already said, but did not affect the masses in the slightest. Dogged by fears of a crisis of disillusionment and of extremist speculation, they clung even more stubbornly than Bernstein to an indefensible justification of their own Marxist purity, refusing to take their critiques to their logical conclusion. In practice, weakened perhaps by the noisy and sterile negative attitude of the revolutionaries, they settled in the end for fragmentary reforming action, a policy of compromise and bargaining, in the course of which the more distant and general goals of the struggle were increasingly lost to view. Besides, in order to win the revisionists would have needed large numbers of youthful supporters, but the youth of the epoch, if they were socialists, gravitated almost unanimously to the revolutionary end of the spectrum, particularly toward the syndicalists. On top of that Bissolati, Bonomi, and Salvemini,[13] who had been the strongest

---

[12] Leonida Bissolati (1857–1920), Ivanoe Bonomi (1873–1951), and Angiolo Cabrini (1869–1937) were the leaders of the first generation of the Italian socialist and unionist movement.

[13] Gaetano Salvemini (1873–1957) was born in the Puglia region and studied history at the University of Florence. He was one of the most brilliant and stimulating intellectuals of the time. Attracted by Marxism in his youth, he soon abandoned this ideology in favor of the democratic and federalist ideals expressed by Carlo Cattaneo. Salvemini brought

proponents of the revision, split off from the party or were expelled and lost any influence they had had on the masses. Graziadei was almost the only one left who kept faith in the credo of revisionism, even when, after twenty years, he switched to communism.[14]

It was the revolutionary syndicalists and two quite junior members of the movement, Arturo Labriola and Enrico Leone,[15] who can take special credit for a serious revival of Marxist studies at this time. In the pages of a whole flock of journals could be found exegetical writings and polemical discussions that clearly demonstrated independence of judgment and flashes of genius, though they were vitiated by their all too evident dogmatism and slippery methodology. Labriola, more than any other Marxist of his time, devoted the resources of a brilliant intellect to the creation of a patently voluntaristic interpretation that was intended to turn Marx into a precursor of syndicalist ideas. But his eloquence had very little power to convince, and he never succeeded in demonstrating that Marx had even thought of, much less committed to

to the Socialist party an interest in the southern question, which he interpreted, for the first time in Italy, as a question of the emancipation of agricultural laborers. On this he challenged the official ideology of the party, which was totally devoted to the central role of the industrial workers of the north. The central and noninstrumental role that Salvemini assigned to democratic institutions was another reason for disagreement with the socialists. He based his divorce from the party primarily on this question. After that he founded *L'Unità* (1911), the first Italian democratic journal. His critique of corporatism, statism, and protectionism found supporters among both the liberals and the leftists, such as Rosselli, Gramsci, and Gobetti. Within the Left he was one the few to take a position in favor of the war and became a "Wilsonian." Salvemini was one the first to insist on a vigorous reaction against Fascist violence, and along with Rosselli founded the first clandestine journal in Florence (*Non Mollare*). He was also part of the first nucleus of the movement Giustizia e Libertà, even though he disagreed with its socialist stamp. After Rosselli was arrested, Salvemini left Italy and lived in France, England, and finally the United States, where he taught Italian civilization at Harvard University. In 1947 he went back to Italy and to his position as professor of history in Florence. Among his works are *Magnati e popolani in Firenze dal 1280 al 1295* (1899), *La questione meridionale* (1898–1899), *Le origini della reazione* (1899), *Il pensiero religioso e politico-sociale di G. Mazzini* (1905), and *La dittatura fascista in Italia* (1927).

[14] Antonio Graziadei (1873–1953), from Ferrara, was with Antonio Gramsci and Amedeo Bordiga a member of the Communist wing, which split from the Socialist party in 1921 at the Congress of Livorno.

[15] Arturo Labriola (1873–1959) was born in Naples, where he studied economics. In spite of his socialist ideas, he drew close to Vilfredo Pareto, with whom he shared strong antiprotectionist and antistatist ideas. From within the Socialist party he opposed Turati's reformism, becoming more and more sympathetic to Sorel's revolutionary syndicalism. During Fascist rule he spent many years abroad, though he never found a modus vivendi in the movement of the exiles. Labriola had been a contributor to the journal *Divenire sociale*, founded in 1905 by Enrico Leone (1875–1940), who was also born near Naples, and looked on Sorel's voluntarism as a viable answer to scientific socialism. Only in 1923 did he reject Sorel's myth of violence and irrationalism.

writing, the notions about revolutionary idealism, direct action, federalism, and so on, that he, Labriola, so brazenly attributed to him. Unhappily, this movement turned in practice into an extremely unruly escapade by intellectuals with too much time on their hands and not enough of the discipline necessary for a mass movement. An exotic *feu follet* (will-o'-the-wisp), it wilted as rapidly as it had flourished, leaving few vestiges behind except an overwhelming defense of human liberty in history—an understandable reaction against the dull formalism of the pure Marxists. Many energetic young people who had joined out of natural extravagance and faith in creative violence either went off on their own or switched over to such other extremist movements as anarchism and syndicalism.[16] Thus it was that the only effort at revisionism conducted on a large scale and without hypocrisy or base calculation in mind came to nothing, undermined by its glaring failure in practice and the vulgar way in which too many of the leaders used it as a bandwagon. Old-style conformism was correspondingly strengthened, for it was able to point to theoretical indiscipline as the reason for the practical failure of the attempt. After it ended in 1908 there were no more revisionist movements worth mentioning. The vivacity that had characterized Marxist studies declined, and only rarely did one come across a book, for example, by Salucci, that took up the themes of Bernsteinian revisionism in a way pertinent to the Italian situation, seeking to reconcile Marx and Mazzini, economics and morality.[17] From 1910 to the present only one name of real importance stands out in the field of Marxist exegesis, Rodolfo Mondolfo, a man with the character of a calm and conciliatory scholar, whom we must necessarily examine at greater length for two equally important reasons: he sums up all the motifs of previous criticism, and his exegesis still constitutes the best, and in fact the only, vehicle of Marxist education for the rising generation in Italy.

Mondolfo was no more able to avoid the typical defects of revisionist authors than anyone else: he concocted a stylized Marx, very much revised and corrected; he smuggled his own ideas and current needs into Marx's thought by means of dialectical acrobatics and displays of erudition, renouncing at the outset any attempt at originality; he reviewed that thought in the unique light of the juvenile position of its author, tacitly rejecting as "dross" whatever did not fit into his new interpretive scheme, even though Marx had shown that he attached fundamental importance to "dross" of this kind.

[16] The word "syndicalism" here means "revolutionary syndicalism," the movement inspired by Georges Sorel.

[17] Arturo Salucci, *Il crepuscolo del socialismo (critica delle tendenze e delle soluzioni)* (1910) (2d ed., Milan: Edizioni Corbaccio, 1925).

Like all revisionists, Mondolfo boils Marxism down to the materialistic view of history and reduces that in turn to one central concept, the inversion of praxis. The theory of value, the belief in catastrophe, everything else is thrown *ad bestias* (away). Mondolfo's purpose is to extract from Marxism a philosophy of socialism fully reconcilable with an activist vision of the historical process but without falling into the excesses of extreme voluntarism.

The relation between man and his historical-social environment, he says in substance, is not a relation between two things each external to the other, but a relation of action and reaction, a dialectal relation within a single reality. The subject knows the object inasmuch as he produces it; the subject is social man, who, driven by his needs, by his perpetual dissatisfaction with the reality in which he lives, strives to alter the previously existing forms and social relations. It is in this striving, and thanks alone to this striving, that he gains consciousness of reality and its inadequacy. In order to interpret the world, as Marx said in one of his notes on Feuerbach, it is necessary to change it.

The concrete historical process consists in the unfolding of human activity in a continuous internal struggle, in which the continual coming into being of contradictions to be overcome constitutes the very condition and essence of history. The results of preceding activity become the condition and limit of successive activity, which comes about as opposition to that which is already in existence and tends to overcome it dialectically. The past conditions the present and the present conditions the future, but at the same time it is a stimulus and an impulse to further modifying action. Humanity struggles first against natural conditions, and then against the social conditions that it has created, which in time turn into an impediment to further development.

The struggle takes place between the forces of expansion and the forces of conservation, under the spur of need. What are these forces of expansion? They are, replies Mondolfo, all the energies and activities of men, and they can all be reduced (this is the delicate point that he never proves and the artificial link to Marx) to the concept of *forces of production*. The forces of conservation, however, are represented by groups, strata, and classes that have a stake in the preservation of existing forms and social relations. The struggle thus concretely assumes the aspect of classes battering against classes, and in this sense it can be said that class struggle is the essence of history.

Historical development thus results from the confluence of and at the same time the opposition between two elements: actual conditions and human will.

History therefore has no room for arbitrary actions and creations:

action takes place in the context of its own conditions and its own limits. Even when the moment for revolution strikes, there is an intrinsic necessity at work that, just as it makes revolution inevitable when its time has come, makes it impossible when the fullness of its conditions is absent. This concept of historical necessity, Mondolfo concludes, is the same as the concept of the inversion of praxis and is the essential core of historical materialism.

Unhappily, however, the views of Mondolfo cannot be made to fit those of Marx. As long as Mondolfo limits himself to bringing out the generically dialectical vision of the historical process embedded in Marxism, there is nothing to take exception to. But there is everything to take exception to when he tries to slip human will in among the opposing terms and to turn men, as beings who are aware, who will, and who operate, into the true actors in history, because in the Marxist system the opposing terms are purely and simply technical development (in the broad sense) and social relations. When these two ambient elements are not in conflict, the will to fight against the social formation in which they are living is absent in humans (Longobardi).[18] In order to defend the opposite view, which in itself is perfectly acceptable but does not conform with Marx's thought, Mondolfo is compelled to twist Marx's statements in an amazing manner, substituting for the expressions "forces of production" and "system of production," which are not equivocal in Marx, the expression "men" in the totality of their being. He accomplishes this with a great deal of erudite apparatus and plenty of developmental elaboration, on the basis of scattered phrases arduously quarried, Engels's second thoughts in old age, and especially the famous fourteen glosses on Feuerbach, two pages of juvenile jottings that Marx never published during his lifetime and that record a very interesting phase from which he moved on. But Mondolfo never proves his case, nor could it be otherwise, given that Marx is deaf to this kind of pleading. A typical example of Mondolfo's approach is the attempt to reconcile *Capital* no less, a book impervious to even the faintest inklings of voluntarism, with the concept of *the inversion of praxis*, which Marx embraced as a youth.

Mondolfo says that when Marx wrote that the relations of production are independent of the will of men, he meant to refer to the single phases of economic life, in which men discover these relations already in place and cannot modify or shape them as they wish. But the moment Marx passes from this sort of anatomical and isolated examination of individual epochs to consideration of the continuity of the historical process of development, we observe that the "necessary

18 See n. 24.

relations of production," relations that are already defined and are the determining *base* and *condition* of social and spiritual life, are transformed not into the demiurges of history but into a crystallized and inert material, against which the true living force that is moving and that needs continual development, man in other words, exerts itself.[19]

There is not a shadow of proof, only a gratuitous affirmation. Marx never even came close to letting it be thought that he held such an incomprehensible idea as that there could be a law true in general and false in particular cases, an individual free in the abstract but not in the concrete instance, in eternity but not in the moment.

Besides, if Mondolfo's were really the authentic interpretation of Marxism, and the whole system really rested on the concept of the inversion of praxis, it seems clear to me that it would boil down to liberalism. Marxism as interpreted by Mondolfo, and all Marxist revisionism along with it, is in fact increasingly at odds with any sort of teleology; or rather, from that interpretation one cannot derive any conclusion for or against the socialist solution. One might accept the theory of class struggle as a fact and maintain that it will have a different outcome from the one Marx predicted or that it will constitute a leavening agent in the human community for all eternity. But what vanishes is the thing that was and is the real fulcrum and reason for being of the whole system—the scientific proof of the historical necessity of a socialist solution. The necessity of socialism metamorphoses into the necessity of the socialist movement, of the struggle between the proletariat and the bourgeoisie, a struggle that at this point appears to be open to every possibility and every denouement.

[The Intellectual Crisis]

With Mondolfo the story of Italian revisionism comes to an end—provisionally, one hopes. A sad story, alas, because the twofold critical current that had seemed at first to be taking shape did not succeed in achieving lasting results or influencing the masses, much less coloring the program of the party. Like a desert watercourse, it vanished at last into mysterious underground channels, which were often the channels of ignorance, indifference, and insincerity, or else banal utilitarianism.

With the party having rid itself of the double heresy of Left and Right, both of which evaluated Marxism without blinkers—rid itself, that is, of whatever youthful, lively, and spiritually independent forces

[19] Rodolfo Mondolfo, *Sulle orme di Marx* (1919; 3d ed. Bologna: Cappelli, 1923), p. 221.

it possessed—there was no more talk of the crisis of Marxism, as though it had been definitively resolved. People continued to talk merrily about "scientific socialism" and to reinforce their own positions with indistinct citations from Marx; they continued to refer to *Capital* as the great and untouchable book of socialism, but there was no more real research, no more thinking through to acceptance. In the revolutionaries hypocrisy, or superficiality, was at work, while in the reformers it was a matter of weakness. The socialist elite, which had risen in such a short time from the shadows of conspiracy to the light of parliamentary oratory, felt imprisoned by its own initial propaganda and by the religious needs of the crowd. Everyone surrendered passively to a movement that by now proceeded according to laws of its own, ones very different from those codified in Marxist doctrine, and everyone was careful not to take the bearings of the course they were all steering, for to do so would have revealed to each his state of crisis and that of his neighbor. As many "pure Marxisms" were constructed as there were tendencies. Every so often there was a wrangle over the meaning of the texts, and clever formulas, all more or less "integralist," "centrist," or "unitary," were excogitated in order to avoid schisms and baffle the revolutionary minorities at the congresses. The latter, which had once been assemblies of vibrant and effective forces, were shriveling into a species of academy in which everything was discussed except the vital problems of the movement. In less than twenty years socialism went from the thunderous revelation of Marx to a monotonous chorus of rehearsed lessons. Words continued to flutter, but deeds were few, and the spirit was increasingly utilitarian and mean. There was almost no one who in his heart still believed in apocalyptic prophecies. The living word had been transformed into a dead letter, faith into a rite, the rebel into a priest. After 1908 the intellectual and moral crisis had taken on such an alarming character that a few of the best men, like Rigola,[20] Salvemini, and Modigliani,[21] were forced to

[20] Rinaldo Rigola (1868–1954) was born to a working-class family and was a worker himself. Persecuted for his political activities, in 1900 he was elected deputy. Rigola was one of the founders of the Italian trade-union movement and advocated the independence of the union from the party. He was a critic of Gramsci's idea of workplace councils, which he saw as a form of politicization of the unions. He became a timid supporter of Fascist corporatism.

[21] Giuseppe Emanuele Modigliani (1872–1947) was born in Livorno to a Jewish family (his brother was the painter Amedeo Modigliani) and studied in Pisa, where he became a lawyer and a socialist. He was particularly active in the committee in charge of uncovering the Fascists responsible for Giacomo Matteotti's assassination. Within the Socialist party he had a reformist position, worked on social legislation, and was for many years a member of the municipal council of his city. Along with Rakovsky and Trotsky, Modigliani wrote the document of the Zimmerwald Conference of the Second International

turn their helpless attention to it; among them was Turati himself, who observed that the strength of the party was less both qualitatively and quantitatively, that its groups of members were carrying on listlessly, that its ideas were uncertain, that the fervor of its propagandists had subsided, and that the feeling of being in a slump was widespread. There was a general and progressive paralysis, and the few brains still functioning were on strike. The young people of the country—I refer to the intelligentsia—were experimenting in all directions except that of socialism, which in the hothouse of the Giolitti era appeared to be intellectually finished, with all true passion spent.[22] Youth was by turns Crocean, "vocian" (from the paper La Voce),[23] liberal, futurist, nationalist, and Christian, but it was no longer socialist. No one was interested in socialism anymore.

When I asked one of the best-known representatives of the socialist movement of the period for his explanation of this, I received an ultra-deterministic reply, which showed the inability of many people to grasp the primary and most profound causes of the defeat they had suffered. The young intellectuals, he said to me, almost all of them bourgeois in origin (as he himself was, for that matter), are deserting our ranks because socialism has shifted from its ingenuous, romantic, enthusiastic, but inefficient phase to a very prosaic but positive phase in which the struggle it is waging for higher salaries is hurting the investment portfolios of their fathers. In his book La conferma del marxismo Longobardi takes the same view, though his analysis is more complex.[24]

(1917), precisely before the Leninists split. Assaulted many times by the Fascists during the 1920s, he went to Paris, where he was a member of Giustizia e Libertà, even though he never left the Socialist party. After Pétain took power, he left Paris, where Rudolf Hilferding, the leader of Austrian social democracy, was arrested in his house by the SS.

[22] The era was characterized by the governments led by Giovanni Giolitti (1842–1928) between 1903 and 1913 and based on compromises and easy bargains among all the political parties in order to have large coalitions and minimize social conflict. For this reason, the phrase "Giolitti era" generally had a negative meaning, both for political and moral reasons, even if it was the first quasi-democratic era in Italy because of the extension of the right to vote to all adult males. This was one of the reasons that the political and intellectual opposition to Giolitti took an antidemocratic form.

[23] La Voce was founded by Giuseppe Prezzolini in 1908. Along with the Neapolitan La Critica, founded by Croce, this journal was one of the first important nonacademic intellectual enterprises, conceived as a reaction against the official philosophy of the time, positivism. In this sense, it was also the symbol of a new generation eager to become the protagonists of the national cultural and political renovation. Through La Voce, Prezzolini made possible the dissemination of new philosophical currents (such as idealism, Bergsonism, James's pragmatism, mysticism) and political ideas, for instance, syndicalism, democracy, and nationalism.

[24] Ernesto Cesare Longobardi (1877–1943) was born in Salerno and taught English in

Now this opinion is absurd. It might serve as a way of expressing resentment, not as the conclusion of a dispassionate assessment of the problem. It makes no sense to imagine that only between 1890 and 1900 did there exist enthusiastic young people capable of sacrificing their personal interests and their careers for an ideal. The Risorgimento witnessed profound uprisings and a host of sacrifices among the young and was not in fact guided by a sordid vision of the interest of the bourgeoisie in national unification. Were there no more examples, of the kind absolutely inexplicable on egotistical grounds, of devotion to causes after 1900? On the contrary, it is the almost unanimous opinion that in the generation of intellectuals destined to offer itself up to the war, one could see a growing state of dissatisfaction and moral impatience, a need, whether it was a good thing or a bad one, to escape from a life of refinement and cerebration and to immolate oneself body and soul for a cause, any cause, provided it had the ability to transcend the petty routine of daily life.

If young intellectuals deserted socialism, it was not because they all became utilitarians and philistines overnight. Quite the opposite; it was because the socialist movement itself, in the person of too many of its senior people and in the spirit that guided its work, was losing much of its original ethical fire. There is no reason to think that young people failed to see the deep unease and insincerity of the leaders of the movement, the culpable superficiality with which they thought they could overcome the so-called crisis of Marxism. Young people have a need to believe in the nobility, the purity, and the clarity of the ideals they profess. To strike a bargain, as too many had done, with one's own conscience or to duck the summons and the reproach of reason by concealing one's inner distress under an equivocal formula arouses deep repulsion in them. And deep repulsion is what they felt at the bleating of socialist journals and books, which lacked vigor of thought and moral radiance. To this moral impatience was joined a growing impatience on the intellectual level with dogmatic and materialistic Marxism, and even more with the mental and cultural stance that distinguished the leading exponents of official socialism and the Socialist party.

The new generation was idealistic, voluntaristic, and pragmatic. It did not understand the materialistic, positivistic, pseudo-scientific language of the elders, and they, for their part, rather than make an effort

---

Naples and in Venice. He was an active socialist organizer, engaged in the political rather than the intellectual life of the party. Sympathetic to Sorel's ideas in his youth, later he was among the founders of the Italian Communist party. His most important work (to which Rosselli is referring) was *La conferma del marxismo: Il comunismo scientifico e le recenti esperienze storiche* (1921).

to penetrate the intimate reasons for this reaction, immured themselves in blind sectarian incomprehension, deriding the new attitudes,
rejecting a priori any socialism that was not positivistic, and defining
the idealist philosophers reductively as servants of the bourgeoisie. At
the Congress of Rome it had been solemnly declared that the party
program bore "the specific character of a democratic and positivistic
socialism," so that to adhere to it signified an implicit acceptance of that
particular philosophy. Along with your official membership card you
had to show your philosophical membership card too, and if it did not
have all the right stamps, if you did not display total admiration for
Comte or Spencer, Darwin or Ardigò,[25] you were lectured to or suffered veiled ostracism, even loss of citizenship, until finally you realized that you were out of place where you were and departed for
brighter shores and vaster horizons. It would have been one thing if
the intellectual stance of the elders were strong and fresh, professed
with real passion and profound conviction. In fact it was corroded and
eaten away by a basic strain of criticism of which the young were
perfectly well aware. Criticism is not the road that leads to faith, and no
one had ever bothered to answer that criticism, those weighty refuta-
tions of orthodox Marxism and positivism, with solid arguments, only
with facile irony and stupid accusations.

As a result, the elders understood nothing of the secret travail of the
young, and the young abandoned the glorious old allegiance, marking
a rupture that was fatal for the future of Italian socialism. I use the word

[25] Roberto Ardigò (1828–1920) was born in Lombardy and became a priest. He devoted himself to philosophy, particularly Renaissance naturalism. His essay "Pom-
ponazzi" (1869) can be considered a milestone of Italian positivism, which Ardigò did
much to orient toward a metaphysical naturalism. In his *La psicologia come scienza positiva*
(1870)—which immediately became the textbook of more than one generation—he opposed to spiritualism and Thomism a phenomenistic interpretation of knowledge, however contaminated with the presupposition of a foundational psychophysical substance.
This linked him—and many of his numerous followers—to the German materialists,
Ludwig Büchner and Jacob Moleschott. Only years later did Ardigò begin to study
Herbert Spencer, whose philosophy was similar to his own. This philosophical position
caused Ardigò so many difficulties with the Roman Catholic Church, that he decided to
leave the priesthood. Censure against him was immediate and so strong that it was not
until ten years later, when politics became more secular, that he succeeded in getting a
professorship at the state university. Although he never took an active part in political
life, his philosophy and his life experience helped him become the spiritual leader of all
sorts of oppositions—the republicans, the radicals, and the socialists. When at the turn
of the century positivism came under attack, Ardigò and his followers lost prestige and
soon became the respresentatives of an old-fashioned materialism (commenting on a
collection of his essays published in 1922, Gramsci spoke of a "shoddy book with no
value"). The feeling of having outlived himself was, perhaps, among the reasons of his
two attempts at suicide.

fatal because this break contained the nucleus of many of the reasons for the defeat that lay in the future.[26] The only practical attempt at renewal made from within the party before the war was by Mussolini. As much of an adventurer in the world of culture as he was in that of politics, he had no strong and coherent thought or honest intellectual concern. Only one thing mattered to his frenetic desire for action and command: the affirmation of his own self. Ideas, values, faiths, all had validity to the extent that they could be made to serve his ambition. But being gifted with an uncommon degree of intuition, he—almost alone—realized how the old socialist position no longer satisfied the needs of the young and claimed that he was just the man to revitalize it by throwing it open to idealism on one hand and pragmatic voluntarism and Bergsonism on the other. Despite his intrinsic immorality and the utter superficiality of his revolutionary stance, he succeeded in a short while in putting himself at the head of a large section of socialist youth and gaining control of the party quite unexpectedly. Mussolini's victory was due in large measure to the constitutional incapacity for renewal of the old cadres who led the movement, and who did indeed condemn this sudden and absurd return to Blanquist insurrectionism but were quite unable to meet it with a constructive program animated by an ample long-range vision of the problems of Italian life.[27] Their reformism, tainted by the blight of electioneering and the fight for detailed social improvements, gave off an echo, or so it seemed, of profound skepticism, as of people who no longer believe in the ideals of their own youth but do not dare to admit it.

Let it not be said that in those years there was a shortage among the young of groups with a healthy, realistic outlook, groups capable of furthering a strong and effective reformism. But they were systematically whittled down and eliminated. The most typical example remains Salvemini's journal *L'Unità*,[28] which succeeded in gathering about it an authentic general staff of tendentiously socialist young people—proof that the decadence was not due to the flight of the rising generation from socialism, but to the inability of the party to adapt itself to their demands. The urgent need for a program of action was articulated, which instead of trying to win reforms predominantly economic in nature that only benefited narrow categories of workers, would fight for a series of great *political* reforms of general relevance:

[26] Rosselli means the 1922 defeat in the face of fascism.

[27] Rosselli is referring to the years when Benito Mussolini (1883–1945) was a leader of the Socialist party and, as a representative of the maximalist wing, edited the national newspaper *L'Avanti* between 1912 and 1914. But because of his campaign in favor of the war, he was expelled.

[28] See n. 13 of this chapter.

reforms of taxation, of customs dues, of the communes, of the army, reforms able to create the sort of political consciousness in people that is an indispensable premise for the birth of a modern democracy. Salvemini's critiques often went too far, and he wound up, through love of the concrete, being concerned exclusively with problems. But there is no doubt that he, more acutely than anyone else, diagnosed the crisis that was undermining the foundations of Italian socialism.

The truth is that in the years leading up to the war, Italian socialism was intellectually dead. If it felt any stimulus at all, it must have been the drive to self-destruction, so much did it do to unite all youth groups against it. It caused the intellectual reaction against Marxism to join forces with the convergent reaction against democracy and the parliamentary regime that in Italy took the form of opposition to Giolitti. Reformist socialism, not even realistic but simply out to make a deal, was also identified with the degenerate parliamentary regime, and revolutionary groups guided by Sorel and Mussolini, and nationalist groups as well, grew stronger as a result, since they both influenced this reaction and drew new vigor and justification from it. These two groups aligned themselves with one another at the outbreak of war and gave potential life to fascism.

The attitude of the party during the war, expressed in the unhappy slogan "Neither sabotage nor consent," confirms the uncertainty and the spirit of compromise that animated it.

The war swept over this already fragile intellectual edifice like an avalanche. The febrile postwar period, with its spinning vortex of new experiments, was lived from day to day, but in a reversal of the normal process of drainage, all the muck was saved, and all the most vital elements were sluiced away. Alongside the few solid representatives of the old leadership who were left, there was not even a shadow of any genuine youthful energy. The party plodded wearily along in its accustomed rut; it had a premonition of the final quagmire but kept marching forward. And now it is seven years since it has marched at all, the weeds grow thick in the deserted fields, and not even the feeble ancient voices reach us anymore.

Once and for all a rude intellectual shock is needed to dislodge the Italian socialists from their ideological passivity, to force them to think for themselves and to achieve, through the hard personal travail of search, of doubt, of conflict, new values to take the place of blind faith in the thaumaturgic virtues of the Marxist-materialist nostrums.

The time has come. Even the socialist church is calling for rebellion in the form of free inquiry and an end to all catechisms.

FOUR

CONCLUSION OF REVISIONISM

$\left\langle \text{I}\right.$T WILL BE evident from what has been said in the preceding chapters that although revisionism can take credit for splitting open the hardened crust of dogma in its effort to bring theory in line with the new practice of the workers' movement and separate the aspects of Marxism that were still living and fruitful from those that were sterile and outmoded, it was unable or unwilling to pursue the process of revision to its logical conclusion. In the end it got bogged down in a debate over interpretation that canceled much of the good it had accomplished.

What it did not do the new generation must now attempt, in full sincerity and independence of judgment and without fear of shattering idols made of papier-mâché or of printed paper, and without deluding itself that it will immediately gain a large following. So much critical material has accumulated in thirty years—both in the realm of deeds and in that of ideas—that we are required not to utter novelties or advance yet another interpretation of Marx so much as we are to lay out clearly the objective, and largely concordant, results already attained by revisionism. In short, what has to be done is to draw up a balance sheet of Marxism in relation to the workers' movement.

The task is an urgent one, very urgent, particularly in Italy. For too many years now the ideological outlook of socialism has been frozen, divorced from practice. We are still back with Bernstein, at the stage the debate had reached in 1900, while from 1900 to the present the world has not just moved on but actually hurtled forward. The workers' movement has arisen, becoming a formidable presence in places, while the socialist parties are transforming themselves into parties of government and are on the road to winning majorities. Political democracy is by now part of the patrimony (a patrimony that is not exclusively their own, but fundamental for them nonetheless) of the laboring masses, while the state has been progressively losing its class character. The bourgeois economy has been organizing and rationalizing itself; wealth has multiplied, even for the working class. A tremendous war and a tremendous revolution have taken place, bringing into existence a world of extraordinary new experience . . . everything around us has changed, everything except the socialist program and ideology. They, it is claimed, sprang forth into the world fully formed for all time, through the prophetic genius of Marx.

Throughout the world the Communist schism has certainly helped to give socialism its own face, if for no other reason than the reciprocal necessity for each to distinguish itself and create a completely autonomous identity. But the clarification was of an entirely practical and polemical kind, imposed by circumstances, and it was not accompanied by an equally clear ideological reordering. The leaders of the socialist parties of Europe (England excluded) still lay claim, like Kautsky, to an entirely nonexistent and risible Marxist purity. In fact one could say that the schism and the burden of government responsibility have brought out a rather ambivalent ideological conservatism in the socialist chieftains, making them even more refractory, goaded as they are by the Communist competition, than they were in the past to serious ideological analysis. It is incredible to witness the fear that pervades most of them when they are faced with having to separate openly from the Marxist tradition, and the way they more or less consciously sabotage even the most timid non-Marxist trend. Marx is taboo. The less he is discussed, the better. One concentrates on one's daily experience, on the things life has to teach, and carries on as best one can. The socialist mind thus oscillates between formal orthodoxy and down-to-earth empiricism.

I know many socialists, even young ones, who agree in their hearts with the most extreme points of revisionist thought, who recognize the necessity for a serious attempt at ideological renewal; they will even go so far as to proclaim Marx antiquated. But normally they are prepared to concede all this *in camera charitatis* (in private), within four walls and among friends, and the moment the question arises of taking an official position, they turn reticent and equivocal and are quick to glide away on the smooth surface of the standard familiar order of business. Laziness? Insincerity? Fear of losing the masses? A faint and abject premonition of the perils and responsibilities that come upon us when we take a more autonomous and therefore more subjective, arduous, and critical stand? Probably all of these things at once. In sum, those who ought to exercise leadership, those whose task it is to think for the countless others who are too caught up in the daily problems of existence, ended by making themselves prisoners of the ingenuous fetishism of the masses, which they had created and which they could destroy without too much trouble. It would require only an act of will. And one could understand if the leadership tiptoed around this issue in countries where the socialist movement was developing in a progressive and orderly fashion and was on the way to winning, or reinforcing, positions of power, for in these cases the desire to avoid too much heated debate at the delicate moment of transition from negative criticism to positive action would be more excusable. But the worst of it

is that this is happening primarily in Italy, where the socialist movement has been literally swept away, and where tomorrow it will have to
start again from scratch, with a new spirit appropriate to the great
heritage of the past and the change of generations.

It is imperative to rebel against this fatal advance—which is not an
"advance" at all, but a movement in reverse, or a death agony—and to
combat all forms of intellectual hypocrisy and senile weakness, all
resort to the line of least resistance, which is the worst of examples. We,
the young in years or in spirit, have an obligation to impose a forceful
ideological resolution that will finally clear away all the dead branches
that are blocking the path in such an absurd fashion, that will rid us of
the weight of all the old catechistical baggage that did so much to cause
our defeat. We will be few at first and will have to struggle a good deal.
But the struggle is a vital one, and for those who believe that one of the
principal reasons for the crisis through which socialism is passing lies
in the spirit of compromise and the timidity of the present thinkers and
leaders, it is an obligation of conscience. ⟩

The logical conclusion to which revisionism leads is the splitting off
of socialism from Marxism. Revisionism has in fact refuted or tacitly
abandoned all features of Marxism that were most closely tied in to
socialism, at the same time buttressing the genuinely philosophical
and sociological features of Marxism (historical materialism, class
struggle), features that can no longer be the exclusive appanage of a
single political party because they are on their way to acquiring a
more universal and objective value. The consequences that logically
follow from the interpretation of Marxism furnished by the revisionists
are these: (1) one may be a Marxist without being a socialist; (2) socialists who still believe that they can find a shaping principle in Marxism
or concrete guidance for the socialist movement are fooling themselves.

Proof of these seemingly paradoxical propositions is not difficult to
supply. We have already seen that the true originality of the Marxist
position with respect to the other varieties of socialism did not lie in the
fact that it foresaw a different outcome or proposed that radically different methods be adopted. It lay rather in the concept of the historical
necessity of the coming of socialism through the working of the inner
laws of development in capitalist society. Whereas pre-Marxist socialism denounced social injustice and postulated a socialist society in the
name of an abstract and absolute principle of justice, Marx as a historicist intended to show that the socialist solution exists as a potentiality
in present society and constitutes the synthesis necessary to overcome
the contradiction that is eroding the base of the capitalist system of

production. He arrived at this conclusion through the objective study of the historical process, with the aid of the materialistic approach to historical interpretation. Logically ordered (a posteriori), this is how the sequence of Marxist thought works: first the materialistic approach, then its application to the study of capitalist society, and third the objective prediction of the inevitability of a socialist outcome. A really coherent Marxist is thus a socialist by pure deduction. If the premise, that is, the theory of historical materialism, fails, or if there is a change in the results to which the application of the method leads, the socialist conclusion automatically fails too.

Now what did the revisionist reaction purport? It said that in Marxism there is an original fundamental nucleus, which is historical materialism. Around this nucleus a pseudo-theoretical carapace has formed, which is no more than the product of Marx's first clumsy attempt to apply the materialistic method to the society of his time. Then it was highly meaningful. But today, with the method perfected, and in light of all the transformations that have taken place, it can no longer withstand close scrutiny. This hardened crust, this dross, comprises the belief that a crisis is coming, belief in progressive impoverishment, belief in the concentration of wealth in fewer and fewer hands, and belief in the heightening of the class struggle until a final violent clash occurs. Let us get rid of the incrustation, the fallacious applications of the method, and we will be able to salvage the primordial core, the pure nucleus of Marxism.

But getting rid of the incrustation amounts to throwing out the socialist conclusions to which Marxism led; and since Marxism is a socialist theory solely in virtue of its conclusions, to do so amounts to excluding Marxism from the category of socialist theories. And excluded it was. From that moment Marxism lost the attribute of being socialistic. But such a paradoxical event could not really be owned up to, given the close identification that most people had grown used to making between socialism and Marxism. Since the socialist conclusion had fallen, socialism had to be reintroduced into the premises, and so the revisionists wrestled to make room in historical materialism for the moment of liberty, for an activist vision of the historical process. And so the theory of the inversion of praxis arose, or arose again—a theory that is not socialistic per se and that contains no particular sanction for the socialist solution, but that by making room for human will in history thereby makes room for socialism. Clearly, however, the relation between historical materialism and socialism had been turned upside down. That which had previously constituted a necessary conclusion now became a contingent premise. The revisionists followed Marx's trail in reverse, and from socialist science they returned to faith, to the position, that is, of the pre-Marxist schools.

It is scarcely necessary to point out that they were not clearly aware of what they were doing, and that they have continued to maintain absurdly that Marxism is the socialist theory par excellence, making the principle of the inversion of praxis the essential pillar of their socialism. The depressing result is that the moment socialism tries to deepen the theoretical underpinning on which it rests, it feels the ground slipping out from under its feet and finds itself wavering between the abyss on one hand and dogmatism on the other.

In order to get from the theory of the inversion of praxis to the . . . frozen praxis of socialist society, socialist revisionists are forced to deny themselves by embracing the vulgar economic determinism and the extreme simplification of sociological diagnosis against which they had quite rightly rebelled. That is to say, they must: (1) reduce all social contradictions to the unique contradiction between the system of production and the system of appropriation; (2) impose an obligatory role on human free will; (3) fix one categorical direction for the evolution of production; and (4) postulate a static and perfect social state.

They must, in other words, deny the dialectical vision of history as an indefinite series of struggles, not only or always struggles between classes, and not only or always economic in nature, which is the basis of their revision, and which is also, for Marx and Engels, the only a priori law of history. They must deny history itself.

In truth, the Marxism of the revisionists is averse to making strong predictions about the future, or to put it another way, no consequences for or against socialism flow from their theoretical position. One could accept that history is a never-ending conflict between classes and envision a variety of different outcomes; one might even take the view that the bourgeoisie does not act solely to preserve its gains. In order to derive a socialist conclusion, one has to feed in empirical data (the Marxist belief in catastrophe), or else an element of faith. For that matter, it has to be remembered that in the dialectic of history the moment of the thesis is no less important than that of the antithesis; indeed, neither can be conceived without the other. Any political conception that one wishes to derive from historical materialism must adopt, justify, and embrace both the conservative function of the bourgeoisie and the revolutionary function of the proletariat, placing itself always at the juncture of these two forces.

I hold that it is sterile to try to tie philosophical positions too closely to practical programs. But if one does wish to establish this tie for the theory of historical materialism, the revisionist interpretation of it leads not to socialism but to full liberalism—a more concrete and realistic liberalism that looks to the substance of the social movement and the dialectic of things and identifies with more precision and realism the agents of progress and the driving forces of the movement, that brings into the picture the groups and the classes that today, in these social conditions, with this form of production, this psychology, these needs, this ideological baggage, gives first place to the social problem, to the struggle between proletarians and capitalists, ⟨but always within liberalism.

With revisionism, therefore, the objective and rigorous proof that socialism is the solution, which had given the Marxist system its distinctive character, fails.⟩ From Marxism the road leads to revisionism, and from revisionism to liberalism. This progression is inevitable. Thirty years ago Bernstein let it be understood that this would be the conclusion. The socialist movement means everything, he said, and the end means nothing. ⟨Or the end is valid to the extent that it sustains the movement.⟩ This was the formulation of a liberal socialist. At the time it caused a scandal. Today it is on the way to becoming the characteristic point of view of the entire new socialist generation.

About the value of historical materialism there has been much discussion in recent years. Many Marxist writers are disposed to concede that it provides no support for the belief that socialism must come, but they all insist on emphasizing its immense value as a guide, as a "compass" for the socialist movement, so much so that they speak of it as the specific philosophy of the socialist *movement*. Only historical materialism, Mondolfo proclaims, only the concept of the inversion of praxis, can reconcile the two extremes of fatalistic materialism and antihistorical voluntarism, thus rescuing the movement from glib revolutionism but also from getting bogged down in reformism. It alone gives the revolutionary an understanding of the possibilities and limits of action at any given moment. Mondolfo states without hesitation that the fundamental defect of the Italian socialists has lain in the incongruence of their philosophical premises, in the lack of a coherent theoretical orientation, in the neglect of the essential principle of historical realism on which they believed they stood, which consists in the inversion of praxis.

Now I must confess that in all the well-known formulas dear to Marxist revisionists, from "the inversion of praxis" to "reality that conditions and is conditioned," from "man creating his history within the limits of pre-existing conditions that are beyond his control" to "the present, offspring of the past and progenitor of the future," I find nothing specific, nothing capable of satisfying the needs of the socialist movement, nothing that might guide socialist action in any concrete historical situation. In all of this I find only a generic transposition of the dialectical principle from the conceptual sphere to the real world and a generic counsel of prudence for revolutionaries, one infinitely less persuasive than what one learns by living and experiencing freely. I would note, however, that while in the Marxist system this dialectic of things had a perfectly clear significance and a well-defined direction (leading to the socialist solution), in revisionism its value becomes increasingly vague and evanescent. When the time comes to put the compass to use, the instrument that was so greatly extolled turns out to be immune to the magnetic influence of history as it unfolds. In any actual situation the employment of the materialistic method depends, evidently, on an evaluation of the state of *things* (the mechanism of production) and of *consciousness* (men engaged in their struggle against the physical and economic environment). Now within certain limits this interpretation will always be vitiated by subjectivism and a priori assumptions. The antithesis between voluntarism and fatalism, which one thought had been vanquished in the realm of theory through the concept of the inversion of praxis, springs up again in the world of action. Even unbridled voluntarism (when it is proclaiming simplistic theses and invoking miraculous leaps) can imagine itself in good faith to be suffused with the sense of history. If room is made for the will in the historical process, the voluntarist can always, with majestic intuition, maintain that the appeal to the will is valid and may even think it a good idea to exaggerate intentionally the role of the will in order to force blind and sluggish mankind to make reasonable use of it. When we enter the complex realm of psychology, historical materialism shows itself to be helpless.

In substance, the whole of historical materialism, once interdependence is substituted for determinism, boils down in practical terms to a lesson in historical realism, to a banal truism that was known to men of action a long time ago: Don't bite off more than you can chew. When this lesson was first delivered in Marx's time it had a salutary effect because it contrasted sharply with the frenzied utopianism, and all the other deductive schemes for social palingenesis, to which the abstract rationalism of the eighteenth century had given birth. But today it tends to do more harm than good. All the European socialist movements, under the incubus of this *necessity* that they have all helped to bring to light, have lost all faith in the creative élan of the masses. Perhaps the time has come to put the emphasis on the moment of *liberty*, to remember that in any case it is the business of reformist parties to exaggerate the voluntarist element, just as it behooves the conservative ones to exaggerate the obstacles in its way. Marxist determinism, and also the corrected interpretation of it that the revisionists offer, leads to the acceptance, or at least to an excessive respect a priori, for existing reality just because it exists. It humiliates mankind by reminding it continually of its littleness in comparison with the formidable forces of the environment, nature, and society, and it can easily lead to forms of resignation similar to those found in Catholicism. All gods are dangerous, including those of the forces of production. Let me say something that may appear paradoxical: it seems to me that at the present stage of social relations, historical materialism is a philosophy much better suited to the capitalist class than to the proletariat. The capitalist, particularly the entrepreneur, being in charge of the production process, dominating and linking its elements, sharing actively in technical progress, possesses an awareness of his active participation in the transformation of the process of production. He is able concretely to insert his will into history, and his relation to economic life is typically one of action-reaction. The proletarian (and the intellectual who joins the cause of the workers on his behalf), however, since he only feels the effects or is forced to assist passively in the process of production, sees the forces of production merely as controlling factors against which, at present, he is powerless to react. Historical materialism, when he applies it, becomes not a liberating philosophy but a philosophy that shows him his chains, and in doing so induces him to make vain attempts to get free of them. At times of unusual exaltation it may serve to cool down overheated illusions, but it cannot be the basic philosophy for a workers' movement that is still in the age of minority when it comes to directing the economy. Psychologically speaking, it is inevitable that historical materialism should assume, among the masses, a deterministic hue.

More generally, we could postulate that all those in power have to draw attention continually to limitations, whereas all those who are dominated have to deny them or reduce their import. The Communist party in Russia thirsts for historical materialism; scientific socialist-Marxist parties in Europe thirst for voluntarism—not voluntarism as something to chatter about, but a voluntarism nourished by virile faith in the capacity of the will to build, to renew the world.

The vicissitudes of Italian socialism unfortunately constitute the most striking confirmation of what has been said. The philosophers of historical materialism complain of the insufficient theoretical and philosophical preparation of the Italian socialists and their lack of rigor, thinking that they have thus identified one of the reasons for their defeat. I would advance the opposite complaint: they are too preoccupied with theory and pseudo-theory, too worried about conforming to Marxist "canons," too fearful of showing themselves to be empirical, resolute, and pragmatic. That false preoccupation with being historicist that comes to us from Marx, and even more from the Marxist cohort in general, is unbearable sometimes, and especially so at times when action and urgent decisions have to be taken. There is a fear of being antihistorical, of diverging from the main route marked out on the Marxist maps, of not conforming perfectly to the historical physiognomy of one's time. We are historians when we should be making the news and news reporters when we should be making history. And so there are analyses, studies, debates, brain-racking sessions in order to pin down with deceptive and scholastic exactitude the "civil state" of our time, diagnoses and prognoses of the phenomena before our very eyes. This professorial mentality has nothing to do with the mentality of men of action who intend to take an active part in the historical process. In Italy the common dwelling was on fire, the flames from the houses of the workers were turning the sky red, and the inhabitants—the socialists—were squabbling among themselves about whether it really was a fire, what had caused it, whether it fell into this or that category, whether it had been foretold in the sacred books, whether it was burning only in Italy, and so on.[1]

During periods of rapid change especially one sees how illusory and deleterious it is to claim to be following the *guiding thread* of historical materialism: a real condemnation to impotence. Action requires timeliness, intuition, adaptation, creation. The concrete historical process, as the devotees of historical materialism have depicted it, is history lived by nobody, history a posteriori, history for professors. Its vaunted compass works only after the ship is in port. It can be a great help to the historian, but it is often useless and sometimes harmful to one involved in making history. The gross predictive errors Marx made in applying his method simply confirm what I have said.

Historical materialism has planted too deeply in the minds of the majority the notion that the historical process is a mechanical process, an automatic compounding of clearly determined, quantifiable forces that cannot be modified through the voluntary actions of men. Remember Bernstein, with his admonition that from now on the problem is merely that of ascertaining with precision the quantitative relation of the factors at work, of the preponderant historical forces! The attitude of too many eminent socialists faced with the phenomenon of nascent fascism was either Buddhistic or Stoic. They spread their arms disconsolately and prepared themselves for martyrdom, convinced that there was little or nothing they could do to oppose a fatal progress that they had analyzed in all of its components. They had already rationally

---

[1] Rosselli is recalling the years of Fascist violence, which occurred after the end of World War I, and whose preferred targets were the workers' institutions and circles.

justified their own loss when the enemy had not even begun to dream he could win. How easy it is to resign oneself to defeat when it seems to emerge from the "force of things," from the "immaturity of capitalistic development," from the "phase of necessary bourgeois expansion," and so on and so forth. And if these slogans cannot bear the weight, then low-grade Hegelianism fills the bill admirably, with its rationalization of the real, of all realities, of even a reality that, since it runs counter to the inner laws of historical development, ought to extrude itself from . . . reality.

Once again the comparison with Catholic belief comes to mind. The believer, stunned by the loss of a loved one, sees the secret hand of the Lord in even the most atrocious trials. The historical materialist, bowing down before the dark god of capitalism, behaves in the same fashion.

The Marxists' constant failure to give full weight to ideologies and to so-called irrational factors (the passions) is especially serious. It is enough to reflect on the really remarkable way in which nationalism stands up under economic pressure. While calm spells last, the damage done by this failure is not great; but in dynamic times of crisis or revolution, the consequences can be decisive. At those times political life turns incandescent, and it can be shaped in the most contradictory ways just because of the immense part played by the "irrational" elements. This normally escapes the historical materialist, so that he ends up making a very wrong estimate of the forces in play. This happened in a typical manner at the beginning of the Fascist movement. It cannot be said that the first Fascist associations began to take action exclusively out of class interest or under class guidance; nor were they composed only of bourgeois. They were groups of deranged misfits, of idealists (and also criminals), seized by a patriotic and romantic delirium. Only later did they become the tool of agrarian-plutocratic reactionaries. Historical materialists (or those who pass for such . . .) were accustomed to deal with man as a type, with the historical process as typical, with the primary causes and the vast waves of the movement of history; they had grown used to considering ideas as travesties of class interests and class relations and had no idea of the autonomous and powerful force that passion, beautiful or ugly as it might be, aroused in the souls of their rivals. They did not realize that when the clash comes, one's level of critical awareness counts for less than spontaneity, living force, inner conviction, the active spirit of struggle and sacrifice. And so it was that while the explosive power of the Fascist movement was growing in a stunning fashion, pure critical capacity held sway among the leaders on the other side. Between the fighters and the historians the contest was never in doubt. The fighters won.

To conclude, the trust the socialists place in their historical materialist compass is a naive illusion and a contradiction. It is an illusion because in the best of cases historical materialism enables one only to identify a very general line of development in the life not of one but of many generations, and it always has to be used with the greatest caution, if for no other reason than that no one is in a position to know what future developments of technology there will be and thus what the characteristics of the "system of production" will be. Any forecast we can make, being merely a projection into the future of present conditions, which will certainly change, is misguided. At most the faithful user of the historical materialist compass will succeed in plotting not a real course but a simulation—the course that society would follow if nothing changed, if technology, social relations, culture, ideology, sensibility, and so on, all remained as they are now. His predictions will be generic and inaccurate, of no use to anybody who has to take concrete action.

And if only that were all, the projection of the present into the future! What in fact happens all too often is a projection of the past into the future—the past out of which Marx constructed his system and made his forecasts eighty years ago.

But to entrust themselves to the historical materialist compass is also a contradiction for socialists. What they wish to do is to bring a completely critical and rational consciousness to bear on the movement, and on the method that presides over the movement, not on its end. The end, socialism, is something they postulate for sentimental and often quite arbitrary reasons, from principles held on faith. If they want to exercise their critical acumen, they should start by applying it to the end first, and then to the method. To mobilize all of philosophy in order to decide practical questions that experience and common sense were meant to resolve, and then carefully switch off this critical consciousness when dealing with the largest problems connected with socialism's goals, is a grotesque piece of nonsense.

But it was not theory in any case that gave the coup de grace to Marxist socialism. In theory all theses, even the most strongly grounded, are open to debate, and any solution can be accepted. Even if one could prove categorically that revisionism had broken the logical link between socialism and Marxism, there would always be people who would attempt to maintain the contrary through habile and knowing exegesis. No, the rude awakening came from actuality, from the progressive erosion of two myths that underlie all Marxist propaganda and that have been the main reasons for its success: (1) communism as ordained by the ineluctable necessity of the system of production, the fated outcome of the contradictions and the crises that are undermining the organism of capitalism; (2) communism viewed as the only social structure able to guarantee, through the rational ordering of production and distribution, an immense increase in productivity and well-being, freeing mankind from enslavement to material need.

The first myth has been greatly undermined by the profound transformations capitalism underwent between Marx's time and to our own, the second by the fact that workers have acquired an imposing array of experience in economics and politics. Capitalist rationalization on one hand and the Russian experiment on the other have only furthered the erosion.

Let us begin with the first. In his works Marx had delineated a typical phase of capitalist development, the anarchic and explosive one that occurs at the beginning, of the kind seen in England—reckless individualism, free competition, the ferocious exploitation of factory hands. In this phase production is terribly unplanned, and the factory system functions with enormous waste and wear, at the cost of unspeakable suffering on the part of the masses, who are violently despoiled of their trades and their tools and reduced to the rank of a commodity, the victims of recurrent economic crises and of the unemployment that appears to be a functional necessity for capitalism.

Marx's error was to have mistaken the prologue for the entire course of development, to have given transitory phenomena long temporal duration, to have laid down the progressive impoverishment of the masses and the accumulation of riches in the hands of a few as the "law, general and [absolute," of capitalist accumulation, thus compromising his entire conception with] a theoretical deductivism and [with] the dialectical schematism so dear to Hegelians. The fact is that capitalism succeeded in getting out of the impasse into which it seemed to have driven itself. The workers' movement, social legislation, countless other forms of intervention by society, all put an end in the most advanced countries to the most disgusting abuses. The refinement of the production process and of the capitalist mentality revealed that increasing profitability required better-qualified, better-fed, better-paid workers, capable of consuming as well as producing the gigantic mountains of products that were flooding the market. Limited-liability public companies democratized capital within certain limits, and capitalist coalitions reacted to the harm done when production was governed by the caprice of profit and the decision of individuals. From a policy under which the state abstained from interfering in the economy there was a shift, by imperceptible degrees, to a policy of intensive and growing state intervention, with the nationalization of essential public services (the railways, post office, banks, insurance companies, and so on), controlled prices for many commodities (light, bread, water, housing, and so on), supervision of markets, professional bodies, foreign trade, awards and subventions, expropriation in the public interest, public works, enforced regulation of salaries and conditions of work . . . there was a burgeoning of initiatives on the part of public bodies, of which we do not yet have an adequate picture. The experience of England, the Mecca of individualistic libertarianism, is typical. There we currently find an enormous range of services provided by social organizations absorbing almost half of the budget, aid to the unemployed and to the owners of mines, customs tariffs, the determination of salaries, and so on. The sector of nationalized, seminationalized, or state-controlled enterprises comprises a variety of companies worth 315 billion lire, equivalent to about two-thirds of the total capital of the great English business organizations.

Even more typical is the process that has led, in the most important branches of industry, to the replacement of individual private enterprises with huge anonymous firms, gigantic coalitions of capital and expertise linked among themselves horizontally or vertically (trusts, cartels, and so on) on an international scale and forced much more often than people realize to seek an increase in profit through cost reductions achieved through mass production and a dizzying rate of progress in the methods of production. In America especially the process of economic rationalization has assumed such a rapid pace in recent years that it has eliminated the worst effects of unrestrained competition and fragmentation, realizing an extremely high level of productivity.

The old Marxist argument against the culpable level of waste in capitalism has lost much of its force in light of this progress. The productivity attained by many companies in Germany and America is such that it is hard to imagine its being surpassed by state or collective management. Imagine, for example, the abrupt socialization of the German chemical industry. The best that could be hoped for as a result of such a takeover would be to maintain the current level of production and rate of progress. The workers' wages would be enhanced only by the part of the profit that was not reinvested in the industry, which would become disposable income.

The process of reorganization that large-scale capitalist industry has been forced to undertake certainly confirms the accuracy of much of the criticism made by Marxists, and generally by the reformist schools of thought in the last century, of the regime of anarchic competition, and it represents notable progress toward a more rational production, no longer dominated by the blind egoism of a tiny minority. But by the same token the habitual denunciations of Marx are fatally robbed of

their efficacy and their relevance, and so is his conception of the socialist movement, a conception based on the kind of anarchic capitalism
that he thought was incurable. Likewise, the events of the war and the
postwar period have overturned Marx's predictions. The social revolution broke out in Russia, the most backward country, while the most
advanced country, the United States, survived the crisis with the least
turmoil. England is another example: for ten years one-tenth of its
working population has been unemployed. This is an appalling level,
which in Marx's time would have brought on social chaos or some
attempt at revolutionary expropriation. Instead we see nothing of the
kind. The high standard of living of the population, in other words, its
escape (which Marx denied could ever take place) from subsistence at
the margin, has allowed England to meet this crisis.

This does not cancel the fact that the capitalist regime is still showing
serious deficiencies, and not just in the economy: war and class struggle are the darker areas in the picture. But we have to get used to
considering the overall picture and not just the shadowy parts. At the
moment the Marxist mentality is too dominated by the contrary critical
prejudice: Marxists inevitably concentrate on the negative aspects of
the modern world, which enable them to confirm the pessimism of
Marx. Observe, for example, their attitude to the phenomenon of rationalization. They fail to realize that truly advanced forms of technology-
based, rationalized capitalism are not very different from what they
would be if socialism were brought to industry. The differences no
longer lie in the sphere of production (as in Marx), but in the sphere of
distribution and that of morality. Capitalist rationalization contains
within itself many of the elements of socialist rationalization; the huge
differences between them of spirit and intention shrink rapidly if we
look at practical results. Today it is possible to imagine the transfer from
one to the other coming about through a gradual and peaceful
process—a process capable of preserving the proven qualities of the
first while progressively reinforcing them with the best values of the
second. But for this shift to happen, the socialists will have to abandon
their old habit of automatic criticism and take a sober look at the new
capitalist reality.

For anyone who really wants to do something constructive, it is a
dangerous mistake to keep on stubbornly contrasting a pure, ideal
social form (socialist society) with an entirely applied one (present
capitalist society). All pure forms are by definition superior to applied
ones. In theory even total libertarianism—the Newtonian harmony of
individual egoisms, celebrated by Bentham—is capable of ensuring
the maximum degree of collective well-being. We have to get from
theory to reality and put up with inevitable disappointments. Life is

chock-full of bruising encounters and unknown quantities, and the only values it produces are relative ones.

The point of reference for Marxist socialists is an ideal social form that arose out of a critical and sentimental reaction to the analysis of the deficiencies and the moral and material miseries of a phase of capitalism that has been *superseded* in the most advanced countries. To the extent that capitalism has resolved the problems and the contradictions signaled by Marx, or has actually realized socialist principles, Marxist criticism is obsolete. A hundred years ago the vision of rationalized production, liberated from the caprices of individual egoism, was spellbinding. Today, in the face of rationalization by the great capitalist industries, the spell is much weaker, and only an attachment to the old commonplaces and ignorance of the new economic reality are able to keep it alive in the minds of European socialists.

In a debate between Marx and a cotton spinner from Lancashire or a producer of cauldrons from Birmingham, Marx would certainly have come off best. Despite his exaggerations, he and not his opponent was ahead of his time, and it was he who felt the direction of economic progress. But try to imagine an orthodox Marxist today engaged in a debate with Ford, and you will see how all his demands and denunciations relating to production are thwarted by the things Ford has actually done. Indeed, the Marxist finds himself constrained to shift his denunciation onto the moral plane, to defend qualitative values, moral factors, the rights of the workers to autonomy and intelligence, against the appalling uniformity and leveling discipline of standardized production. In a word, he has to become liberal and resuscitate the old formulas of utopian socialism and the libertarian revolt. There is really no end to the irony of history . . . !

The great weakness of contemporary socialists lies precisely in their steadfast resistance to the evolution of reality, in the way they always refer to outdated factual situations even when they are trying to illustrate their ideal form of society, in their use of old, worn-out arguments that have very little to do with the reality of modern economic life. They are going to have to realize that the old clichés about the unquestionable superiority of production when disengaged from the profit motive will not do any longer. They are going to have to descend to a detailed analysis and produce solutions that correspond to the problems at hand, to match ideals to reality. They are finally going to have to open their eyes to the countless episodes involving workers that have taken place in recent decades, and especially the episode in Russia.

In Russia, twelve years after the revolution, they have scarcely regained the prewar level of industrial production, while in agriculture the level of production still lags behind. Even in the best-organized industrial firms they are very far from the levels of productivity and pay in comparable firms in capitalist countries. The mental outlook of the workers has certainly not changed—the Soviets confess this themselves—with the rapidity that was desired and foreseen. Indeed, following an initial period in which Communist formulas were rigidly applied, they have been forced to put much of the old disciplinary framework back into place, in other words, differentiated grades of salary and status. In sum, they have had to accept that the optimistic forecast of the old socialists could come true only if its accomplishment depended on the efforts of those rare individuals in whom the transformation of the companies from private to public ownership creates very strong feelings of personal responsibility, of what the Anglo-Saxons call a sense of "public service." But the truth is that output depends instead on the average level of awareness and capacity in the great mass of the workers, a level that changes extremely slowly, through a profound and protracted effort to educate them. The numerous and very interesting experiments in forming rural cooperatives tried in Italy prove the latter point. For every ten that turned out well, at least another ten failed. And the ten that succeeded did so because of the marvelous self-sacrifice of those who ran them, through struggles and sacrifices lasting decades, in which the masses were called upon to participate globally.

After what has happened in Russia, a socialist is no longer free to view socialist rationalization with the ingenuous and utopian eyes of times past. The Russian experience reveals clearly, even leaving aside the dictatorship, what enormous importance political and psychological elements have. The Russian five-year plan is dominated by the entirely political aim of enhancing industry, and with it the growth of the proletariat, the backbone of the regime, at the expense of agriculture and the great majority of the population. The prices of industrial products are set at a level artificially higher than those of agricultural products, which greatly reduces the purchasing power of the rural strata. The allocation of resources itself is carried out according to political criteria, with the aim of promoting heavy industry and raw materials production in the resource sector. Never was there a more deliberate sacrifice of the evident interests of the economy to a political dogma; never was a conflict more artificially created, a conflict that one has every right to call a conflict of classes. The peasant is no longer exploited by the great landed proprietor, to whom he once was forced to hand over a part of his harvest; today he still has to hand it over, but to the representatives of the state and the urban dwellers, in the form of a brutal reduction of his purchasing power.

From the Russian experiment—an experiment fundamental in any case for the history of world socialism—there emerges a great lesson that no one can deny: a violent revolution and an abrupt disruption of the entire system of production, though they may seem to clear the way to rebuild the structures of production afresh, on rational principles, bring in their train a tremendous crisis. The more developed and refined the financial and industrial arrangements are, the more tremendous the crisis is, and it imposes sacrifices and suffering past all naming on the revolutionary generation. Paradise is forbidden to the revolutionary generation. It will labor and sacrifice for its offspring. But—and this is the crucial point—did the proletarian masses in Russia go knowingly to their sacrifice? When the workers conquered the workplace, did they have any notion what was waiting for them? And if they had had a glimpse, if they had had before their eyes—as other proletariats do today in the wake of their experience—a depiction of the unspeakable sufferings to come, would they actively have supported the revolutionary movement, the party of total and immediate socialization? In order to answer yes, one has to assert that the Russian working class was endowed with a sublime moral force, with a heroic will for self-immolation usually found only in a few elect spirits; in sum, that it held to a conception of life resolutely antithetical to that which Marxism instills. This is another way of saying that after the Russian experiment the facile propagandists of the revolution will no longer be able to move and arouse the masses with a vision of the Communist paradise within easy reach. Instead they will have to repeat the words of Garibaldi before Aspromonte[2]—"I promise you hunger, pain, and death"—and, abandoning the old Marxist platform, appeal first and foremost to moral idealism.

---

[2] In the summer of 1862 Garibaldi (1807–1882) led, spontaneously, a military campaign to "liberate" Rome from the Vatican, which was protected by the French army. Unwilling to be drawn into a conflict with Paris, the Italian government ordered Garibaldi to withdraw; when Garibaldi refused, it ordered an attack on him in the Calabria mountains (Aspromonte). Garibaldi was wounded. The incident created a stir all over Europe; in Italy it aroused a radical opposition toward the newborn Italian government.

FIVE

OVERCOMING MARXISM

THE TITLE of the present chapter ought not to mislead. In saying that Marx has been overcome, I really do not mean to imply that nothing living or profound remains in his thought; quite the contrary. No one dreams of proposing a total (and totally absurd) denial of Marx in order to go back to the age of utopianism, or to movements of solidarity and to historiographical theories that have been rightly cast aside because of their formalism. The hundred-year history of the proletarian movement cannot be forgotten. The son emancipates himself, but he cannot deny his father. Modern socialists are Marx's children, even if at present they refuse to assume his legacy in other than a very guarded manner.

I would even go farther and maintain that today it is impossible to conceive of a modern individual, one endowed, that is, with a strong awareness of the problems of his time, who is not, within certain limits, a Marxist—meaning someone who has not incorporated into his being a whole ensemble of truths that, though they might with good reason have appeared revolutionary in Marx's time, have been comprehended by modern systems of knowledge and modern consciousness to such an extent that they have become almost banal. These include the preeminent importance attributed to economic forces, and among these to the forces of production and their articulation; the close ties that exist between the system of production and social relations, and the consequent historical relativity of the latter; the organic development of the mode of production and the impossibility of bypassing the essential phases of economic development; the gradual spread of mechanical technology and industrialism; the reality of class struggles and the part these struggles have played in the past; the advance of the proletariat as a result of capitalistic development and the overriding conflict between capitalists and proletarians; the frequent shaping of ideologies on the basis of class interests or the interests of a specific social group; and so on.

In the end, this is where Marx's real triumph lies: in having permeated all of modern social science with his own thought and his own powerful brand of realism, in counting even his fiercest adversaries among his pupils, in seeing many of his intuitive glimpses of the future treated as commonplace. Even with a due regard for proportion, we can say that Marx occupies the position in social science held in philosophy by Kant. As it was after Kant, so it is after Marx: certain positions have been left behind for ever, and the course of research has been altered in a decisive manner. Is there any longer a historian able to write about history without taking into account the forms of production and the level reached by technology, economic relations, and class structures? Without portraying, in addition to the political, moral, and religious aspects, what Marx called the economic structure? And are there still people active in politics who are able to shut out Marx's realistic and dialectical vision of social life and actually to delude themselves that the floodgates of class struggle, or rather class struggles, can possibly be dammed by protestations of fellow feeling or by calling in the riot police? Today even antiproletarian reaction is carried out in the spirit of Marx, that is, it has a much clearer notion of the forces that it wants to control. And the points at issue in something like 75 percent of political debate are still today ones that first emerged in the thought of Marx. But that is just the point; these are truths and as such cannot be described as the monopoly of socialists, much less give the socialist movement its distinctive character and direction. They are truths, and as such are neither bourgeois nor proletarian.

⟨ The real problem for socialists does not therefore consist in denying Marx but in extricating themselves from him, accepting what is vital and rejecting *openly and definitely* everything erroneous, utopian, and contingent in Marxism. To make of Marx, as so many socialists still do, the supreme beacon who must guide them, *saecula saeculorum* (for eternity), on their perilous navigation across the oceans of history is completely equivocal and anachronistic. If their intent is to invoke the properly tactical and political aspects of Marx, that is, his specific theory of the social upheaval and the coming of socialism, they are doing nothing but invoke errors that have already been refuted by thirty years of socialist criticism, and more than by criticism, of socialist practice. But if they mean to invoke his central theory of historical materialism, they are invoking a viewpoint that is no longer specifically socialist, or at any rate a viewpoint so generic that it is no longer capable of supplying a precise guide to concrete action. ⟩ Marx would be the first to deride the ridiculous claim of his epigones to make the history of social doctrine in general and socialist doctrine in particular come to a halt within the regions of his own brain: ⟨ he who refused to concede the most sensational "closures" of history to even Moses and Jesus; ⟩ he who gave the most typical example in his own time of rebellion against traditional, accepted ideas. The example of the youthful Marx is the best defense against those who will accuse us of committing treason against Marxism. It is to him, to his corrosive prose style and his ferocious intransigence, that we owe the disdain still felt for all non-Marxist currents within socialism ⟨and the sectarian and violent manner of combating them that the Communists have so willingly embraced. No one was ever more cruel, heedless, and unjust than he.⟩ After having made generous use of the work of his predecessors and rivals, he did not hesitate, for the sake of enhancing his own decisive contribution, to magnify the points of difference between him and them and to double the dosage of polemical violence so that his own scientific edifice would loom in splendor over a field covered with rubble.

⟨Such behavior is understandably human; at the limit we might even be prepared to allow that in a man of his genius such overpowering and exclusive pride has its uses. But the belief that all the fantasies and whims, all the acts of spite and incomprehension perpetrated by a malicious polemicist, should be taken for pure gold is simply astounding. Luckily a reaction is starting to take shape in Europe, and blind adoration of Marx is vanishing. Indeed, it is slowly and inexorably turning into detachment. But in Italy, at least until a few years ago, the devotion shown for Marx was like that shown for the Virgin of Pompeii or the relic of San Gennaro. Indeed there were some who averred that the Marxist ampule was destined to liquefy to all eternity, in every case and on all occasions, when in fact there was very little left in it capable of undergoing the miraculous transformation. . . . I have known many young people who, without having grasped the rudiments of political economy, went ahead and lost themselves in the meanderings of Marx's theory of value, or who preferred subtle exegesis of endless contradictory passages in the works of Marx to the study of actual reality, or who channeled all their zeal into mastering not his spirit but his style, a style woven out of *saississantes* (striking) oppositions and *tranchants* (trenchant) pronouncements. . . . But let us hope all that belongs to the past by now.

In conclusion: Marx the socialist is a figure refuted in theory and progressively abandoned in practice. He belongs to a phase that was certainly essential but that is now outmoded in the history of the socialist movement.⟩ His thought constitutes one of the strands—the most precious, perhaps—in the intellectual background of socialism, and there will always be those who will continue to build on his foundation, but it can no longer aspire to the exclusive and overriding position it enjoyed down to our time. It was he who made the socialist movement take its first giant step, who sent it down the high road of politics, who gave it its point of departure; he who showed it what its raw material was, what its essential instruments and tactics were to be. More than any other political agitator he helped spread the threefold tactical program of the socialist parties: class struggle, self-emancipation by the proletariat, the conquest of political power. But it still remains a point of departure. To invoke him today amounts to circling around in a closed orbit, freezing the historical process at a phase that is long past. Marxism was elementary pedagogy for the proletariat, a fit doctrine for its tormented infancy, when the *porro unum et necessarium* (fundamental and necessary thing) was simply to awaken the brutalized and derelict masses. There is no doubt that it was admirably suited to those preliminary requirements. The hedonism, the materialism, and the utopianism that pervade it reflected exactly the material and mental condition of the masses. It makes no attempt to force open the narrow limits within which the life of the masses was constrained, no effort to open up a wider and truer spiritual horizon to them. On the contrary, it completely adopts the proletarian frame of mind. It converts proletarian interests and states of mind, proletarian language, outlook, and sensibility into theory and extends it to all mankind. The crowd, virgin and rebellious, has two faces, indistinct religiosity and material appetite, which find a perfect correlative in Marx's doctrine: on one hand a mythic, apocalyptic vision, including a momentary glimpse of a happy and rich society, without struggle and without history; on the other hand the brutal realism of his approach, the relentlessly negative critique of a world already marked by fate. All these elements worked together to heighten the sense of oppression and thus of rebellion. Indeed, we know that in the minds of Marx and Engels the proletarian uprising had very lofty and symbolic associations, so much so that as young men they used to talk of the proletariat as the heir of classic German philosophy—of a proletariat that in its movement of emancipation would progressively realize the idea of liberty. But this was a point of view that could be grasped only by small groups of initiates, never by the masses.

By mocking all the categories of ethics, ignoring the problems of consciousness, and postponing the problem of the formation of character until the revolution was over (and the environment transformed), by going so far as to deny that there existed a principle of liberty, Marxism shut the masses off from any leap of idealism, any attempt at inner improvement, and any capacity to envision the promised paradise as a higher order of things.

Those who keep stubbornly trying to disprove the intrinsically materialistic, deterministic, and hedonistic character of Marxism, who attempt all sorts of interpretive acrobatics in order to prove to us that Marxist humanism leaves room for ethical valuations, must admit at any rate that as propaganda the Marxist point of view runs inexorably to degeneration. The misconception that always arises between the propagandist and those he is addressing causes the latter, despite all the reservations and cautions of the former, to prize the most vulgar, unilateral, and erroneous aspects of the corpus of Marxist doctrine, the ones that connect most easily with their own limited sensibility. This is the famous "dross" (economic determinism, belief in catastrophe, the theory of surplus value) that the revisionists try in vain to get rid of. Anyone who has been present at Marxist propaganda meetings knows full well the fate that awaits the poor wretch who undertakes, for example, to divulge an idea as cerebral and complex as the theory of the inversion of praxis. I have attended such meetings, and they taught me a lot. Now clearly the Marxism that really interests us here is not the more or less pure Marxism of a coterie of initiates, but the spurious Marxism of their followers. What counts, in the final analysis, is whatever bit of truth, stimulus, and idealism one is able to convey to a mass with the help of a doctrine. Marxism is not the doctrine of Platonic contemplation. It is the doctrine of the proletarian movement. And as such, it has to deal with the psychology, the needs, and the deficiencies of the proletariat. What does it matter to me, after all, that the fourteen notes on Feuerbach, or the *Critique of Hegel's Philosophy of Right*, are the antithesis of any purely materialistic and fatalistic set of views, and that in them the skies part, revealing the golden uplands of speculative philosophy? What does it matter? The masses read and understand the *Manifesto*, not the notes, and the *Manifesto* speaks for itself, without a mass of commentary. To try to present the *Manifesto* through the filter of the notes on Feuerbach would simply be a waste of time. Stripped of his belief in catastrophe, his determinism, and his prophetic utterance, Marx is no longer a vehicle for propaganda but an object of study. The *Manifesto* attracts the masses a hundred times more than do all the high-wire displays of exegesis by Marxist revisionists, in which, under the onslaught of the dialectic of things, of praxis inverting itself, of anthropological naturalism—volatile, generic, and amorphous concepts, useless as propaganda—the beautiful myth slips from one's grasp and melts away like snow in the summertime.

In sum, Marxism is no longer a force for good in our world. It was once the only way to pry poor people out of their own passivity and channel them into a civic, organic movement of liberation. But today its influence leads people astray and coarsens them. It leads them astray because it feeds their fantasies and their minds on a reality that has in fact been superseded. It coarsens them because it appeals to a vulgar conception of life, to motives of an inferior type that are typical of masses still shut off from any ray of spiritual illumination but are absolutely antithetical to those that a socialist society presupposes.

Once you have summoned the utilitarian demon, it is not so easy to send him away: the more you make use of his services, the more he enslaves you. This demon corrupts the proletarians, undermines attempts at liberation, and turns the movement bourgeois in the worst sense of the word by gradually locking it into the position of its adversary.

Henri De Man, in his celebrated work *Au delà du marxisme*,[1] has depicted this nemesis in the most graphic and potent manner possible.

The truth is that one could apply to Marxist ideology its own principle of the inversion of praxis. This same ideology, which once had the power to galvanize, has become an obstacle and a deterrent.

Marxist philosophy, De Man proclaims, is simply a result of the social status of the proletariat, an indicator of its inferiority and its subjection to the spirit of capitalism. The Marxist ethic ⟨—which does not really exist, since there is only one ethic, with no adjective attached, the ethic of Socrates, Christ, and Kant—⟩ is merely the liberal (utilitarian) ethic based on homo economicus. The disguised religion of proletarian cynicism and materialism is only capitalism with the polarity reversed. The Marxists have never understood that the strengthening of the economic movement to which their own doctrine fatally contributes, though at first it accomplished exactly what it was meant to, is today hindering the building of a new civilization and steering the movement toward corruption. In too many cases the elite among socialist workers, under the influence of Marxist materialism, does not

---

[1] Henri (Hendrik) De Man (1885–1953) was born in Belgium to a family of petite-noblesse origins and studied at the University of Brussels. In 1902 he enrolled in the Socialist party and changed his ideological commitment from anarchism to scientific socialism, which he assumed as a life choice. He was in contact with August Bebel, Karl Kautsky, Karl Liebknecht, and Rosa Luxemburg and played an important role in the unification of German socialism and in the creation of the youth branch of the Second International. The First World War marked his detachment from Marxism. In the International he took a position against the war, but Germany's violation of Belgian neutrality drove him to the volunteer service. Because of his participation at the Zimmerwald meeting of the International, he was arrested and tortured. His experience in Russia during the revolution and the impression of fanaticism left on him by Lenin and Trotsky increased De Man's distance from Marxism. Between 1919 and 1920 he was in Washington, where he taught social psychology at George Washington University and studied the phenomena of Taylorism and American unionism. Back in Europe, he taught at Frankfurt for several years, during which he studied the socialization of public services and the problems of a planned economy. He then started collaborating with the Belgian government in the job sector. During the Second World War, while he was in Switzerland, he maintained contact with "collaborators" of both the Nazis and members of the French Resistance. To avoid prison and public denouncement, he was forced into exile. His most famous book, *Au delà du marxisme*, appeared in French in 1927 as a translation of the German edition, entitled *Zur Psychologie des Sozialismus* (1926).

herald a new civilization and new cultural values; on the contrary, it runs the risk of being transformed into a new bourgeoisie in waiting, though a very retrograde one if its intellectual tastes are compared with those of the bulk of the bourgeois army.

I do not mean to imply that the Marxist ideology has brought us to this pass all by itself. Prior to all ideology there exists man the beast, proletarian or bourgeois as he may be, with his sad burden of weakness and misery. But as the socialist movement passed from its ingenuous, utopian, and negative phase to a phase of positive accomplishment, Marxist doctrine certainly hobbled and trammeled it by giving its instinctive gross materialism a rational alibi of extraordinary allure, instead of helping the proletariat to raise itself up spiritually and project pure and original values.

Where is all this leading? The answer is simple. Socialism has to rectify, on pain of paralysis, its own national, material, deterministic, and economic bias. It has to return to its origins, dive back down into the heart of the masses, and refresh itself anew on the vital sap of the movement. Whether gradualist or revolutionary, it needs an injection of ethics and a voluntaristic orientation. Until now it has talked almost exclusively of interests, rights, and material well-being. From now on it must talk more often of idealism, duties, and sacrifices. Too many of the attributes of divinity have been assigned to the proletariat by making it the bearer of all the purest virtues, and all its deficiencies and miseries have been too simplistically attributed to the depravity of the social structure. Rousseau's man in the "state of nature" became, in the nineteenth century, Mazzini's "people" and Marx's "proletariat." The "proletariat" has risen to the rank of a philosophical category; history has become an epic poem in which the proletarian hero defeats the bourgeois monster; the proletarians all appear naturally good and just, corrupted only by their environment and by social injustice. By reasoning in the abstract, flesh-and-blood humanity, the living and breathing proletarians, have been lost sight of. The social structure is no doubt largely to blame; but the imperfections, the limitations, and the weakness of the proletariat, which are prior to and independent of all social status or class division, derive from the fact that they are human beings, and this has been forgotten. *Homo homini lupus* has much deeper roots than the ingenuous Marxist psychology, which deliberately ignores all the problems of consciousness and moral formation, supposes. It is an illusion to believe that it can be conquered on the external level only, through purely environmental reforms. By taking deterministic formulas, which describe man as a function of his environment, as the basis for all of its propaganda, Marxism has ended up by seeing only the problem of means and of material change, with the result that too often it has confused the means with the ends, compromising or obscuring the genuine goals of socialism. For the last fifty years it seems that all of socialism has been reduced to the dogma of socialization: the socialist spirit will increase as property is socialized. No one wants to admit that socialization of property might take place without any transformation of the psyche or of morality necessarily following in its wake. And yet there is no longer a socialist or even a Communist to be found who seriously foresees the possibility of a thoroughgoing suppression of private property in the area of production. But be that as it may, Communists continue to repeat the mythic formula as though the supreme ideal were somehow wrapped up in it.

As with the end, so with the means. Just as socialism has been resolved into socialization, so the socialist movement is too easily resolved into the principle of class struggle, in which the substance of the whole process of proletarian emancipation lies, according to some. Once again a tactical principle of indubitable pedagogical and instrumental value has been mistaken for the essence of the movement, which lies in something more profound and positive than opposition and struggle, no matter how self-aware. The greatest mass movement in history has been forced to fit the parameters of a brief historical phase, eternalizing a given situation and contingent motives. No one has noticed that as the great plebeian river, swollen continually by fresh tributary streams, advances toward its debouchment, the narrow boundaries of its ancient watercourse are no longer sufficient to hold it.

What is needed, finally, is a free, noble, and frank reaffirmation of the essence of socialist idealism, quite apart from the prejudices of any particular school or method. Socialism is not socialization; it is not the proletariat in power; it is not even material equality. Socialism, grasped in its essential aspect, is the progressive actualization of the idea of liberty and justice among men: an innate idea that lies more or less buried under the sediment of centuries in the marrow of every human being. It is the progressive effort to ensure an equal chance of living the only life worthy of the name to all humans, setting them free from the enslavement to the material world and material needs that today still dominate the greater number, allowing them the possibility freely to develop their personalities in a continuous struggle for perfection against their primitive and bestial instincts and against the corruptions of a civilization too much the prey of the demons of success and money.

[But—it will be said—all this is not socialism. Socialism desires the abolition of classes and economic equality. But here, for the sake of transcending Marxism, you are sliding into vagueness, disinterring the whimsies of the past and fixing your gaze on one thing only: trends.

I admit without hesitation that the position I have taken does not permit naive faith in changeless republics or cities of the sun. The adepts of that sort of categorical and utopian teleology must simply make a clean break with socialism. But would that mean excommunicating only a few unhappy nonconformists, or would all of socialism be anathematized? That is the question before us. If instead of entrusting ourselves to an abstract definition of socialism we struggle to arrive at one by induction grounded in a century of experience, what definition will we come up with? If instead of socialism we analyze the actual socialist parties, their actual organization, the demands and the real stimuli emanating from the masses, the mentality of political and syndicalist leaders, are we quite sure of being able to reconnect with the classic definition of socialism? In my opinion, the question supplies its own answer. The utopian tendency of the parties to oversimplify is proportional to the level of moral culture in the masses. Once the masses could be stirred to life only by virtue of extremely elementary propaganda. But at present a large segment of the masses, in Germany, France, and England at least, finds itself in a position to adopt a less primitive notion of what the political contest means.

The Communists today are what the socialists were fifty years ago, with this difference: then the masses were extremely rude and impoverished, but today only a part of them are still so.

To the extent that economic progress and political experience for this still considerable percentage can be realized, the Communist movement will lose strength, and the socialist movement will be able to rid itself of its utopian residues.]

For socialists, too, there is only one final goal in sight: the single person, the concrete individual, the primary and fundamental cell. Or rather, society comes first, but only to the extent that by this name we designate an aggregate of individualities and concentrate on the majority. For, as an organization, society is a means to an end, an instrument in the service of mankind, not of metaphysical entities like the land of one's birth or communism. There exist no purposes of society that are not at the same time purposes of the individual as a moral personality; indeed, these purposes are lifeless except when they are lived out in the inner depths of human consciousness. Justice, morality, right, and liberty are realized only to the extent that they are realized in separate individualities. A just state is not one in which laws are inspired by an abstract criterion of justice, but one whose members are inspired in their concrete activities by a rule of justice. A free state requires first and foremost free men, and a socialist state socialist spirits. I do not hesitate to declare that the socialist revolution will come about, in the last analysis, only to the extent that the transformation of the social structure is accompanied by a moral revolution—by the conquest, that is, a conquest perpetually renewed, of a qualitatively better humanity, more good, more just, more spiritual.

The problem that confronts all reforming movements boils down to this alternative: transformation of *things* or transformation of *human consciousness*? Marxism, with its hedonistic and deterministic outlook, has always put the problem of means foremost, and so it responds categorically: the transformation of things, the transformation of the pattern of production and distribution. It has little or no interest in the ultimate goal. Its historicism combines with its utopianism to make it theorize about the means—socialization—and depreciate the end: humanity. It postpones all problems of moral formation and culture until power has been won and the transformation has taken place. Because only then will true history begin, only then will the famous passage "from the rule of necessity to that of liberty" occur, and only then will men become masters of their own history, which will no longer be history but stasis. Before that the only problem is the one of struggle and redemption and the formation of fighters.

There could be nothing more utopian and mechanical than this sudden inversion of philosophical stance, which is explicable only by the messianic nature of Marxist prophecy. But we, who find ourselves face-to-face with the problems of the transformation of the material order of things, who observe the transformation taking place, however slowly, before our eyes, can no longer give our assent to this negative and simplistic solution; we suffer all the torment and all the immediacy of problems of morality and culture. The transformation of the material world has to proceed in step with that of consciousnesss, for material victories are worth very little, especially when they impose new and grave responsibilities on the victors, without adequate spiritual preparation.

The important thing in this reaction against Marxism, clearly, is not to swing too far in the other direction—not to lapse automatically into the ethical exaggerations of the utopians and the Christian socialists (the often unwitting allies of the reactionary elements of society) who abolished any difference between the end and the means by reducing the whole social question to a moral problem. We have to find the golden mean, the fusion between two different points of view, the harmonic equilibrium between end and means. We accept the realistic Marxist critique of capitalist society, albeit with the reservations made necessary by the transformations that have taken place; but we do not share the teleology of Marxism, and we assert that there has to be a moral component to counteract the degeneration to which overreliance on the dogma of class struggle can lead.

Though the problem of distinguishing between the end and the means is an essential one when the focus is political (or technical), and indeed the success of any movement depends on the exact choice of means, there is no reason to make such a distinction when the focus is on morality, inasmuch as the means and the end then fuse with one another. The means must not only suit the end (which is a technical problem), it must also be permeated by it. This principle, the *ABC* of idealism, was expounded with sovereign authority by Lassalle,[2] as it is today by De Man. It leads us to recognize that the principle of class struggle (the heart of the socialist movement, according to many modern socialists) is not in itself sufficient to allow us to intuit our ultimate purpose, especially when it is preached in black-and-white terms. The universality of the end is what guarantees ethical value. Can rigid antagonism between social classes on its own provide proletarians with an understanding of the universal and ethical value of socialism? It is doubtful, to say the least. For the masses, who are unaccustomed to soar in this fashion into the stratosphere of philosophy, it is likely that strongly class-based discourse will cause a degradation, a contamination of the ultimate end. For them the concept of class arises out of shared interests and a common destiny more than it does out of ideals. Class is, in fact, something palpable, distinguishable from humanity as a whole. It is difficult for those who belong to one class and who share in the sufferings occasioned by that belonging to idealize class to the point of including by a leap of idealism all of humanity. In this regard, it is interesting to note that the Labour party has always refused to make class struggle an essential plank of its platform in the way that the socialist parties on the continent typically have done. It does not make the proletariat a lone protagonist; the protagonist is society, which the Labourites try to transform as a whole and in each of its component parts. They come to this project more easily because the concept of the separation of classes is not, and cannot be, as absolute among the English as it is among us, since there persists among them a religious and moral patrimony that individuals of all classes feel they have in common.

---

[2] Ferdinand Lassalle (1825–1864) was one of the first leaders of German social democracy. In his youth he was close to Marx and Engels; later his reformism alienated him from Marxism. Lassalle bargained with Bismarck for universal male suffrage; he shared with the chancellor a Hegelian conception of the state and a deep aversion for liberalism. Lassalle was convinced that the party should have only a short-term program to implement social legislation. This reformist attitude generated hostility among German socialists, particularly August Bebel and in London Marx and Engels.

De Man thus takes his analysis even farther, actually denying the importance of the ultimate end when contemplated in isolation or recognizing it merely for whatever role it succeeds in playing in day-to-day life. "It is the present motive and not the future aim which is decisive," he writes. "That does not imply any denial of the importance of the final aim; for this, in so far as it has a value, is one of the causal elements of the present. Consequently, its worth can only be that of the actions to which it gives rise." "I am a socialist," he concludes, "not because I believe in the realisation of a socialist vision of the future more than I believe in any other ideal you like to mention, but because I am convinced that the socialist motive makes human beings happier and better here and now."[3] He makes a marvelous pronouncement at this point: "Mankind can assuage its deepest nostalgia, the victory over time, only by transforming its future ends into drives in the present, and thus incorporating a fragment of the future in the present."[4]

Just so. De Man has spoken well and has perfected, by sublimating it, Bernstein's famous formula: the movement is everything, the end is nothing. Yes. The socialist movement is everything, to the extent, however, that the volitions and motives that guide it are permeated with socialist purpose. Thus the end lives in our present actions. This is as much as to say that socialism is not a static and abstract ideal that can one day be completely realized. It is an unreachable, limiting ideal, which is realized in the small portion of it that succeeds in penetrating our lives.

Socialism, more than an external state to be realized, is, for the individual, a plan for living to be actualized.[5]

[3] H. De Man, *Au delà du marxisme*, English edition with the title *The Psychology of Socialism*, translated from the German edition by Eden and Cedar Paul (London: Allen & Unwin, 1928), pp. 472–73.

[4] This sentence does not appear in the English edition; see H. De Man, *Au delà du marxisme*, ed. Michel Brelaz and Ivo Rens (Paris: Editions du Seuil, 1974), p. 401: "L'homme ne peut calmer sa nostalgie la plus profonde, la victoire sur le temps, que s'il transforme ses buts futurs en mobiles actuels et incorpore ainsi un fragment de l'avenir au présent."

[5] See G. Sorel, "The Ethics of Socialism" (1899), in John L. Stanley, *From Georges Sorel: Essays in Socialism and Philosophy* (New York: Oxford University Press, 1976), pp. 107–8; De Man, *The Psychology of Socialism*, p. 498.

SIX

LIBERAL SOCIALISM

THE SLOW but inevitable erosion of Marxist socialism has not been accompanied, unfortunately, by a vigorous effort at reconstruction. The old faith is shaken, but the new one has not yet appeared. Socialism slowly went adrift, and when the time came to take fresh bearings, the majority of socialists shrank back, appalled at how far they had come. The old guard sank its dialectical claws into the sacred texts and held on tight, while the young oscillated between a mortifying dogmatism and the most painful uncertainty. The monopoly Marxism enjoyed for almost half a century meant that too many people lost the habit of thinking for themselves, in full independence of judgment, about the problems of socialism. As a result, the forced emancipation now taking place makes them dizzy.

Once again it proves easier to criticize than to reconstruct. But of what use is a critique if it is not accompanied by an attempt, at least, to rebuild? Here we are not in the realm of pure science. The socialist movement *exists*, prior to and independently of any theory and any theoretical justification. Twenty-five million human beings have organized under the banners of socialism and are struggling in the name of socialism for their own emancipation. Denial will not do; it is necessary always to keep in mind this immense factual reality. To put it briefly: until we figure out how to replace the old, worn-out Marxist view with a new one that satisfies to the same extent, though with the necessary modifications, the fundamental demands of the working masses, our work, if not completely futile, will certainly be of very little interest.

Now this fresher, more fruitful, and up-to-date view does not have to be created out of cerebral introspection. It already lives potentially in revisionist criticism and is gradually being realized through the workers' movement. Rather, the problem consists in making explicit what is implicit and getting rid of the residue that still clings to its ideology, in having the courage to call things by their real names. Revisionist neo-Marxism and workers' praxis are respectively the theoretical face and the practical face of a new liberal socialist conception in which the problems of social justice and living together can and should be put on the same level as those of liberty and individual life. Socialism must tend to become liberal, and liberalism to take on the substance of the proletarian struggle. It is not possible to be liberal without joining actively in the cause of the workers, and there is no way to serve the cause of labor efficiently without coming to grips with the philosophy of the modern world, a philosophy founded on the idea of development through oppositions eternally overcome; here lies the core of the liberal point of view.

All of European, and not just European, social democracy is moving toward a form of renewed liberalism that is absorbing into itself elements from movements that would seem to be opposed (bourgeois enlightenment and proletarian socialism). It is fighting everywhere for individual freedoms, political freedoms, freedom to vote, and freedom of conscience. The messianic and teleological aspects are receding into the background while problems of the concrete movement to emancipate the workers are coming to the fore. The ideal of a perfect society of free and equal persons, with no classes, no struggle, and no state, is being transformed more and more every day into a limiting ideal that in itself is worthless but that serves as a stimulus and a focus for the spirit. The new faith nourishes itself on the proletarian struggle and the proletarian ascent, on the effort of the entire society to supersede the narrow and unjust terms dictated by bourgeois society, on the eternal thirst for justice and urge for freedom. And more generally— rising to a detached contemplation of the social movement—it feeds on a vision of life as an inexhaustible clash of forces and ideologies that overcome themselves through mutual negation in order to accede to higher forms of social structure and spiritual activity.

The phrase "liberal socialism" has a strange sound to many who are accustomed to current political terminology. The word "liberalism" unfortunately has been used to smuggle so many different kinds of merchandise and has been so much the preserve of the bourgeoisie in the past, that today a socialist has difficulty bringing himself to use it. But I do not wish to propose a new party terminology here. I wish only to bring the socialist movement back to its first principles, to its historical and psychological origins, and to demonstrate that socialism, in the last analysis, is a philosophy of liberty.

In any case, the time when bourgeois politics and liberal, free-market politics were one and the same has passed. All over the world the bourgeoisies no longer defend free markets and are no longer necessarily liberal. The more the proletarian movement takes hold and an active sense of liberty gains strength among the masses, the more the bourgeoisie, in its most backward sectors, tries to escape from the discipline and pattern of liberty. Even the new directions that modern production—rationalized, mechanized, technocratic—is taking as it sacrifices the human personality of the worker are forcing socialists to assume a liberal function in the quite traditional sense of the term. The day will come when this word, this attribute, will be claimed with proud self-awareness by the socialist: that will be the day of his maturity, the day when he wins emancipation, at least in the domain of the spiritual.

Liberalism in its most straightforward sense can be defined as the political theory that takes the inner freedom of the human spirit as a given and adopts liberty as the ultimate goal, but also the ultimate means, the ultimate rule, of shared human life. The goal is to arrive at a condition of social life in which each individual is certain of being able to develop his own personality fully. Liberty is also the means in the sense that the final stage cannot be bestowed or imposed; it has to be earned through hard personal struggle, as the generations succeed one another in time. Liberalism conceives of liberty not as a fact of nature, but as becoming, as development. One is not born free; one becomes free. And one stays free by retaining an active and vigilant sense of one's autonomy, by constantly exercising one's freedoms.

Faith in liberty is at the same time a declaration of faith in man, in his unlimited perfectibility, in his capacity for self-determination, in his innate sense of justice. A true liberal is anything but a skeptic; he is a believer, even though he opposes all dogmatic pronouncements, and an optimist, even though his conception of life is virile and dramatic.

In the abstract, this is how matters stand. In historical terms, the question becomes more complicated because liberalism has both a conceptual history and a practical one, and in the course of its unfolding it has produced an extraordinary harvest of practical experience and successive degrees of conceptualization. It was born of modern critical thought and made its first mark on history at the time of the Reformation. The subsequent ferocity of the wars of religion, in which men slaughtered one another in the name of opposing faiths and opposing dogmas, was the matrix of the notion of liberty of religious conscience, which blossomed as a flower does amid ruins. Catholics and Protestants, incapable of exterminating each other, agreed to a truce and acknowledged the right of all individuals to profess the cult that each preferred. Liberty as a principle then spread to the sphere of cultural life in the seventeenth and eighteenth centuries through the influence of scientific progress and as a result of the economic and intellectual ascendancy of the bourgeoisie. The latter reached a high point with the publication of the *Encyclopédie* and finally achieved its political triumph with the revolution of 1789 and the accompanying Declaration of the Rights of Man. In our age the liberal idea has revealed its tendency to structure every aspect and every part of social life, especially the economic sphere. The result is that liberty, from being a notionally universal prerogative that in fact corresponded to the interests of a minority, is truly becoming the patrimony of all.

Socialism is nothing more than the logical development, taken to its extreme consequences, of the principle of liberty. Socialism, when understood in its fundamental sense and judged by its results—as the concrete movement for the emancipation of the proletariat—is liberalism in action; it means that liberty comes into the life of poor people. Socialism says: the abstract recognition of liberty of conscience and political freedoms for all, though it may represent an essential moment in the development of political theory, is a thing of very limited value when the majority of men, forced to live as a result of circumstances of birth and environment in moral and material poverty, are left without the possibility of appreciating its significance and taking any actual advantage of it. Liberty without the accompaniment and support of a minimum of economic autonomy, without emancipation from the grip of pressing material necessity, does not exist for the individual; it is a mere phantasm. In these circumstances the individual is enslaved by poverty, humiliated by his own subjection; and life presents only one aspect to him, gives him only one illusion to pursue: material satisfaction. Free in law, he is in fact a slave. And the sense of servitude is sharpened by bitterness and irony the moment the virtual slave becomes aware of his legal liberty and of the obstacles that society places in the way of his actually gaining it. Now the socialist contends that when socialism was born, modern society was full of individuals in this situation; and individuals in this situation still compose a large segment of the working class in the capitalist world today, deprived as they are of any control over the tools with which they work, of any share in the process of decision making that guides production, of any sense of dignity and responsibility in the workplace—dignity and responsibility, the first steps on the ladder leading from slavery to liberty.

In the name of liberty, and for the purpose of ensuring its effective possession by all men and not just a privileged minority, socialists postulate the end of bourgeois privilege and the effective extension of the liberties of the bourgeoisie to all. In the name of liberty they ask for a more equal distribution of wealth and the automatic guarantee for every person of a life worth living. In the name of liberty they speak of socialization, the abolition, that is, of private ownership of the means of production and exchange. They want social life to be guided not by the egoistic criterion of personal utility, but by the social criterion, the criterion of the collective good. If the choice is between an intermediate grade of liberty that applies to the whole collectivity and an unbounded liberty furnished to a few at the expense of the many, an intermediate liberty is better, a hundred times better. Ethics, economics, and right all lead to this conclusion.

The socialist movement is, in consequence, the objective heir of liberalism: it carries this dynamic idea of liberty forward through the vicissitudes of history toward its actualization. Liberalism and socialism, rather than opposing one another in the manner depicted in outdated polemics, are connected by an inner bond. Liberalism is the ideal force of inspiration, and socialism is the practical force of realization.

The bourgeoisie was, at one time, the standard-bearer of this idea of liberty; the liberal function was in its hands when it broke open the rigid, frozen order of the feudal world and sowed the seeds of fecund life. In its battle against the dogmatism of the church and monarchical absolutism, against the privileges of the nobility and clergy, against the dead realm of static, forced production, the bourgeoisie embodied, over a long sequence of centuries, the progressive impetus of the whole society. That is no longer true. The bourgeoisie has won; it has captured the dominating heights, but as it triumphs, its revolutionary function and its progressive ferment fade away. It is no longer driven by a restless urge for liberty and progress to surpass the gains it has already made; it is no longer abetted by a universal ideal that transcends its class interests, as in 1789. Bourgeois liberalism, so called, has forged a closed and rigid system propped up by the array of economic, juridical and social principles that are synthesized in the expression "capitalist bourgeois state." It still harks back to the old principles of the French Revolution, but those principles have the appearance of being crystallized, embalmed, bereft of their inner significance; they now seem to be in contradiction to the spirit that inspired those who proclaimed these very principles in a rush of generous enthusiasm.

Bourgeois liberalism attempts to halt the historical process at its present stage, to perpetuate its own commanding position, to transform into a privilege what was once a right deriving from its undeniable pioneering work; it obstructs the entry of militant new social forces onto the stage of history. With its dogmatic attachment to the principles of economic libertarianism (private property, rights of inheritance, full freedom of initiative in every field, with the state as the organ responsible for internal policing and external defense), it has managed to shackle the dynamic spirit of liberalism to the transitory pattern of a particular social system. The truth is that liberalism is by definition historicist and relativistic; it sees history as a perpetual flux, an eternal becoming and overcoming, and nothing is more contrary to its essence than stasis, immobility, categorical certainty, and faith in the possession of absolute, definitive truths, of the kind that now characterize the bourgeois liberals.

Bourgeois liberalism is powerless to understand the problem posed by the socialist movement; in other words, it does not understand that political and social liberty by themselves are incapable of bringing about liberalism's true goal. It arbitrarily extends its historical experience to the proletariat and makes the absurd claim that the problem of liberty presents itself in the same terms for all social classes. It is clear, for example, that while the conquest of political liberty constituted for the bourgeoisie the sublimation and fulfillment of its own power, which had already come to dominate the economic and cultural sectors, the demand by the proletariat for political liberty and the achievement of it signified no more than the commencement of the struggle for economic emancipation, since it still had no real influence on the control centers of economic life. The process in the latter case is inverted, and this is probably one of the principal reasons for the crisis tormenting the socialist movements of Europe, especially since the war—the terrible disproportion between their economic force, technical capacity, and cultural level on one hand and their political power on the other. The proletariat came to possess a formidable political weapon, to which there did not correspond then (and does not correspond now) the sort of linkage needed to make it work.

Only a few components of the bourgeoisie still exercise a useful, in fact a practically indispensable, progressive function. Which ones? The ones that, quite apart from their privileges of birth, are doing creative work in the spheres of pure intellectual endeavor and managerial technique: the intellectuals, the scientists, the least corrupt and most active sector of the industrial and agrarian bourgeoisie, and also those imposing figures of the modern world, the entrepreneurs, the great captains of industry, those who play the same role in the economy that active politicians do in politics. No matter what the economic system, such persons will still have the task of coordinating the various factors of production and making sure that the rhythm of economic progress does not lag.

The proof of the liberal function that a few sections of the bourgeoisie still carry out is the existence, in all modern democracies, of democratic bourgeois parties that are not insensitive to the pressure of progress and that offer a hand, however cautiously and hesitantly, to the rising working class. But the bourgeoisie in the sense of social class (though it is really more a social and mental category than a class) that obtains the largest part of its income from accumulated capital and privileges, or at any rate that defends this system of privilege as being the one most fitted to preserve its dominance and most favorable to the development of social life, is no longer liberal and can no longer be liberal.

For the bourgeoisie still to be able to make any plausible claim to perform a liberal role, it and the economic system that conforms to its interests would have to show themselves capable, through the sheer innate virtue of basic principle, of meeting the demands of the new class, the Fourth Estate. The bourgeoisie would have to show that, for the sake of remaining faithful to its great historical tradition, it was capable of sacrificing the position of wealth and power it had won and of giving in voluntarily to the demands of the new social forces. But this amounts to asking for a superhuman act of disinterestedness and heroism! An appetite for self-immolation of this kind might be found in one or two exceptional and superior souls so divorced from the fate of their own social class as to attain the serene objectivity of the philosopher, or better still to embrace the cause of the oppressed, but certainly not in an entire class, holding on tightly to its possessions, its privileges, its power.

Where then is liberalism alive, where is it being implemented? In all the active, revolutionary (in the full sense of the word) forces of history; in all the social forces that—without perhaps fully realizing it themselves—exercise an innovative function, in all the forces that aim to transcend the present condition of society and to open up ever new domains and new horizons for liberty and progress.

The poor, the oppressed, those unable to adapt themselves to the present state of affairs because they are suffering under it and feel limited and mutilated and are conscious of their mutilation: the new armies of liberalism will be these. The working class in modern capitalist society is the only class that, as a class, *can* be revolutionary. The socialism that conveys their demands, that fights against the actual state of affairs in the name of the needs of the greatest number and of a higher principle of liberty and justice, that awakens the masses from their ancient servitude and gives them a new consciousness of the inferior position they find themselves in, is the truly liberal and liberating political movement.

In the words of Saragat, one of the most thoughtful representatives of the new Italian socialism, "The proletariat is not trying to remake history from its inception; on the contrary it is doing no more than bring to completion an age-old task that was begun at the beginning of human society. . . . The idea of liberty is not born with the proletariat but with mankind, with the first ray of spiritual self-awareness in man. The task of the proletariat is to bear higher and farther the torch that was passed on to it, in the dramatic turmoil of history, by the classes that came before."[1]

---

[1] Giuseppe Saragat (1898–1988) was born in Turin, where he studied economics. He was a member of a reformist socialist party (PSU) and collaborated on the clandestine

In sum, the proletariat can rightly say that the legacy of the liberal function has passed to it.

On one condition, however: that the poor, the working class, and the socialist movement demand the transformation of bourgeois society inasmuch as they become able, thanks to both the theory to which they adhere and the capacities they possess, to make it really better.

Their long opposition has made the socialists too accustomed to conceiving of socialism in polemical terms and in terms of pure force: bourgeois society is rotten, bourgeois society is full of discord, vice, and injustice, so let us smash it. One wants to say to them, Steady on. In dealing with society, the only people who smash things are those who know how to build them; or put another way, you get rid of the old only by building the new—if for no other reason than that social life cannot admit periods of arrest and regression, from which the first to suffer are the proletarians. It is no longer enough to demonstrate on paper that socialist society is more just and rational. It has to be made to work in practice, and to do that abilities are necessary, and abilities cannot be improvised, nor is it enough that they are present in tiny minorities.

From being an abstract problem of justice, socialism is changing every day into a problem of abilities. The return of Proudhon. . . .

The objection has been raised, against this effort to express socialism in terms of liberty, to recognize in the socialist movement the heir of the liberal function, that liberalism sorts ill with a program of reconstruction as precise and categorical as the one that distinguishes the modern socialist parties. Liberals, it is always said, cannot by definition know how future states of equilibrium will be arrived at. Like bourgeois conservatives, who call themselves liberal, the socialists too would end by imprisoning liberalism within a closed and predetermined system, within the limits of the collectivist system. Now the liberal spirit is essentially dialectical and historicist; struggle is the very essence of its life; history is the result of a perpetual confluence and collision of forces, and therefore there is nothing more illiberal and utopian than to want to assign it an obligatory path to be followed. For the liberal no principle or program, however mythical and however remote its descent, can have the sort of absolute and categorical flavor that the

---

journal *Il Quarto Stato*, founded by Pietro Nenni (the leader of the Socialist party after World War II) and Rosselli. Saragat was active in the clandestine movement in France and then in the Resistance. From 1935 on he pointed out the danger of Soviet dictatorship, even while trying to preserve unity among the Italian Left for the purpose of combating fascism. Between 1964 and 1971 he was president of the Italian Republic.

teleological program of the socialists has for them. Their way of looking forward to, indeed, their fervent hope of achieving, the future Kingdom of Heaven on earth, a kingdom of justice, peace, and equality, in other words, a static and perfect social state, is profoundly repugnant to the liberals' conception of life.

These objections are perfectly valid if directed against the old mythic and utopian socialist worldview and against the frame of mind still widely diffused in socialist ranks. The *Communist Manifesto*, for all that it has contributed to furthering the demand for freedom, the liberal demand, in other words, among the masses, is in itself, in the messianic outlook that informs it, profoundly illiberal. The same is true for the traditional Marxist conception and for most of the socialist parties' teleological programs for rebuilding society. But here it is necessary to make a distinction and recall that the concrete socialist movement is one thing, and its program, or rather its former program, is another. What I do want to claim here is that the socialist *movement*, on account of its real motivating drives and the results that up to now it has attained in social development, normally exercises an unquestionable liberal function in the society in which we live today. The proletariat can declare whatever it wishes in its programmatic statements. But as long as it continues to find itself in a situation of moral and material inferiority and feels the powerful urge to liberate itself from this situation, and in liberating itself uses the right means and instruments, that is, those that point the way to further progress, it will be carrying out a substantially liberal task—whether it wants to or not and realizes the fact or not. No one can deny that in all countries the workers' movement, once the initial period of desperate rebellion was over, has demonstrated that it very much understands the exigencies of progress. Not only does it no longer struggle against the introduction of more refined methods of production, or against machinery, it even goes so far as to request that they be introduced, seeing clearly that the possibilities of improvement and raising standards are closely linked to a higher level of social productivity.

⟨ Marx always pointed out to socialists that socialist society will come about not through an internal reform of capitalist society and its system of distribution, but through the evolution of the forces of production. To develop these forces of production and to develop them as rapidly and integrally as possible will be the best means of bringing the new society within reach. Marx, however, believed that this process of development was extremely rapid and would bring about within a brief span of time a catastrophic crisis in the system of capitalist relations, whereas reality has shown that this development does not necessarily lead to a socialist outcome. From this flows the crisis of socialist doctrine, the sensation that the economic machine is not following a set course, the revision of socialist programs, and the gradual appearance of a more complex and realistic vision in all socialist movements. Like a wayfarer who sees a distant mountain on the horizon, its features standing out in strong and simple relief, and who then discovers as he draws closer that it is sinuous and jagged, all ridges and undulations, likewise the socialist, observing economic and social life from up close, came to realize the excessive tendency to simplify and the one-sidedness of the original socialist program.)

Throughout Europe we are witnessing in these years a profound transformation of the socialist movement, which is showing an ever stronger grasp of reality and according an ever more decided primacy to the workers' movement and to concrete, immediate programs. One after another the residues of utopianism and messianism that played such a large part at the outset are being cast aside, and in socialist literature the old manuals of catechism or apocalypse which set them-selves the task of delineating the hypothetical socialist state in the most risible details have rightly fallen into oblivion.

Even for socialists, the simplistic formulas and bold, miraculous pre-scriptions that were meant to unlock the secret of the future have had their day. By now there are numerous socialists who concede that the goal, or rather a goal, an intermediate stage, can be set only in very general terms, and that what has to be done is to adapt to circum-stances and to a world in continuous, vertiginous transformation; that it is necessary to measure ourselves against actual experience and hold on tight only to a few fixed points of reference, for the truth is that only out of movement, out of experience freely undertaken, will we receive any guidance for tomorrow.

The events of the war and of the postwar period, especially in Russia, have led to the abandonment of the old centralizing, collectivist program that made the state the administrator and universal controller of the rights and liberties of all. No one any longer believes, as he once did, that the simple fact of expropriation, by which productive enter-prises are transferred into the hands of the collectivity, will bring about an apocalyptic transformation—with levels of production and wealth multiplied; work loads lightened and made a source of delight; man-kind freed at last from material enslavement; struggles, social classes, and wars abolished automatically; and brotherhood, justice, and peace triumphant. . . .

For serious, intelligent, educated socialists—indeed, for society's entire management elite—these things are by now viewed as fairy tales which it is healthier not to discuss. Above all, everyone now sees clearly the dangers of bureaucratic elephantiasis, the intrusive state, the rule of the incompetent, the stamping out of all individual autonomy and liberty, and the loss of any incentive for managers or their subordinates. Let us not even dwell on the problem of human happiness.

At this point the prevailing tendency in the socialist camp is in favor of forms of management that are as autonomous as possible, untrammeled and suited to the various types of enterprise, forms that take into account the whole gamut of different needs. These forms might include municipal management, cooperative management, guild management, management by trust, mixed management in which the general interest is incorporated into particular interests, individual and, accordingly, family management as tradition, technology, and the environment dictate, and so on. The notion of an industrial, commercial, and agricultural state has grown faint, except when the discussion turns to essential public services. Indeed, I would go farther: no socialist any longer makes any attempt to defend a priori, in general terms, the prescription that property must be socialized. Many eminent thinkers (I note the recent striking conversion of G.D.H. Cole, one of the most perceptive British socialists)[2] are beginning to adopt the view that for some branches of industry the most important problem is democratizing the command structure of the factories and the control of their technical and social management in the interests of the collectivity. Even in the most progressive and routinized areas, in which by now the possibility and the utility of socialization is evident, care is taken to state that in any event it can be implemented not at a stroke, but only gradually, in slow stages, with an adequate corollary of experience and capacity. In sum, it appears to me that the quite justified reservations that, in the name of liberalism, might once have been advanced against the abstractness and the utopianism of the old socialist programs are on the way to being extinguished through the victory of common sense, experience, the practical lessons learned by the movement, and above all assumption of the responsibilities of government.

[2] George Douglas Howard Cole (1889–1959) was born in Cambridge, England, and studied and taught at Oxford. By 1906 he had become a socialist and joined the Oxford Fabian Society. Between 1911 and 1914 he was critical of the Labour party and an advocate of guild socialism: the establishment of workers' control in industry through self-governing guilds based on industrial trade unions. Critical of the bureaucratic approach of Sidney and Beatrice Webb, Cole emphasized the importance of ideas in the movement and the necessity of unleashing creative energies from below. This led him to resign from the Fabian Society in 1915 (he rejoined it in 1928). In the 1950s he focused on local and regional communities, which he saw as the answer to statism through local self-government. Cole's major writings known to Rosselli were *The World of Labour* (1913), *Self-Government in Industry* (1917), *Guild Socialism* (1917), *Guild Socialism Re-stated* (1920), and *Workshop Organization* (1923).

I have noted that the liberal position is distinguished by faith in liberty not only as an end, but also as a means. Liberty can never be won through tyranny or dictatorship, or even through being granted from above. Liberty is a conquest, a self-conquest, which is preserved only through the continual exercise of one's faculties and individual autonomies.

For liberalism, and hence for socialism, observance of the *liberal method*, that is, the democratic method, of entering the political contest is fundamental. This is the method that in its essence is utterly permeated with the principle of liberty. It can be summed up in a single word: self-government. The liberal method intends peoples and social classes, like individuals, to administer their affairs by using their own capacities, without coercion or paternalistic intervention. Its great pedagogical virtue consists in making sure that there exists a climate that compels all men to exercise their highest faculties, in putting in place institutions that induce them to participate actively in social life. It bears as its fundamental premise the principle that the free conviction of the majority, just as it is the best way to arrive at truth, is also the best means of guaranteeing social progress and protecting liberty. On the political level, it can be defined as a complex of rules of the game that all the parties in contention commit themselves to respect, rules intended to ensure the peaceful coexistence of citizens, social classes, and states; to restrain competition, which is inevitable and indeed desirable, within tolerable limits; to permit the various parties to succeed to power in turn; and to guide the forces of innovation that will arise from time to time into legal channels.

More than a system of political mechanics, it is intended to be a sort of *pact of civility* to which men of all faiths bind themselves in order to salvage the attributes of their own humanity out of the struggle. For all that it is not susceptible of a rigid definition, it could be said to be crystallized in the principle of popular sovereignty, in the system of representative government, in respect for the rights of minorities (in practice, the right to opposition), in the solemn recognition of a few fundamental rights of the person that have been definitively accepted by the modern conscience (freedom of thought, freedom to meet, freedom of the press, freedom of organization, freedom to vote, and so on), and in the explicit disavowal of recourse to violence.

The liberal method of taking part in the political contest cannot be qualified; it is not and cannot be either bourgeois or socialist, conservative or revolutionary, though its very nature tends to make it favor the forces of progress. As a bond prior to any political tendency, it requires of those who enter into it faith in reason, sacred respect for mankind, the recognition that each citizen enjoys an infrangible sphere of autonomy, and the rooted conviction that nothing strong and lasting is built with brute force, even when it is employed in the service of fine ideals. Like all refined instruments, it naturally implies a high degree of civilization; rather, it is itself the product of civilization. Sabotage on the part of a single player in the game is enough to prevent the method from functioning properly. But from that it follows that any violence used by the others to keep that individual player in line would be fully legitimate. For example, violence that the proletariat was forced to employ if it found itself under attack by reactionary forces following a great election victory that prepared the way for it to come to power, would be totally justified and completely liberal violence.[3] Liberalism does not exclude violence, but it transforms it into strength by giving it the sanction of morality and right.

Acknowledgment of the liberal method and faith in that method are the practical core of political liberalism.

Sadly, there are more than a few socialists who belittle or even deride the democratic method. With a display of realpolitik, they remind us that all great historical transformations were accompanied by violence and that it is ingenuous to indulge in the delusion that the bourgeois class will allow itself to be despoiled without offering resistance, out of respect for liberal dogma. They add that the democratic method is the method proper to bourgeois society, that it answers to the conservative and governmental needs of the bourgeoisie. Of course, they say, the proletariat can and should make use of democratic institutions as long as it is weak and needs to build up strength, but as soon as it is strong enough to engage in battle, it ought to kick all that democratic, utopian, and humanitarian gimmickry to one side and have recourse to violence, the sole determinant at supreme periods of crisis and transition.

This sort of talk, which democratic socialists have been hearing for thirty years, reveals a complete incomprehension on the part of those who utter it of the spirit and the essence of the liberal method, a physiological incapacity to cut themselves loose from notions that may have had some rationale at the origins of the socialist movement, when the proletariat was without political rights and had nothing to lose but its chains, but that have no more reason for being now that the proletariat has attained its political adulthood in every country. The working class in Europe today finds itself face-to-face with a bourgeoisie that, drawn along by the logic of its own principles and above all by the irresistible pressure of the proletariat, has been forced to give itself (what it did not have in the first place) a democratic constitution. The bourgeoisie today acknowledges explicitly that power has its only

---

[3] Rosselli is referring again to the Fascist assaults in Italy between 1919 and 1920.

source of legitimacy in the people, in the entire people, which expresses its will in parliament, through universal suffrage. The party or the parties that have a majority govern, and fortified by the consensus of the greater number, they have, in principle, the right to modify as they see fit the social constitution, with the sole stipulation that the right of opposition be respected.

For present purposes there is no need to discuss whether the bourgeoisie at present adheres to this principle in good or bad faith, out of conviction or necessity. What is past doubt is that this principle can be greeted only with profound joy by socialists. Do they not claim to want to serve the interests of the great majority of the population? Do they not advance a claim to represent specifically the demands and the ideals of the entire working class? So how can they hesitate to accept fully a way of engaging in the political contest that is bound, sooner or later, to place power in their grasp and that legitimates a priori all their demands?

No reform will be too audacious provided it receives the support, elicited through propaganda, of the majority. No transformation will be too radical, provided it rests on a stable consensus. The problem of problems, for all the socialist parties, has now become that of providing themselves with a program able to satisfy the necessities of an organic majority of the population in their respective countries.

No one believes that by entrusting himself to the democratic method he will miraculously expel violence from history or basks in the illusion that the bourgeoisie will placidly resign itself to its own decline. In the aftermath of so tragic a war, in the aftermath of the experience of fascism, such beliefs are out of the question. No one can dismiss the possibility that the bourgeoisie, or the most backward section of it, may attempt acts of armed oppression, terrorized by the implacable rise of the proletarian tide and hemmed in by a workers' movement made formidable by its own gradualism, by intelligent conformity to the realities of the time, and by respect for legal methods. But note that, first, the bourgeoisie is not a uniform bloc; much more often than people realize, its pretended unity is an abstract fiction. It is just this vulgar dichotomy on the part of many socialists that contributes to the creation, in moments of crisis, of an artificial bourgeois bloc. Second, arms need human consciousness and human will to operate them. As far as I know, the army and the police are part of the people, the proletariat, not the bourgeoisie. And third, should this eventuality occur, the purest orthodox liberalism, from Blackstone to Mill, not only legitimizes the use of force on the part of the majority, but even requires it.

In other words, this is not the angelic dream of cherubim who live only for utopia; it is an awareness of the weight of morality and right in the great conflicts among classes and peoples. What we have to do is to legitimate this eventual violence, to situate ourselves so that we will not be the transgressors of the pact of civility and will have resort to violence only if forced to do so, in the name of the principle of legality and majority that even our adversaries, as long as they controlled a majority, had announced that they accepted, for which indeed they enforced respect.

Not a few will smile at this point and accuse the "formalists" of the democratic method of losing themselves in Byzantine distinctions. But in doing that they demonstrate that they are still beyond good and evil, for they do not know that all right lies precisely in these distinctions, and they have not the remotest idea of the impact on the imagination made when right is violated or with what energy it is able to infuse its defenders.

⟨The paradox is that those who are so fond of mouthing resonant summons to insurrection and to violence as equalizing, as necessary, as historic, are normally the least capable, in part because of their upbringing and the humanitarian motives that actuate them, of seriously organizing a revolutionary movement. Their urge to man the barricades is for the most part a memory of things they have read, a sentimental, romantic, and Jacobin tradition taken from the annals of the French Revolution—when it is not merely an abstraction of self-consciously cerebral thinkers. For as soon as the bourgeoisie, taking clever advantage of their rabid statements, engage in illegal action, they are ordinarily helpless to do anything except appeal to the sacred constitutional charters that have been violated, to the innate rights that have been trampled, to the sense of humanity that has been offended. They solemnly reprove those who wield the truncheons on behalf of the bourgeoisie—all too often authentic proletarians, alas—for not remaining faithful to the spirit of their *own* civilization, which is apparently the only one that is obliged—who knows why?—always to be faithful to the democratic method.⟩

Hard as it is to believe, many socialists still have not understood the fact that the reservation with which they usually accompany their oath of allegiance to the democratic method (to the effect that they will make use of it as long as it is to their advantage, later to reject it) does nothing but authorize the reactionary strata to adopt illegal means *immediately* in order to strike down while there is still time a workers' movement that is threatening to become dangerous.

The Italian example of 1919–1920 is painful proof of this. The Socialist party, though it had won a striking electoral success, had gathered no more than a third, in fact rather less than that, of the votes. Hence it did not dispose of a majority, although the elections had been held, for the first and last time in Italy, in a completely orderly fashion. Still, it solemnly declared to the bourgeoisie that its ultimate hour had sounded, that it should prepare to disappear, that the revolution in the streets was about to break out, and that it would be followed by dictatorship and the moral and physical suppression of all dissenting minorities. It is true that all it did in the sequel, except for sporadic episodes, was to erect barricades made of index cards and committee resolutions. But meanwhile it had played right into the hands of reactionary elements, which by pointing to the follies of the extremists were able to pass themselves off as paragons of innocence, as the restorers of threatened freedoms and violated right, with consequences that are superfluous to recall.

Let us hope the lesson did some good and that socialists will quit playing at being Machiavellians and philosophers of history and will abstain in the future from trying to insert a little of everything into the socialist program—legality and violence, peace and war, democracy and dictatorship—for the sake of never being caught "unprepared." In politics it is important always to speak clearly, even at the cost of appearing a little simplistic.

And let them also quit playing the eternal skeptics and believing that the law of Cain, the law of violence and blood, must forever reign among mankind on earth. One might ask these eternal skeptics what answer in Greece and Rome and even in the slave-owning colonies of the eighteenth and nineteenth centuries the slave owners, the sociologists, and even the slaves themselves would have given concerning the possibility that one day the institution of slavery would disappear; or what the response of the Huguenot in France and the Jew in Spain would have been to one who had prophesied that the day would come when the different religions would live together in peace: easy scornful grins and lectures on realism. And yet humanity today can record these two sublime victories: the abolition of slavery and freedom of conscience. ⟨ If the voices of the skeptics of every age had been heeded, no effort would ever have been made to supersede the existing state of affairs. And so today, if we were to give any weight to the reflex skepticism of many reactionary and revolutionary extremists, we would lose hope of finally securing that minimum of civilization which is the democratic method. But there is nothing more grotesque than this stubborn, radical pessimism in those who, like intransigent socialists, intend nothing less than the realization of socialism, the instantiation of a perfect, eternal justice among men. Their optimism concerning ends ought to make them a little less pessimistic about means. ⟩

But in recent years, sovereign reality has stepped in to deal with the last tergiversations and Machiavellianisms of the theorists. The force of circumstances, even more than their explicit acceptance, has turned socialists throughout Europe into the most intransigent defenders of democratic institutions. They find themselves having to defend an immense patrimony, material, juridical, and moral, acquired over long decades of struggle and sacrifice. Their movement has its soundest base not in their political party but in an immense network of interests (leagues, cooperatives, mutual societies, and so on) that requires and demands constant vigilance and protection. The socialists understand well that if they did not fulfill this protective function, they would end up being supplanted by other currents, toward which syndicalist and cooperative forces would inevitably gravitate. Also, living through the immediate postwar period they realized that, no matter how one cared to argue, it is far from being the right moment to challenge the bourgeoisie on the terrain of force: since the proletariat, as a political force, is still in the minority, it is better to cling openly to the rights that bourgeois liberalism recognizes for minorities. But the strongest warning was given to the socialists by the Communist experience. The rise, on their extreme left wing, of a movement that denies any right of expression and life to socialist forces in the name of dictatorship and the persecution that the socialists have suffered in Russia have given them a Froebelian demonstration of the essential, intrinsic value (not only as an instrument but as a climate) of liberty and democratic institutions.[4] Trotsky, who inveighs from his forced exile in Turkey against the tyranny of Stalin and the dictatorship of a handful of bureaucrats, after having derided "bourgeois" liberties and democratic methods for so many years, is perhaps the most comforting example of the unquenchable vitality of the liberal postulate.

Within a few years socialist support for the liberal method and the liberal climate—explicit, total, definitive support—will be a fait accompli. At that point there will be one last step for the socialists to take in order to enter the logic and spirit of liberalism; this step too is inevitable, but it will require a long period of inculcation in the masses; it is that the socialists accept that the democratic method and the liberal climate constitute such a fundamental conquest of modern civilization that they will have to be respected even, and especially, when there is a stable socialist majority at the helm of the government, even when the essential points of the reform program are on the way to being realized. This does not mean giving up the teleological goals of socialism; it means only showing respect for a few essential forms of life in com-

---

[4] That is, a pedagogical demonstration. Friedrich W. A. Fröbel (1782–1852) one of the founders of modern pedagogy and a pupil of Johann H. Pestalozzi (1746–1827).

mon. The socialists too will have to commit themselves to respecting
the rights of dissenting minorities and the right of opposition, no matter what the circumstances. They should not be afraid of appearing
doubtful or weak by doing so. On the contrary. No faith is more solid
than one in which the believer is not afraid of the criticism of his
adversaries, which he seeks out as both a stimulus and a boundary. No
party or movement is as strong as one that recognizes the right of its
adversaries to exist and that declares that on the day of its own victory
it will not cast aside the spirit of the liberal method that enabled it to
grow from a small and weak minority into a position of dominance.

⟨ Socialism will be liberal on the day it is able to pronounce a noble
and conclusive word on this subject. ⟩

In conclusion, if I were asked to illustrate briefly the practical consequences of the observations made in the course of these two chapters, I
would put the matter as follows.

Until now socialist action has had a predominantly economic slant.
Probably it had to be like that, since it would be utterly utopian to prate
about morality, spiritual autonomy, duty, support and respect for the
democratic method to someone living in indigence and barely able to
satisfy the elementary demands of subsistence through exhausting
and degrading labor. The permanent attainment of a degree of relative
well-being is a *conditio sine qua non*. Everything else is blocked by the
presence of material indigence. Indigence is the great enemy, no more
or less than privileged wealth. Those who had nothing were always
the servants of the powerful. To be hungry is to be morally deaf, and
moralistic appeals translate fatally into sermonizing.

But step by step, as economic circumstances get better (and they
have already been greatly improved), as the working class proceeds to
affirm itself politically and the state offers an opening to new demands,
as the bourgeoisie, or at least its most progressive components, no
longer opposes with its traditional stubbornness the process of proletarian emancipation, that of culture and morality must come to the top
of the agenda, for otherwise the movement will lose its way and grow
corrupt. Socialism can no longer limit itself to reforming the external
aspects of social life. Any emancipation aimed solely at reducing or
eliminating oppression from the social environment, any liberty that
was purely negative, unaccompanied by a reaffirmation of the eternal
values of the spirit, would mean liberation from one kind of slavery in
the name of another kind. Either emancipation will be total—body and
soul—or it will not occur.

Thus it is some consolation to observe that in recent years spiritual
demands of this type have been finding expression, however hesitant,

within the working class, thanks to the same syndicalist movement that had appeared deaf to all questions except those involving hours of work and wage levels. The ever more insistent demand for worker control, for a share in the management of the factory, for the constitutionalization of the factory regime, the battles over issues of principle and dignity, all these things reveal the rise of a new self-respect in the average worker, who is no longer content with material improvements alone but intends to assert his autonomous personality both inside and outside the factory, not only as a citizen but also as a producer. Even the idea of socialization is no longer advanced in purely utilitarian terms of enhanced productivity. A critique of the traditional conception of centralized, collectivist socialism now being heard from within the ranks of socialism documents the existence of new demands for autonomy and liberty.

Our task must lie in the development of these initial, obscure intuitions of the proletarian soul, in revealing the great importance they have for any revision of the theoretical groundwork of the socialist movement. We have to help the proletariat to come to know itself, showing it the real reasons and the effective remedies for the painful state of psychological and social inferiority in which it finds itself, and we have to formulate the results of this process of collective introspection in concrete political terms. We have to insist that an ideal of autonomy and liberty should increasingly be the beacon of the socialist movement. We have to make it clear that for a revolution to bear fruit, it is not enough to capture the centers of command, that we have to proceed from the bottom up, not the other way around. We have to conceive of socialism not as the result of the imposition of views by an enlightened minority, but as the result of people coming round to a belief in it out of a long sequence of positive experiences. We should not rely overmuch on passing laws; you can pass all the laws you like, but if they do not validate an objective state of affairs that is actually coming about and are not based on actual behavior, too often they turn out to be fruitless efforts. We have to have more faith in our own powers, to work, experiment, and struggle without prerequisites and excessively rigid programs; we only need to be faithful to a few fundamental directives. What really counts in the last analysis is the process of raising the masses and reforming social relations on the basis of a principle of justice that harmonizes with respect for the liberty of individuals and groups. Routine deference to a program that is now a hundred years old is simply irrelevant in too many respects.

Before ending this brief essay on liberal socialism I would like to indicate summarily what appears to me to be, in outline, the mental structures and subjective attitudes of the liberal socialist. The liberal socialist, faithful to the great lesson arising out of modern critical thought, does not believe that it can be scientifically and rationally shown that socialism's empirical solutions are the best ones, nor even in the historical necessity of the advent of a socialist society. He does not delude himself that he possesses the secret of the future, does not think that he is the custodian of the ultimate, definitive truth about the social universe, and does not bow down before dogmas of any sort. He does not believe that the socialist regime must be, and that it will come about, over the course of centuries because of some law that transcends the will of human beings. Indeed, viewing the matter with a cold eye, he might even admit as a hypothesis that the forces of privilege, injustice, and the oppression of the many in the interest of the few might continue to prevail. His motto is: Socialism will be, but it might not be. It will be if we want it and if the masses want it, through a conscious creative effort.

In this doubt, in this virile relativism that gives a powerful impulse to action and wishes to leave plenty of room for human will in history; in this critical demon that obliges one continually to review one's position in the light of fresh experience; in this faith in the supreme values of the spirit and the marvelous animating force of liberty, end and means, climate and lever, lies the state of mind of a socialist who has sailed away from Marxist seas and touched land on the shores of liberalism.

Action is his true standard. He is a socialist because of a whole ensemble of principles and experiences and because of convictions formed in the study of social phenomena; but he is a socialist above all out of faith, sentiment, *active* attachment—this is the point, the real criterion—to the cause of the poor and the oppressed. Whoever adopts this cause as his own can act only in the spirit of liberalism and in the practice of socialism.

SEVEN

THE STRUGGLE FOR LIBERTY

THE ITALIAN PROBLEM is essentially the problem of liberty—but liberty understood in the fullest sense: as spiritual autonomy, as the setting free of the conscience for individuals, and as the organization of the social world (meaning the building of the state) and relations among groups and classes. Without free men, there is no possibility of a free state. If consciences are not set free, there is no possibility of social classes being set free. This is not to reason in a circle. Liberty begins with the formation of the individual and ends with the triumph of a state whose members are free individuals, equal in rights and duties, a state in which the liberty of each is the condition and limit of the liberty of all the rest.

Now it is sad to have to admit this, but nonetheless it is true: in Italy the training of the individual, the formation of the individual as the basic moral unit, is still to a large extent unaccomplished. Because of poverty, indifference, and a long-standing resignedness, most Italians still lack a sharp and deep-rooted sense of autonomy and responsibility. The state of subjection that lasted for centuries makes the average Italian vacillate between the habit of servility and anarchic revolt even today. The concept of life as a struggle and a mission, the notion of liberty as a moral duty, and the awareness of one's limitations and those of others are all missing. Italians take pride in their persona, that is, their exterior values and relationships, more often than they do in their personality. Their inner lives are exuberantly rich but lopsided, overflowing in sentiment that pours out in instinctive and emphatic forms. Calm reflection on the principal problems of life, the habit of attending to the voice of one's conscience, the fecund spiritual torment that gradually creates a whole, a prodigious interior world (and this alone can supply a sense of oneself as a distinct and autonomous unity)—all these things are absent in the majority. The influence of Catholicism, pagan in its cultic practice and dogmatic in its substance, and the paternalism of a long series of governments have for centuries excused the Italians from the burden of thinking for themselves. Poverty has done the rest. The average Italian to this day still surrenders his spiritual autonomy to the church, and now he finds that in relation to the state, which has been raised to the status of an end in itself, he has been forced to surrender even his dignity as a human being; he has sunk to the status of a mere instrument. Conditioned to servitude in the sphere of conscience, he is now being forced into servitude in the social and political sphere: the logical outcome of a series of passive surrenders.

The attitude of *dolce far niente* (sweet laziness) said to be characteristic of the Italians, an insulting myth if we consider the material aspects of life, is unfortunately not without some foundation in the moral realm. The Italians are morally lazy. There is an underlying skepticism and a low-grade Machiavellianism in them that induces them to contaminate all values with ridicule and to transform the darkest tragedies into comedy. Since they are accustomed to letting others think about the chief problems of conscience for them (a real spiritual contracting-out system), it is natural that they should easily resign themselves to contracting out the chief problems of political life. The intervention of a deus ex machina, a *duce*, a commander—whether he goes by the name of pope, king, or Mussolini—often answers to a psychological need on their part. From this point of view the Mussolini government is anything but revolutionary. It is linked to the tradition and proceeds along the line of least resistance. Fascism, all appearances to the contrary, is the most passive development in Italian history. It is the gigantic backwash of centuries, an abject example of adaptation and resignation. Mussolini won because of a long sequence of cunning compromises and because he was met with massive desertion. Only a few small groups of proletarians and intellectuals had the courage to face up to him with radical fixity of purpose right from the start.

Mussolini betrays the measure of his banality when he considers the problem of authority and discipline as the essential pedagogical problem for the Italians.

Good Lord, that's the last thing we have to teach the Italians! For centuries they bowed to every master and served every tyrant. In our history to date there has been no real revolution of the people. From among the Italians at every epoch of their history there have emerged towering summits, solitary and remote: heroic minorities, unbending individuals. But the Italians have never been able to realize themselves as a people. Italy was the great nonparticipant in the wars of religion, which were the principal leaven of liberalism, the birth pangs of modern man. Italian Catholicism, afflicted with the Roman court and with its own state of passive consensus, also remained extraneous to the process of purification that followed the Reformation. Being Catholic in a country where Catholicism has a monopoly is a far cry from being Catholic in lands where religions compete.

Where politics was concerned, for centuries we received only a reflected glare from abroad, and when the great waves of European life washed over us they were already spent and choppy.

Even our struggle for independence was the work of a minority, not the passion of the people. Only a few urban centers in the north took an active part in the revolt against the foreigners. In central and southern Italy, when the first stage of enthusiasm had passed, the house of Savoy was no different from the house of Lorraine or that of Bourbon.

The Piedmontese bureaucracy wrapped all of Italy in its ordered but suffocating coils, extinguishing the last impulses to liberty. The triumph of monarchical and diplomatic interests had the effect, as in Germany, of driving a wedge between the myth of national unity and the myth of liberty. Mazzini and Cattaneo were the great losers of the Risorgimento. Even political freedoms, which slowly arrived as the decades passed, were born of bargaining and tacit compromise. The conquest of liberty is not connected in Italy to any mass movement capable of playing the role of myth or paradigm. The masses took no part. The proletariat did not win its specific freedom to organize, strike, and vote at the cost of protracted effort and sacrifice. Its apprenticeship, around 1900, was too short, and when universal suffrage came, it appeared to be what it was, a calculated paternalist concession. The rule that one loves and fights only for what has cost one much struggle and sacrifice has been proved in exemplary fashion by the experience of fascism. The liberal edifice collapsed like an empty hulk at the first impact, and the working classes stood by uncaring as values still alien to their consciousness were reversed.

When Mussolini today lists the size of his herd of followers and his pack of hounds and vaunts unanimity, the single party, and the disappearance of any substantial opposition or independent initiative on the part of opposing minorities, all in the name of a carnivalesque revolution, he is doing nothing more than revive the pomp of the Bourbons, without even leaving us the consolation of knowing that the dynasty in power is a foreign one, kept in place by its troops.

It is indeed true that the innate factiousness of the native of Romagna would have driven him to engage in battle. But he cannot conceive of battle in terms other than those of brute force. The despotic pride of the dictator compels him systematically to extinguish any will to opposition or struggle. Still and all, his sectarian intransigence serves the cause of liberty. With truncheons and handcuffs, and with more refined torments, Mussolini is constructing modern Italians, volunteers for liberty, by the tens of thousands. His persecuting fury and the overpowering logic of the repressive instruments of which he is by now himself a prisoner are turning into our best allies.

For the first time in the history of Italy, the defense of the inalienable rights of the person and the principle of self-government pose themselves as problems for the people and no longer as problems just for a select group of insiders. No Italian, no matter how poor and uneducated he may be, can ignore fascism and the life-and-death problems that fascism raises. The most miserable laborer in Calabria can today suffer and hope for the same cause for which the most refined intellectual, even the modern industrialist in the north, suffers and hopes. Out of all the hardship and humiliation, awareness of the value of liberty is springing up in a dramatic fashion throughout vast sectors of the Italian people. Today the Italians, in their desperate struggle to regain basic autonomies, are perhaps more free psychologically than they were under the pseudo-constitutional regime of Giolitti, when there were thousands of independent associations.

Everyone views the problem—quite rightly—through the lens of his own interests and his own party, but the focus is becoming the same for all: liberty. Even the Communists, for all their cheap sneers, find themselves constrained to explain the dictatorship in terms of liberty. Fascist oppression is bringing about the moral unity of the Italian people.

Where do the socialists stand in relation to the problem of liberty? Does the Marxist doctrine to which the majority still adheres permit them to view the Italian question integrally, with the sort of ideological and ethical clarity that is an indispensable premise for a movement of renewal?

I would say not. Marxist socialism ignores liberty, to which it assigns an entirely secondary and historically conditioned value. Mistaking its eternal and immutable essence for its transient manifestations, Marxist socialism actually disavows liberty and perceives only individual, concrete, and provisional class liberties—the more or less clever camouflage of class interests. As far as Marxist socialism is concerned, the utterly fundamental problem of mankind's moral liberty does not even exist or does so entirely and solely in relation to the subjection of men to the economic machine. Marxian man, as we saw, is unfree by definition and operates uniquely and totally under the pressure of economic need; he is forced to employ methods of production and to create for himself imperative political, social, and spiritual relations. The core of Marxism lies in the concept of the historical necessity of the advent of a socialist society by virtue of an objective and fatal process of transformation within the material world. Human will appears in a secondary, not to say determined, role. Problems of consciousness, of autonomy, of the formation of free personalities, do not exist for Marx. They are all postponed to the new day following the social transformation. Nothing could be more utopian and antiliberal than this abrupt and messi-

anic shift of position, this switch from a realm where inexorable necessity dominates to one where sovereign liberty reigns.

Morality, like liberty, is seen as historically produced, reflecting
merely the evolution of external conditions. To the extent that there is
liberty in the external world of production, there will be liberty in the
inner world. Only when men are emancipated from subjection to capitalist relations will they become free. Abolish the monopolistic control
of property, abolish the present system of social relations, Marx declares, and you will see a generation of free men appear automatically.

This is an error and an illusion, or at least an exceedingly narrow
point of view. As always happens with innovative theses, Marxism
highlighted only a part, though an essential one, of the problem, but in
order to bring it into greater relief it sacrificed all the others. There are,
in the lives of human beings and of society, essential values that do not
depend on a simple transformation of the environment, values that are
always posed whenever we rise above the level of purely animal existence and that require, in order to be understood, a molding process
and the efforts of a long series of generations: indeed, one might say
that they constitute the prerequisite for the transformation of the environment that the socialists wish to see. If humans have neither a sense
of dignity nor one of responsibility rooted deep inside themselves, if
they do not feel pride in their own autonomy, if they have not attained
freedom in their inner lives, we do not create socialism. We create the
barracks state, the Prussian state, a state that is labeled free but is really
a slave state. If there has not been a period of free inquiry, if there has
not been a 1789 (a cycle through which every generation has to pass),
socialism is reduced to nothing more than a melancholy dream of
bureaucrats.

The impotence of Marxist socialism in the face of problems of liberty
and morality is also shown by its relative inability to see into the phenomenon of fascism. It sees in fascism only a brutal case of class reaction, the typical modern form of capitalist reaction. Fascism is the bourgeoisie *tout court*, turning to violence in order to oppose the rise of the
proletariat. All the rest is an ideological smoke screen, say the Marxists. With facile oversimplification that they try to pass off as realism,
they overlook the whole moral side of the question, everything charac-
teristically Italian that the Fascist phenomenon reveals. But they are
making a grave mistake. Fascism is not explicable purely in terms of
class interests. Its goon squads did not come into being solely because
they were subsidized by angry, reactionary social elites. Factiousness,
the spirit of adventure, romantic inclinations, petit bourgeois idealism,
nationalist rhetoric, feelings aroused by the war, the restless desire for
something, anything at all, as long as it was new—without motives

like these there would have been no fascism. Out of the deeply sedi-mented layers of national character and the experience of generations, the Fascist phenomenon burst into the light; it was stimulated by an evident class interest but has strongly marked traits that are indepen-dent of class criteria. In the Bolshevism of 1919 many aspects of fas-cism, and not just the extrinsic ones, can be seen fully formed. Look at fascism as something emerging from the subsoil of Italy and you will see that it expresses the deepest vices, the latent weaknesses, the miseries, alas, of our people, of all our people. It is a mistake to believe that Mussolini triumphed only through brute force. Brute force on its own never triumphs. He won because he cleverly played the right notes, the ones to which the average psychology of the Italians was extraordinarily susceptible. Fascism has in some sense been the auto-biography of a nation that shrugs at the political contest, that worships unanimity and shrinks from heresy, that dreams of the triumph of facility, trust, and enthusiasm.

To battle fascism does not therefore mean simply battling a ferocious and resolute class reaction; it means battling a certain type of mentality, a sensibility, an Italian tradition to which large sectors of the populace unfortunately belong without their knowing it. It is thus a difficult struggle and does not consist of a simple problem in the mechanics of overthrowing a regime. Above all it is a problem of our own and others' moral and political formation, especially that of our adversaries, and indeed of all the Italians, quite apart from any division into classes. Far from ending on the day fascism falls, our constructive problems will commence only then . . . but the struggle is thus a fine one, and vital, truly worthy of any sacrifice.

Today many socialists, fixing their gaze on the underlying "eco-nomic structure," make a point of ignoring these problems, pure and simple. What does the struggle for liberty signify for them? It serves a higher purpose, it is a campaign to conquer institutions and tactical positions that will be useful but impermanent, because they will later be cast aside with the coming of socialist society. The habit of consider-ing the economic problem the key one, the determining factor, and of measuring all values in utilitarian terms makes them lose touch with the profound and permanent values that only a regime of liberty is capable of sustaining. What interests them exclusively is the *form* of the political contest, not the substance of a liberal climate. When Marxists demand liberty they do so not for its intrinsic value, but only because they think it favors the self-awareness of the proletariat, and in fact capitalist development. Caught in a bind between their use of liberal methods and their illiberal goals, they inevitably feel a little uneasy about the fight for liberty and take part only with an endless number of reservations, qualifications, and subtle distinctions that sap the demands they make (on an interim basis and for quite different ends) of any power to grip the imagination or make converts. Indeed, how does one go about inciting the working class to a revolutionary struggle in the name of liberty when at the same time one is instructing it that liberty does not exist, that the democratic method is of use today but might well be rejected tomorrow, that the struggle in which we are engaged is a socialist struggle only in a very indirect sense? It is like trying to square a circle. From the beginning of history, there never was a revolution created out of values embraced temporarily. Tactics and calculation may well serve to fuel an academic debate, but never a battle in the streets. Without the flash of a supreme ideal for which one is fighting, an ideal that thoroughly permeates the substance and the purposes of the struggle in which one is engaged, without a quivering, burning feeling of the value of the good one is fighting for, no one reaches the temperature for revolution. Until the socialists assert the absolute, intrinsic value of the liberal climate, of democratic institutions, of concrete freedom of the press, freedom of assembly, and freedom of thought, they will be helpless to take part in the struggle for liberty and win.

Hamstrung as it is by a thousand anxieties on this score alone, we can see why Italian socialism, though it commands the essential levers needed to create an anti-Fascist uprising, has not yet succeeded in bringing about a real awakening among the masses. It lacks a profound belief in liberty and is worn down by the contradiction between means and ends.

The superiority of the liberal socialist position outlined in the preceding chapter seems to me to lie in this: it makes us feel that our hearts are fully in this struggle for liberty, and we do not have to reject any part of our program or make trade-offs, adopting notions that really belong to the bourgeois ideology. In our view our entire program is founded on the myth of liberty, because we urge and justify even the most far-reaching social changes in the name of a principle of liberty: full, effective, and positive liberty for all human beings, in every aspect of their existence. Political and spiritual liberty today, because it constitutes the premise, the instrument, and the indispensable atmosphere for our fight, indeed is an immanent part of the fight; and liberty in the future, autonomy in the economy and in the state. Liberty as a means and an end. We are fighting for the means—the democratic method— inasmuch as it is completely permeated by the end. Our position is nothing more than the logical development to its ultimate consequences of the principle of liberty. The liberal socialist has no plans to suspend certain programs, holds no secret doctrines, and is not keeping quiet about any future demands that might conflict with the current stand being taken in the struggle. I see it as a marvelous harmony, a perfect correspondence between ends and means, thought and action, today's struggle and tomorrow's. And today more than ever, when any semblance of liberty is dead in Italy, I sense the supreme beauty of a struggle that is taking place for the first principles of our lives and our faith.

At this point the "old hands," the good old positivistic, realistic socialists, will raise their voices, pointing out to us that these are radiant dreams for poets and intellectuals; that the ideal of a struggle for liberty can animate only a small minority of aristocrats against fascism; that the masses, oppressed by the problems of living and accustomed to attend to what is solid, useful, and positive, will mobilize only for economic motives; that if the outcome of the anti-Fascist battle depended on the deeds of tiny minorities, then we might be right, but it depends on arousing the masses, and this makes it necessary to concentrate on the needs and the psychology of the masses; that we thus have to create a basically economic rationale for our opposition to fascism, making it clear that our appeal is for liberty, because only when liberty comes will the workers see an improvement in their living conditions and respect for their fundamental rights.

Though it may seem persuasive, this line of reasoning conceals a grave weakness and a contradiction. Clearly no one denies the need to explain the content and the consequences of the struggle for liberty in positive terms: the better life it brings, with more bread, and more things to eat with it. One arrives at the ideal only through the real, Jaurès said. The more pressure there is from social and environmental conditions, the more one is shut off from pure contemplation of the ideal.

But this elementary constatation is one thing, and the cliché that the masses respond only to the material aspects of existence is another, since in shifting from the first to the second we lose all the ideal value, all the ultimate goals, of the struggle for liberty.

To turn the masses in this fashion into a new Moloch, the devourer of the best part of our humanity, is a piece of cheap blackmail that has to stop, especially since—much more often than one might think—it is really a handy alibi for the spiritual impotence or the stupid pride of those who use it. It is those who presume to speak for the masses and to teach the rest of us lessons in humility who are truly behaving in an aristocratic fashion. With what right do they hand over to a small minority (in which they include themselves) a monopoly of all disinterested sentiments? With what right do they make this drastic distinction between a few elect spirits on one hand and the multitude, the pariahs of the spirit, on the other? Do they not see that in doing this they specifically condemn the rights of the masses, the rights of the majority, which would automatically give way before those of the elect, the minority, for the very reason that this minority expresses qualitatively superior values? Pessimistic judgments of the masses are pessimistic judgments of mankind, since the masses are only a sum of concrete individuals. If you say that the masses are incapable of affirming, even in their own crude and primitive way, the value of the struggle for liberty, you are saying that mankind ignores whatever instincts it has that are not narrowly utilitarian; at the same time you chop off any hope of palingenesis and social redemption at the roots, and you administer a blow to faith in democratic institutions, a faith founded on the belief that all men are fundamentally identical and on a reasonable optimism concerning them.

The modern utilitarians[1] will reply that it is only to the degree to which human beings succeed in freeing themselves from enslavement to material needs that they start to appreciate ideal values. But this line of reasoning is both false and dangerous: false because in the past, when on the average people subsisted at an infinitely lower level than they do at present and were much more vulnerable to their environment, there were colossal examples of collective fervor for religious, political, and social causes, which are impossible to account for on economic grounds alone; dangerous because it would amount to saying that the bourgeoisie, which enjoys much more economic autonomy than the proletariat, ought to be all the more inclined to profess disinterested beliefs. This, one need hardly add, runs blatantly counter to reality and to all of socialist thought.

The fact is, it isn't true that the masses are deaf to any appeal based on motives not strictly utilitarian. There is a place in the lives of all human beings, even the poorest and most coarsened, for moments of escape and catharsis. We all know that such idealistic moments exist in family life; it is absurd to deny that they exist in the social sphere. In the history of every people there are moments, however brief, of sublime beauty, in which vast crowds show that they are open to an elevated and disinterested vision. The workers' movement, and even the war, showed us examples of this. Why should we suppose that the working class would be incapable of realizing the beauty of the fight for liberty, a struggle that entails having at the outset a sense of respect for oneself and one's fellow human beings?

[1] Rosselli means Marxist socialists. De Man suggested the connection between Bentham and Marx in *The Psychology of Socialism*, pp. 479–86 ("Here, once more, Marxism suffers from the heritage of its philosophic ancestry: it speaks of more happiness, and means more wellbeing" [p. 486])

The persons sunk deepest in slavery are those who, having attained an awareness of their servile condition, resign themselves to it. The most impotent are those who, having caught a glimpse of the value of liberty, are nevertheless willing to adulterate it, laying claim to liberty on totally functional and utilitarian grounds in response to the supposed insensibility of the masses. If the masses (meaning the average person) were really so incapable of feeling the higher value of liberty, that would be the best reason to respond with patient attempts at education and conversion. Instead the Marxists have always taken a special delight in stamping out the first signs of idealistic conviction, which they disdain and which they never fail to trace to supposedly utilitarian origins.

But above all the position of the Marxists vis-à-vis the problem of liberty reveals a contradiction. On one hand they insist that the masses can be mobilized only by material interests, while on the other hand they are asking them, in the actual Italian situation today, to topple fascism by force. They do not understand that no one will be driven to make the sort of sacrifices that are indispensable in a revolutionary conflict out of self-interest. It would not be enough to point out to the masses that they would gain certain advantages from a regime of liberty; they would have to be shown that such sacrifices as imprisonment, exile, and physical harm were producing rewards at the very instant at which they were made, even for those called upon to make them—which is patently absurd. A revolutionary struggle, whatever its aim, requires an altruistic and idealistic disposition in the masses, the capacity to give birth to a heroic minority that sacrifices itself. If the masses can be mobilized only by the sort of motives our utilitarians ascribe to them, for what cause will they sacrifice themselves? That remains a mystery.

It has to be said that the socialists who still remain tied to a formalistic and instrumental notion of the struggle for liberty are fatally cut off from the battle and are heading for a compromise that may perhaps guarantee a semblance of liberty but will stifle the vital spark that gives it life.

We therefore intend to summon the Italian people, the masses, to a revolutionary struggle in the name of the principle of liberty. This principle of liberty does not exclude, indeed it includes, demands of a more positive kind and daring social reforms: the struggle for bread and for more humane living conditions is identical with the struggle for liberty for all classes, especially the working class; but the animating myth of the Italian revolution will be represented by the principle of liberty.

Those who would reprove us for intransigence ought to recall that in the lives of individuals, as of peoples, there are dramatic moments in which the clash of two principles, two moral worlds that mutually exclude one another, does not allow for a compromise solution. Liberalism's practical rule, that of the just mean, lapses, for it can be applied only where agreement on the fundamentals of social life obtains. Fascism took the lead in clearing the ground of all the comfortable, quietistic middle positions with its rigid proclamation of its own sectarian and categorical principles; this opened an ideological and practical abyss between one group of Italians and the rest, between Fascist Italy and modern Europe. Fascism is, first and foremost, war on liberalism; hence coming to terms is out of the question.

In all countries liberty is the daughter of revolution. England with its 1648, France with its 1789, Germany and Russia with the revolutions of 1917 and 1918, all achieved conclusive acts of emancipation. It almost seems as though some historical fatality connects the emancipation of the peoples through the centuries. Gladstone once said that if the English people had obeyed the precepts of non-recourse to violence and the maintenance of order, English liberties would never have been won.

Those belonging to the free peoples who have had the cult of liberty in their bloodstream for many generations invite us to compromise, understanding nothing of the struggle taking place in Italy; unwittingly, they are the best allies of fascism. Fascism has no fear of lukewarm convictions and of the readiness to bargain that its own intransigence forces on others. In eight years of government it has always emerged victorious over attempts to outmaneuver it and corrupt it. What it fears are straight consciences and pure faith in principles, and what it has struck at with barbarity are men whose stoic and puritan lives revealed them to be symbols of the work of regeneration.

No doubt it is very unsettling to have such a tragic problem in Europe as the Italian situation, but there is no point in deluding ourselves: it will be eliminated only when it is resolved. By now there exists, within Italy and abroad, a generation of men who have chosen their destinies and who will not refuse to fight the battle to its logical conclusion for anything in the world. By now it is they who are forcing the dictatorship to follow its destiny by imprisoning fascism within the horrible logic of its own repressive system; ⟨ on the day that fascism leaves them an opening, they will march an army through it. ⟩ These men ask nothing from foreign nations except for the understanding and moral solidarity that ought to be felt as a matter of duty within the community of free peoples.

EIGHT

FOR A NEW SOCIALISM

Ideology

IN THE FOREGOING CHAPTER a brief sketch was given of how the battle against fascism ought to be conducted by a socialism cognizant of the higher claims of morality and liberty. In this one I will try to stake out a few points of reference for the socialist movement of tomorrow.

The issue is anything but esoteric. The tomorrow we envision will not be long in coming, and in any case it will arrive without warning. History does not give advance notice or grant deferrals. If the problems of the socialist revival are not faced up to courageously right now, the socialist movement will run the risk of being bowled over by a sudden demagogic cyclone, as happened after the war.

But before narrowing our focus to these problems, we ought to ask ourselves: What will it be like for socialism to come back to life? Will it simply pick up where it left off, or will this be a modern and original renaissance?

Those who have spent their entire lives in the movement do not understand the gravity of the crisis through which we are passing and delude themselves that nothing substantial has changed. Aware of the deep penetration socialism achieved in Italy and the vast reservoirs of sympathy in the masses, they foresee no radical break. It seems to them that the problems of yesterday will be the problems of tomorrow, that events will confirm this continuity, of which they themselves are the guarantors. . . .

They are drawn to this conclusion by their own analysis of the phenomenon of fascism—which they define as an irrational interlude ascribable to extrinsic and superficial causes—and through a vein of skeptical fatalism. What happened, they say, had to happen. The socialist movement has been what it has been not because of the will of men but because of the force of circumstances and inscrutable events. "Circumstances" cannot be put on trial. The fact that socialism has suffered this abrupt setback along its glorious course does not mean that it could have been avoided or that the socialists are to blame; it is merely a vicissitude of the struggle between the proletariat and the bourgeoisie. Reactionism may have won, but that was not because of errors committed by its adversaries; it was because of the immense advances that had been made and consolidated, advances that provoked the reaction as fatally as atmospheric condensation provokes rainfall. There is nothing essential that needs to be rethought. We just have to wait, hope, and set out again courageously as soon as the way is open. Fascism is only an episode. The losers of today will be tomorrow's winners.

That is not how the new generation sees things. The young do not care for easy absolution through the retrospective appeal to deterministic logic. They demand a frank scrutiny of why we lost, a rigorous process of reexamination and self-criticism. Believing in the role of human will in history, they are not inclined to attribute their defeat to hostile deities or the rhythm of the forces of production. They have the strong sensation that fascism by now is an experience that will leave its mark on Italian life, that it cannot be dealt with as if it were a mere accident or simply an interlude. Combating it does not mean eliminating it. Indeed, the better one understands it, the more effectively it can be fought and overcome. To understand is to overcome. Fascism is almost completely devoid of constructive values, but it has value that cannot be overlooked as experience, as a revelation of the Italians to themselves. In addition, fascism, though it has not solved them, or has solved them badly, has raised problems that cannot be ignored. When fascism crumbles the problems of relations between socialism and the nation, of government in a democratic regime, of political autonomy, will confront us with an entirely new intensity and in an utterly new form.

But decisive renewal will be forced on the socialist movement by the existence of new generations, with whom it must start preparing itself to reckon, rather than by the experience of fascism (a tremendously negative experience but a potent one). The duration of the Fascist phenomenon—which prohibits any sort of ties with the past—and the fundamental experience of living through the war and the postwar period have created a new mentality in the young and a painful split between them and elements of the older generation. This split occurs in every time and place, but the war has made it more acute in Europe, and in Italy it is actually dramatic—for reasons adduced in the chapter on Italian socialism. ⟨ For those who took part in the war while young or were formed in its heightened atmosphere, the war is a tragic point of departure, a chrism, an indelible imprint. For us there is no lived history before 1914, only history learned from books, and it does not sound a deep echo in us. For our elders, with the exception of a few rare spirits who are eternally young, the turning point of their lives, their time of accomplishment, is in the years 1890 to 1915. After that come the shadows. The violent negation that followed, culminating in fascism, necessarily presents itself as an assault on the best part of themselves and on the tenacious and patient labor with which they sought to express themselves. They view tomorrow not as a time when they will step forth with trembling hearts into a future filled with hazard and mystery, but as a return to the world of their youth after a long detour. Thus their longing gaze turns nostalgically to a past that cannot return and that inevitably means nothing to the young. The rupture has been too sharp. The clash of mentalities prevents any real rapport. Old socialists and young ones may love one another, esteem one another, and work together, but they no longer understand one another. This is inevitable: they speak two different languages. Probably such an attitude on the part of the young contains a good deal of injustice to the older generation; this can be corrected and a way found to heal the rift when the time comes to write the history books. But in the meantime it is not bad for them to utilize their own acerbic will for renewal and purification, the faith, however illusory, that they have in their own ability to do better in the future than others did before them, learning all there is to learn from the hard lesson these years have taught them.)

So let us define ourselves in relation to the future.

First, the ideological problem. I have already stated the essential points in chapter 7 on liberal socialism, and there is no need to repeat them here. European socialism is headed firmly toward liberal and Labourite ideas and practices and toward assuming governmental responsibility. This will happen in Italy too. It is desirable that this transition take place in a self-aware fashion, in other words, that it be foreseen and chosen and not appear to be dictated by circumstances and that it be accompanied by a serious effort at ideological renewal. Marxism can no longer aspire to play the role it played in the past. If it continues to do so, laziness and insincerity would be the reasons. There is not one socialist leader who still believes in Marxism in his heart; if there is, he does so with so many qualifications and distinctions that it loses a large part of its pedagogical and normative force. These things have to be said loud and clear, without fear of causing some to feel let down. Those who are not so inclined must allow others to speak out without hindrance and without expelling them from the ranks of socialism for doing so. It is time to throw off the absurd reverential awe that surrounds everything having to do with Marx. We have to dissociate socialism from Marxism, or at any rate to concede that they might be dissociated, and recognize Marxism as one of the many transitory theorizations of the socialist movement—a movement that affirms itself spontaneously and independently of any theory and that is based on elementary human motives and needs.

Here I touch on a point that I believe is fundamental. We talk about liberty, we fight for liberty, but the first liberty we have to put in place is liberty within the movement itself, and that means breaking up these hardened layers of dogma and grotesque monopolies. The socialist movement has to be coherent enough to apply to itself the ideal rules that inspire its attempt to reform all of society. Discipline is essential for action, but it is a mistake to impose it in the domain of ideas and ideologies. The desire to use the party to make everyone put on the same mass-produced intellectual clothes is the most mortifying and dangerous thing imaginable. I have already had occasion to point out what a chilling paralysis Marxist monopoly inflicted on the Italian Socialist party. Agreed, often it was more a formal monopoly, a matter of phraseology, than a real one, because when it comes to Marxism most people are still beyond good and evil; but it needs to be smashed nonetheless in order to promote the free flow of all the currents of belief that in the past fed into the great movement for social emancipation. Among Italian socialists there have been perpetuated divisions and barriers to communication that have no more reason to exist if adherence to Marxist principles is no longer considered a test of faith, and if, along with traditional conception of socialism, we accept the vitality, or at any rate the utility, of other currents of belief particularly open to moral problems (Mazzinian socialists, ethical socialists, Christian socialists) or to problems of autonomy and political structure (republicans, those who favor regional autonomy)[1] or to problems of liberty and individual dignity (liberal socialists, and a good many self-styled anarchist socialists), and so on. In the last thirty years the Italian socialist movement has crystallized, so to speak, and has progressively lost all its power of absorption and transformation. It has carved out a place, indeed a notable place, for itself in the Italian social panorama, but it has been satisfied to cultivate its own plot, implicitly abandoning any attempt to extend its influence and renew itself. Thus it has done an outstanding job of promoting other movements such as the Christian democratic one and has kept itself uncontaminated by any sort of cultural vitality. I am certain that an Italian socialist movement capable of forcing itself to undertake a profound reexamination of its values would succeed in attracting all the youthful forces, wherever they are coming from, that now support the cause of the workers and that will do so more strongly in the future when Italy is free; it would also succeed in causing life and debate to flourish in it. This last is an

---

[1] In Rosselli's time the "autonomisti," supporters of large regional autonomies and even a federal system, were particularly active in Sardinia (the leader of this movement, Emilio Lussu, escaped from Lipari with Rosselli and was a leader of Giustizia e Libertà).

ineluctable necessity for young people, who have a duty to come to grips with the problems of their time as they enter the world of ideas.

What has been said about the necessity of an ideological renewal and of greater liberalism inside the movement can be extended to the whole problem of culture. Socialists in general, and Italian socialists in particular, are terribly backward when it comes to culture—with respect to the views of the best of the rising generation, I mean. This derives in part from the fact that mass movements are by their nature ponderous and very conservative where culture and ideology are concerned; but by far the largest factor, at least in Italy, is the fetishistic attachment to the doctrines of positivistic materialism that characterized the socialist elite thirty years ago. This elite has always violently attacked any deviation from an atheist, materialist, and positivistic socialism and has scorned any youth movement that did not adhere to its habitual views as bourgeois. Such hatred of novelty in fact contained a notable degree of incomprehension and a fair dose of arrogance as well, inasmuch as when it first coalesced this leadership had not only failed to impose any change on the bourgeois mind-set of the time, which was entirely dominated by the high priests of positivism, but had enthusiastically adopted exactly the same mind-set, following (at a distance of many decades) the example of the very bourgeois democratic movements it was preparing to supplant in politics. Hence its members ought not to have been surprised when the more recent generations of socialist youth underwent an evolution in relation to their own time. But no. They carried over into culture the same dogmatic attitude they adopted in politics and claimed that in philosophy absolute, definitive truths had been attained, with no possibility of retreat or self-contradiction. Dialectic was celebrated in the social movement but denied in the world of ideas, or else introduced there in a mechanical form. A socialist had to be, and could only be, a positivist! Idealism and spirituality were "bourgeois" degenerations!

Well, old socialists and new ones are just going to have to accept the fact that a few postulates concerning the human spirit, no matter how contradictory, cannot be avoided. They are eternal, as thought is, being part of the very nature of our intelligence, and they cannot be encapsulated in any set of class relations whatsoever. It is not true that socialism stands in a necessary relation to the materialistic and positivistic strains in philosophy, and it is ridiculous to suppose that the day will arrive when men, having come to an agreement on the principal problems of life and existence, will sweep aside religions and metaphysical systems in order to live exclusively in the realm of sensory experience. That day, which luckily will never dawn, would be a grim one indeed. For as long as the world has existed, this variation and alternation, this perennial advance through contradictions and syntheses, has always existed, and there is not a cultivated individual who has not experienced it personally.

Socialists proceed too boldly when they transfer the terminology of politics, and the division between classes, into the cultural and spiritual realm. This is another offshoot of Marxist determinism, another mistake of the crudest possible kind. Culture is neither bourgeois nor proletarian; only *non*culture fits these categories, or at most a few extrinsic and secondary aspects of cultural life. Class may influence art, but there is no such thing as class art. The culture of an epoch, of a nation, is a patrimony of values that transcends the economic phenomenon of class and declares its universality. And even with regard to those extrinsic and secondary aspects, those class influences on culture, socialists ought to be very cautious, because although it hurts to have to admit it, the average proletarian is no different from the average bourgeois in his attachment to tradition, to custom, to prevailing taste and morality. The proletariat as such has not up to now shown itself capable of producing any really innovative movement in the sphere of culture. All it does is follow, at a distance of one or two generations, the literary, artistic, and philosophical styles of the cultivated bourgeoisie. If one wishes to find movements of liberation, or serious attempts at such, in the intellectual domain, it is rather to avant-gardes of bourgeois *provenance* that one has to look: not bourgeois themselves, but of bourgeois provenance. The fact is that such avant-gardes conform to the mentality and the prejudices characteristic of the bourgeoisie to a lesser extent than anyone else—a truth confirmed by the fact that almost the entire socialist elite comes from their ranks.

This long analysis leads to a precise conclusion, which is that the socialist political movement has to adopt a principle of broad, intelligent tolerance as its philosophical and cultural attitude. It may be understandable that each individual should make every effort to connect theory and practice, thought and action; indeed he is obliged to do so. But the same obligation is a deadly error when it is forced on the movement as a whole. Grief will result from trying to fetter a movement with a development spanning centuries, a movement irrepressibly polyphonic, to a given philosophical creed. Grief will result from laying down, as they once did, an "official" philosophy of socialism. Doing so means creating as many socialisms as there are currents of belief; or else (more probably) shackling the movement, parching it, isolating it. It means failing to understand the extraordinary complexity and intensity of life in the modern world, in which positions, schools, and methods are shifting unceasingly, where beliefs held to be incontrovertible are very quickly worn out, where one cannot even imagine a restful state. Above all it means forgetting that schools of thought and cultural tastes move in much shorter and more intermittent waves than does the social and socialist movement, or at any rate, that they do not coincide. The premises on which the socialist movement is based are so elementary and universal that they do not imply any specific and necessary relation to one philosophy or another. Any real philosophy, being what it is, can always justify conservatism, revolution, or restoration, as circumstances require. One need only ponder the example of Hegel.

The impossibility as well as the erroneousness of binding the great socialist movement to a particular theoretical penchant, especially Marxism, emerges clearly from an analysis of contemporary socialism. Not only is it freeing itself from subservience to Marxism, but as it grows broader and deeper it is taking on different hues in different national settings. Even the blindest believers in the total internationalism of the proletarian class (a belief typical of *bohémiens* and those suffering from persecution, a belief proper to an initial romantic phase) must now recognize the underlying differences among the principal socialist movements in the world. These differences are not attributable to the different degrees of economic development in various countries, as Marxism would have it, but are rather to be explained by reference to complex chains of causality that come together to create the particularity of each national group.

Of all the great socialist movements, only Austro-German social democracy still declares formally that it adheres to Marxism, notwithstanding the clear shift to a more democratic orientation brought about by the revolution of 1918 and the spread of heresy in the youth wing.

The French socialist tradition—romantic, humanistic, and libertarian—has always escaped Marxist influence. Attempts to bring them together always failed; even an outstanding leader such as Jaurès succeeded only in overcoming their heterogeneity while in full rhetorical flight. Among French socialists the cult of the individual, faith in the free initiative of the workers, contact with the facts of national life, recognition of moral factors, and respect for small property-holding by rural cultivators and artisans were never lost. Proudhon,[2] Sorel, and

---

[2] Pierre-Joseph Proudhon (1809–1865) was born in Besançon to a poor family. His essay "Qu'est-ce que la propriété?" (1840) gained the attention of Marx. From 1846 on he lived in Paris, where he socialized with socialists and economists and met Marx, Bakunin, and Blanc. In 1848 he was elected to the National Assembly, and after Louis-Napoléon came to power he went to exile in Belgium. Soon after, he returned to France and published *La Révolution sociale*, with which he hoped to convince the emperor to lead the social revolution; instead he was jailed and exiled again. After the publication of his

Jaurès, not Lafargue and Guesde,[3] are the legitimate representatives of the mentality of French socialism.

The originality of British socialism is even more pronounced. It is decidedly anti-Marxist, anti-ideological, antisecular, and almost insensible of the competition of intellectual trends; with its typically English empirical mentality, it loves concrete problems. The Labour party—a very clever federate union of forces fighting for the cause of justice and labor—practices class struggle but has always refused to elevate it to the status of a supreme tactical maxim. Its aim is the gradual and peaceful reform of society, without creating dramatic conflicts or abrupt convulsions. If one fails to grasp not just the insularity of the British, but the manner in which they are cemented together by religion, one will not understand either British socialism or the fiasco suffered on that island by every intellectual trend arriving from the continent, from Rousseauism to Leninsm. The interest they all share in problems of the spirit favors mutual understanding and tolerance and strictly limits the division among classes, and their internal friction, to the material sphere, where it is absorbed. In the House of Commons the parties divide and regroup along new lines, independently of economic criteria, as soon as the debate touches on matters of religion. . . .

The Italian socialists instead, and I am referring especially to political leaders, in their internationalist zeal and their slavish acceptance of Marxist guidelines (Marxism ignores frontiers and recognizes only classes) too often have distorted the unmistakable features of the Italian environment and Italian history. ⟨ The native, albeit slender, socialist tradition (Pisacane, Cafiero, Ferrari, Mazzini)[4] was almost entirely

new book, *De la justice dans la révolution et dans l'église* (1858), Proudhon was sentenced for the second time and forced to emigrate again. His social theory was influenced by Fourier and Saint-Simon, and particularly Rousseau and Smith. His aim was to implement the liberal utopia of total enfranchisement and equality among individuals so as to take the principles of the French Revolution to their full conclusions. By developing Smith's theory, he realized that to establish a perfect equivalence between value and labor it was necessary to abolish money and to return to the direct exchange of work and goods, money being the primary vehicle of capitalist accumulation. Proudhon's socialism was primarily a "mutualism" with strong antistatist implications. He refused to subordinate the political moment to the economic one and was accused by Marx of bourgeois moralism, particularly after the publication of his *Système des contradictions économiques, ou philosophie de la misère* (1846), against which Marx wrote his *Misère de la philosophie*. At the end of the century Proudhon's ideas (and in particular his book *La philosophie du progrès*, 1853) attracted many socialists (Georges Sorel among them) and inspired syndicalist, federalist, mutualist, and pacifist movements.

[3] See n. 1 of ch. 2.

[4] These four Italian men of the Risorgimento have been particularly admired—not all to the same degree—by intellectuals and politicians who identifed with a non-Catholic

disregarded. If not for the syndicalist and cooperative movement that continues to do magnificent, original work, especially in the country-side, one would almost be forced to deny that Italian political socialism has any serious connection with Italian life.)

Italian socialism in the future must pay much more attention to specifically national problems and break the absurd monopoly on patriotism held by so-called national parties. As the different socialist movements in the different European countries grow more specific and individual, we must guard against seeing this as symptomatic of the failure of the universalistic ideal of socialism. On the contrary, it must be seen as a sign of the shift from the abstract to the real, a fundamental and unavoidable step on the ascending pathway of the masses, who are not capable of climbing instantaneously from a highly segmented and local existence to a full experience and understanding of world solidarity. For there to be a community of peoples, the peoples must be self-sufficient entities, with their own inner course of development: only an organic synthesis of various national communities will lead one day to a federation of all nations. Anything else is utopian. The initial denial of national values by the precursors of socialism was a natural reaction to the profound inferiority and oppression inflicted on the masses. Their internationalism was primarily polemical, not constructive. The working class, accustomed to see the state as an instrument of class oppression, inevitably lumped their national homeland together with the other things they condemned and hated, when in fact it is a symbolic expression of the undeniable fact that a people shares a common history and destiny. Today, when the masses in the most advanced countries have been granted full parity in political rights and have come to possess extremely powerful means to make themselves and their own material and ideal concerns felt in the life of

---

culture. Their political ideology included a wide range of options, from liberalism (whether libertarian or not) to radicalism (democratic or anarchic) to republicanism (unitarian or federalist) to socialism (Marxist or non-Marxist). Giuseppe Mazzini was the most popular among them, and his legend and ideas were (and are) widespread among the common people (particularly in some regions of the central-northern peninsula). The other three were known only among a tiny elite—indeed, in some cases they faced hostility from the Italian people. This was the case with Carlo Pisacane (1818–1857), a republican with a deep sensibility for social justice who led an expedition to liberate southern Italy from the Bourbons and was killed with his companions (three hundred political prisoners he had liberated from the island jail of Ponza) by the very populace that was supposed to participate in the insurrection. Carlo Cafiero (1846–1892) was an anarchist-idealist and a committed internationalist who, after an adventurous life, spent his last years in an insane asylum. Giuseppe Ferrari (1811–1876) was a political theorist who shared Mazzini's republicanism and after 1848 aligned himself with the socialists, particularly Louis Blanc, Pierre Leroux, and Proudhon.

the state, the outdated internationalism that denies or even reviles the national homeland is nonsense, a mistake, just another ball and chain shackled to socialist parties by the Marxist fetish. The war has shown the power with which the national myth is endowed. Unwilling peoples were flung against other unwilling peoples in an atrocious war that lasted for years, without a single serious attempt at rebellion taking place in the democratically organized countries. And even more than the myth, all too often it is national prejudice that prevails. A football game or a boxing match will suffice to reveal, alas, what a grip the instinct of factious patriotism has on even the most disabused masses. They are still living in a primitive and extremely dangerous phase of patriotism that easily makes them fall victim to any sort of adventure, provided it is cloaked in the false trappings of national honor and so forth. If, for the sake of combating these primitive or degenerate or selfish forms of devotion to country, the socialists persist in ignoring the highest values of national life, they will be doing nothing but playing into the hands of other groups that base their success on exploiting the national myth.

Practice

Italian socialism needs, indeed I should say requires in the most imperative fashion, a dose of realism; it has to make closer contact with the country by doing away with the mediation of schematic Marxism and all the various distortions that mediation entails. The materialistic theory of history undoubtedly served a valuable purpose at the outset by providing an alternative to views of the historical process that were excessively formalistic and narrow, but when it had fulfilled this critical function and was forced into slavish obedience to a preconceived thesis, it paved the way for dire excesses.

Marxist realism is a false realism much more often than people think. It is misleading about the weight of the various forces at work and their interrelations, and especially about historical development, to which it assigns a set course and a fixed outcome. Marxist socialism has succeeded in rising above the utopianism of its goals by abandoning its plans for perfecting society, but it still applies it to the analysis of development. Development must always necessarily take place in the direction of the collective economy, through a gradual heightening of tension between social classes. Substantial variations on this program are not contemplated, and if they occur, every effort is made to devalue them by reducing them to the level of exceptions. History for the Marxists is a gigantic and tendentious drama, with scripted roles. The

Marxist socialist always has his gaze fixed on the problems of industrial capitalism, and the only legitimate forms of production in his eyes are large-scale rationalized industry and large-scale rationalized agriculture. He thinks that the only kind of worker worthy to be cast as a protagonist is the wage worker. The people and the wage workers are the same thing in Marxist thought. The other forms of production and the other categories of worker are seen as amphibious, transitory, relics of an economic world destined for rapid disappearance: the Marxist sees them as having already been enrolled, absorbed by large-scale capitalism and the proletarian army. The industrial wage worker is the only fit soldier for the socialist battle, because only he can rise to a perfect consciousness of class and of his revolutionary duty. Progress is measured by the degree of proletarianization.

This slanted and oversimplified vision of economic evolution imposes serious drawbacks on the socialist movement, especially in a country both agrarian and industrial like Italy, where economic transformation is slow. The worst of them is the movement's inability to set itself a constructive course in the present phase of transformation, though it too has to be lived through in its totality. Great thinkers who are unable to cope with the little problems of everyday life have always been the butt of jokes, and Marxist socialists risk the same derision: accustomed to traffic in "economic categories," "modes of production," "capitalism," and "socialism," they find they are unable to understand the humble but still vital problems of small-scale industry, small agricultural holdings, sharecropping, skilled handicrafts, and tenancies.

This is another example of their illiberalism. It is directed not against ideologies this time but against the real world, and it is certainly not the least of the reasons for the rapid success other political movements enjoyed in Italy—such as the Christian social movement—which are much less tied to rigid a priori formulas.

Sombart has exposed the error of those who predict the exclusive dominion of a single economic system.[5] The whole experience of the past and the nature of economic evolution tend to the opposite conclusion. In the course of history the number of economic forces existing simultaneously has been constantly growing, even though their positions with respect to one another have altered. Sombart foresees that alongside economies of the capitalist type, cooperative economies, collectivist economies, individualist economies, artisan economies,

---

[5] Werner Sombart (1863–1941) was an economist, a historian of economics, and author of important works, such as *Sozialismus und soziale Bewegung im XIX. Jahrh* (1896) and *Der moderne Kapitalismus* (1902–1908).

and small rural landholding will coexist. He does think—and here one may differ—that capitalism will continue to dominate important sectors of economic life for a long time, especially those that are still in a phase of rapid technical change and those dedicated to the production of complicated products. But he is also the first to foresee considerable modifications in capitalism. It is probable that capitalism will have to renounce its hegemony and submit increasingly to limitations and interventions on the part of public authorities and that various forms of regulated economy, in which the principle of satisfying wants will prevail over the profit motive, will appear. Large enterprises not dominated by capitalists will grow primarily where demand has stabilized and manufacturing technology has emerged from the initial revolutionary stage, making sales and production highly predictable and thus rendering the spirit of initiative increasingly superfluous.

This highly variegated picture of economic life in the near future is much less radiant than that of Marx, but it corresponds much more closely to the lines along which present reality is in fact taking shape. We might debate the rate of evolution, the significance of the various economic forms, and the degree of intervention, but not the phenomena themselves. Socialists who want to influence the reality of their time and have an influence on this evolution cannot continue to impoverish themselves by applying an a priori and linear critique to the process, comparing the evolution that is actually taking place to an ideal evolution that is happening nowhere, not even in Russia. Ignorance of the facts, willful or not, might still be tolerable in those who believe in an imminent revolution in the entire mode of production, but not in those who have an organic grasp of the process of development, nor in those who at this point have positive responsibilities to bear.

I have pointed out that this line of reasoning applies with peculiar force to Italy. If there is a country in which facile, simplistic notions collide with an inexhaustible variety of climatic conditions, cultures, and economic structures and forces, that country is Italy. In fact, the peninsula contains at least two Italies, one modern, citified, and industrial, the other ancient and rural, still estranged from Western civilization, its masses still pristine and enslaved. The latter continues to live stubbornly beyond the pale of the sort of existence that is the indispensable premise for the growth and success of a solid socialist movement of the Marxist type. Quite aside from any intrinsic evaluation of Marxism, it is, past all doubt, fitted only to supply the platform for a political movement that hinges on a work force employed in large- and medium-scale industries and on a section of the rural labor force. In the Italian context this means a political movement that for a long time will be able to involve only a fraction, a *minority*, of the Italian working class, which is concentrated in only a third of the national territory. According to the 1921 census, which is still valid, (1) 56 percent of the population classified as laboring was employed in agriculture, and only 33 percent in industry and commerce; (2) more than half of those engaged in agriculture constitute a vast army of small proprietors, tenants, and sharecroppers; (3) at least a third of those employed in industry and commerce are proprietors, independent businessmen, or managers—a very high proportion, one that attests to the small scale of most industries; and (4) the transformation of Italy from a predominantly agricultural country into an agricultural and industrial one has occurred without any noticeable rise in the percentage of the population employed in industry and commerce: 227 out of 1,000 in 1882, 219 in 1901, 200–210 at present.

The result is that on the basis of the Marxist program and Marxist tactics, a majority will not be won in Italy. So the choice is between resigning oneself to minority status for an indefinite number of years, and perhaps even for generations, or calling for a dictatorship. Italian Communists, clinging to the letter of Marxism, are as logical as the Russians in calling for a dictatorship of the avant-garde of the proletariat and an end to liberty. They are less logical when trying to give the impression that their dictatorship corresponds to the interests of the entire working class. The myth of state seizure of property and the fate of proletarianization do not in fact appeal to two-thirds of the Italian workers. In these sectors the Communist appeal, and even that of socialism *vieux style*, inevitably rings hollow, except at times of crisis or excitation. Especially where agriculture is concerned, the Marxist socialists have never successfully interpreted the profound aspirations of the great mass of Italian peasants. Dominated by their own political premises and economic prejudices, they ended by subordinating the whole socialist movement to the interests of the workers of the north, causing socialists from the south to protest loudly.

The Italian socialists must now make up their minds. Do they wish to remain forever the specific representatives of a *fraction* of the Italian proletariat, waiting with Buddhistic calm for economic evolution to transform Italy into a country like Germany or England, with 80 percent of its wage earners in industry? Or do they wish to start getting ready from now on to win the trust of all, or at least a large majority, of actual Italian working people with a suitable and realistic program, so as to be the ones finally to institute a policy really favorable to the interests of labor, peace, and liberty? If they are more attached to programs than to facts, to abstract ends than to the movement, to mythical promises than to real accomplishments, they have only to keep going down the familiar road: they can be sure that the hour of actually assuming the burden of government will never sound for them, or at any rate for their party. Even if they should join a governing coalition, they will do harmful rather than constructive work, controlling and preventing rather than acting, and without wishing to, they will end up being sucked along in the wake of progressive bourgeois groups that are not bound by rigid formulas and invented premises. In any case, by choosing this course they will betray their truer mission, because the socialist movement must, by definition, occupy itself with the interests and problems of the *whole* working class and not just a fraction of it, however large or small. If, however, they feel that before very long they too will have to face up to what is by now imperative for all the socialist parties in the world—the responsibility of holding power—let them start getting ready now for a thorough revision of their program, their tactics, the very structure of their movement, so as to create for themselves a real chance to win a solid majority. In saying this I am not asking the socialists to renounce their ideals, to toss out their dream of a society regulated by principles of justice and liberty as though these things were just leftover pieces of propaganda. Quite the contrary. I ask them not to compromise the chances of real progress in that direction by clinging morbidly to outdated formulas, programs, and methods; I ask them not to transform their technical means, their tools, into ends, or rather always to use means adequate to the limited ends they propose to attain. In sum, I am asking them to get in step with the economic and psychological reality of their country and not to while away their time dreaming of apocalyptic transformations, not to count on sudden mass conversions that are unthinkable. I ask them to replace the old Marxist program with a broader set of goals, less historically and socially conditioned, which by appealing to universal motives and ideals will be able to win over not just this or that fraction of workers, but all the Italian workers together, without distinction.

To the change of program there must correspond a change in forms of organization. The old dichotomy between the party and the workers' movement must come to an end. The more the problems of the movement are brought to the fore, the more the power of the workers' organizations must make itself felt, even in politics. Worker democracy lives in the *sindacati* (trade unions), not in the party: the party always has a certain tendency to dictatorship in the name of an ideology and of distant goals that it wants to impose not because they accord with the desires of most people, but because of their presumed intrinsic goodness. I am explicitly in favor of a reorganization of the socialist movement along lines similar to those of the Labour party in Britain: centered on the workers' movement, which tends toward unity by a physiological law and is highly adept at absorbing internal conflict, especially if its origin is ideological; and accompanied by a constellation of political groups, cultural associations, cooperative and mutual organizations, and so on. This would mean conceiving of the party of tomorrow in a much larger and more generous spirit than was the case in the past, as a federative synthesis of all the forces that are fighting for the cause of labor on the basis of a constructive labor program. Above all it will have to attend to immediate tasks, to goals that are achievable in a reasonably brief span of time. Only one thing should be constant: the acceptance in *practice* (philosophers of history can amuse themselves as they please in their books) of the liberal way of engaging in the political contest. Here there can be no equivocation or contradiction. You cannot be organizing a revolution while demanding that your adversaries resign themselves to your gradual penetration of the state to the point where you take power by peaceful means.

A reorganization of the Italian socialist movement along the lines sketched here, a reorganization that already exists potentially in the alliance of Italian groups on the Left in the struggle for liberty and a republic of labor, would contribute a great deal to the resolution of what will be the most delicate problem of the post-Fascist era: ensuring a stable government for Italy. There is no question that one of the reasons for the Fascist success was the degeneration of parliamentary life, the impossibility of gathering a homogeneous bloc of support around a constructive program. The socialists, who will inevitably be at the center of the future government, will have to be capable of catalyzing the strong support they will certainly enjoy among broad areas of the population by means of a realistic program and a flexible structure. Further, the assumption of governmental responsibility will make it imperative for the socialists to attenuate their excessively rigid concept of class, which is incompatible with the normal functioning of democratic institutions. Parties in power have to govern not for themselves but for everyone, on a basis of universality. With a class-based program, socialism in Italy will have neither a majority nor power. It must prepare to widen its front to include the entire working class and to govern in the name of a value—labor⟨—that can be said with good reason to interest all men, since all men, or nearly all, are involved in some manner in the work of production.

From this point of view as well, it would be desirable that a new political formation should arise. No longer tied to the past, it would be much freer of any obligation to respect the programs and methods of the past and could more freely elaborate, on the basis of the extraordinary experiences of the last fifteen years, a program of renewal. ⟩

BIBLIOGRAPHICAL NOTE

APART from the Italian edition, and now also this English one, *Socialismo liberale* was translated into French and Spanish. The first edition was in French, translated by Stefan Priacel, with the title *Socialisme libéral* (Paris: Librairie Valois, 1930). The Spanish edition was translated by Diego Abat de Santillon and has the title *Socialismo liberal* (Madrid: Pablo Iglesias, 1991).

Carlo Rosselli also wrote numerous articles, many of them published in *Quaderni di 'Giustizia e Libertà'* and in *Giustizia e Libertà*, others in *Non Mollare, La Critica Sociale, Il Quarto Stato, La Rivolutione Liberale*, and *La Riforma Sociale*. Most of his essays have been collected in the three volumes of the *Opere scelte di Carlo Rosselli*, the first of which (*Socialismo liberale*) was edited by John Rosselli (Turin: Einaudi, 1973), the other two (*Scritti dell'esilio*: vol. 1, *"Giustizia e Libertà" e la Concentrazione antifascista. 1929–1934*, and vol. 2, *Dallo scioglimento della Concentrazione antifascista alla guerra di Spagna. 1934–1937*) by Costanzo Casucci (Turin: Einaudi, [1988]; 1992). Another useful collection of Rosselli's *Scritti politici* was edited by Zeffiro Ciuffoletti and Paolo Bagnoli (Naples: Guida, 1988). Zeffiro Ciuffoletti also edited a volume of the letters of the Rosselli brothers and their mother, *Epistolario familiare. Carlo, Nello Rosselli e la madre, 1914–1937* (Milan: Sugar Co., 1979). Two important collections of Rosselli's writings have been published after his death: *Oggi in Spagna domani in Italia* with the preface by Gaetano Salvemini to the first edition and an introduction by Aldo Garosci (Turin: Einaudi, 1967). The first edition, without Garosci's introduction, was published in Paris in 1938 by Giustizia e Libertà. *Scritti politici e autobiografici*, with the preface by Gaetano Salvemini was published by Polis Editrice (Naples) in 1944. Other important sources are the *Quaderni di "Giustizia e Libertà"* (January 1932-January 1935), which were reprinted twice by the Bottega d'Erasmo of Turin: in 1959 with an introduction by Alberto Tarchiani, and in 1975 with a preface by Alessandro Galante Garrone.

The basic works on Carlo Rosselli's life and thought are: Francesco F. Nitti, *Escape: The Personal Narrative of a Political Prisoner Who Was Rescued from Lipari* (New York: Putnam, 1930); Emilio Lussu, "A Thousand to One," and "The Flight from Lipari," *Atlantic Monthly* (June 1930 and July 1930): 721–32, 31–42; Gaetano Salvemini, *Carlo Rosselli: A Memoir* (London: For Intellectual Liberty, 1937); Guido Calogero, "Il socialismo liberale di Carlo Rosselli," in id., *Difesa del liberalsocialismo* (Rome: Atlantica, 1945), pp. 123–26 (a new edition has been edited by Dino Cofrancesco [Milan: Marzorati, 1972]); Aldo Garosci, *Vita di Carlo Rosselli*, 2 vols. (Rome: Edizioni U, 1946; reprinted Florence: Vallecchi, 1973); Benedetto Croce, "Osservazioni su libri nuovi" (review of Garosci's book) in id., *Nuove Pagine Sparse*, vol. 2 (Naples: Ricciardi, 1949), pp. 194–97; Alessandro Levi, *Ricordo dei fratelli Rosselli* (Florence: La Nuova Italia, 1947); Nicola Tranfaglia, *Carlo Rosselli dall'interventismo a "Giustizia e Libertà"* (Bari: Laterza, 1968); Aldo Garosci, Introduction to *Opere scelte di Carlo Rosselli*, vol. 1;

Norberto Bobbio, Introduction to Carlo Rosselli, *Socialismo liberale* (Turin: Einaudi, 1979); the miscellany *Giustizia e Libertà nella lotta antifascista e nella storia d'Italia. Atti del Convegno Internazionale organizzato a Firenze il 10–12 giugno 1977* (Florence: La Nuova Italia, 1978); Paolo Bagnoli, *Carlo Rosselli tra pensiero politico e azione* with a preface by Giovanni Spadolini (Florence: Passigli, 1985); Franco Invernici, *L'alternativa di "Giustizia e Libertà." Economia e politica nei progetti del gruppo di Carlo Rosselli* (Milan: Franco Angeli, 1987); Santi Fedele, *E verrà un'altra Italia. Politica e cultura nei "Quaderni di Giustizia e Libertà"* (Milan: Franco Angeli, 1992).

INDEX